AF496598

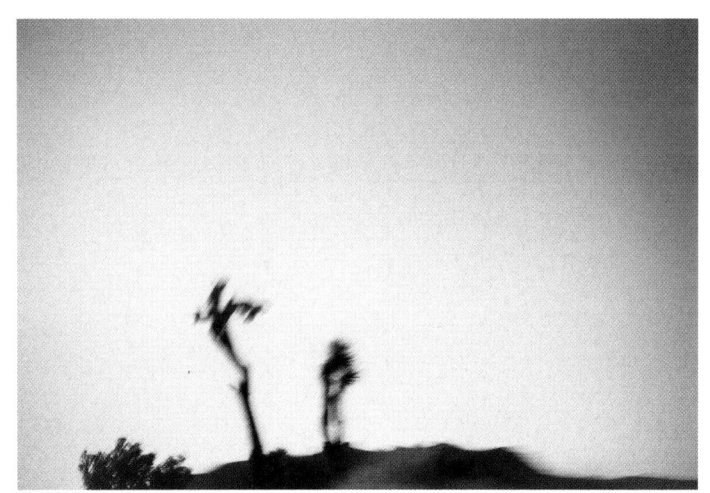

AMERICA SERIES/ FLORENCE MONTMARE

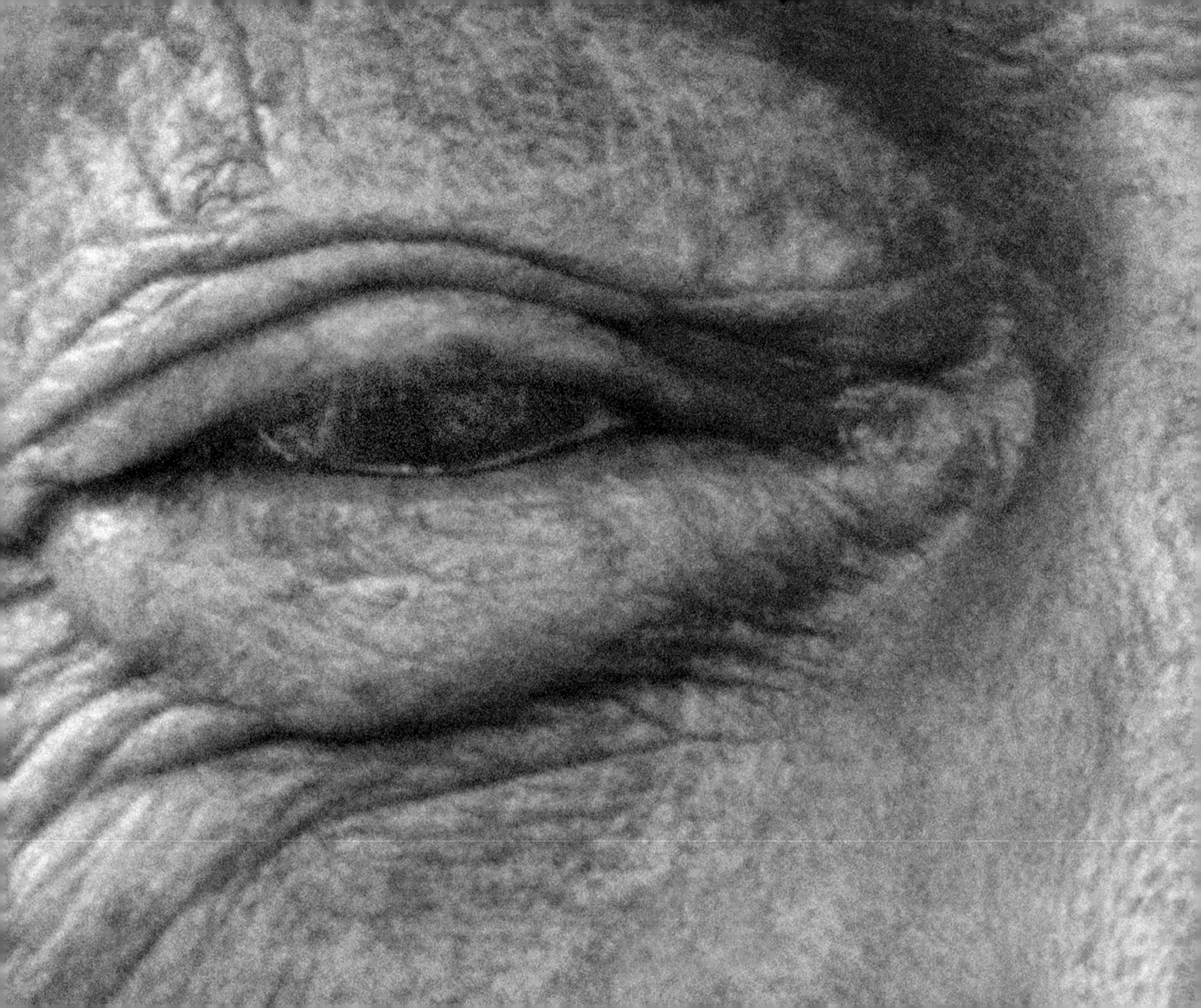

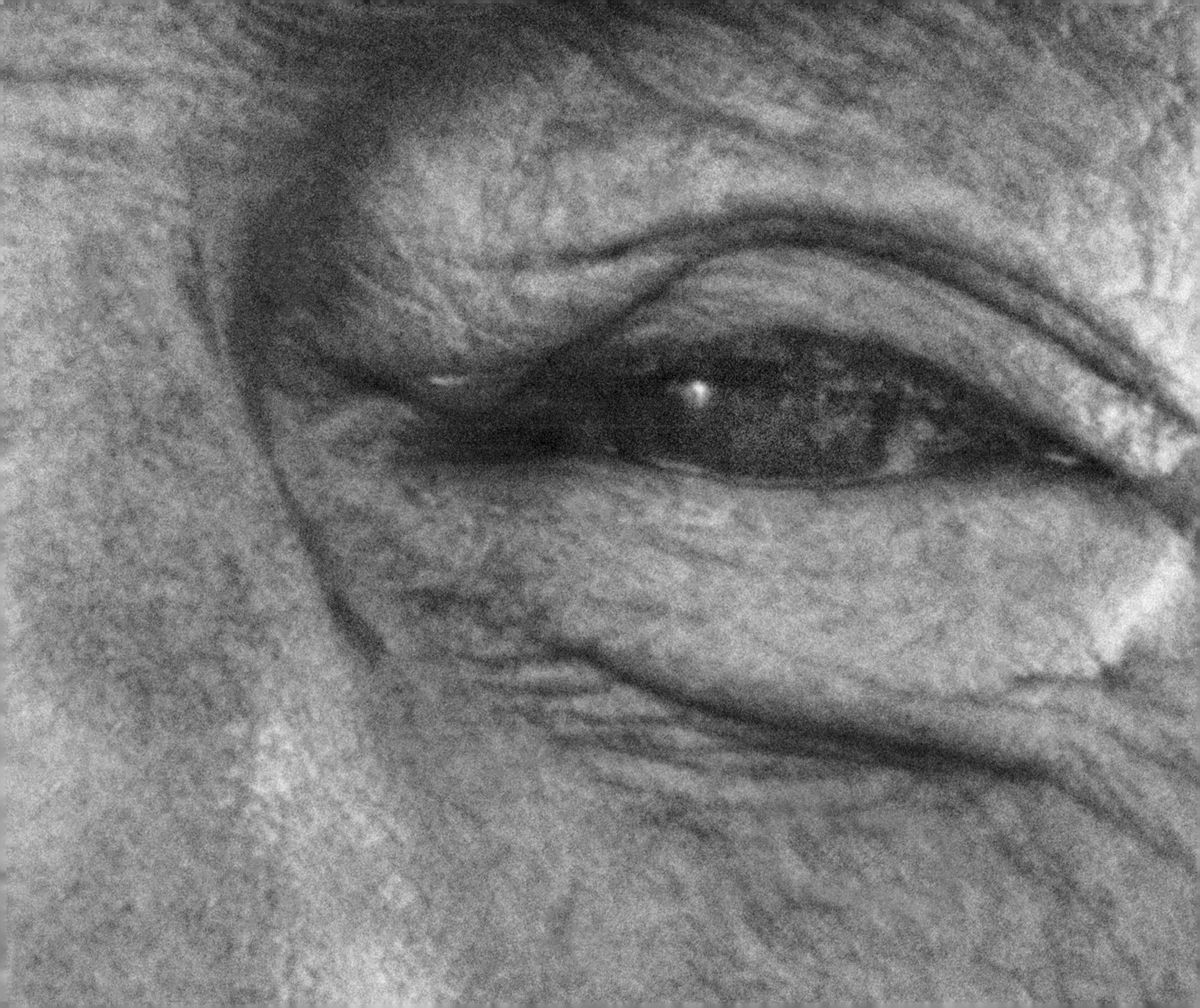

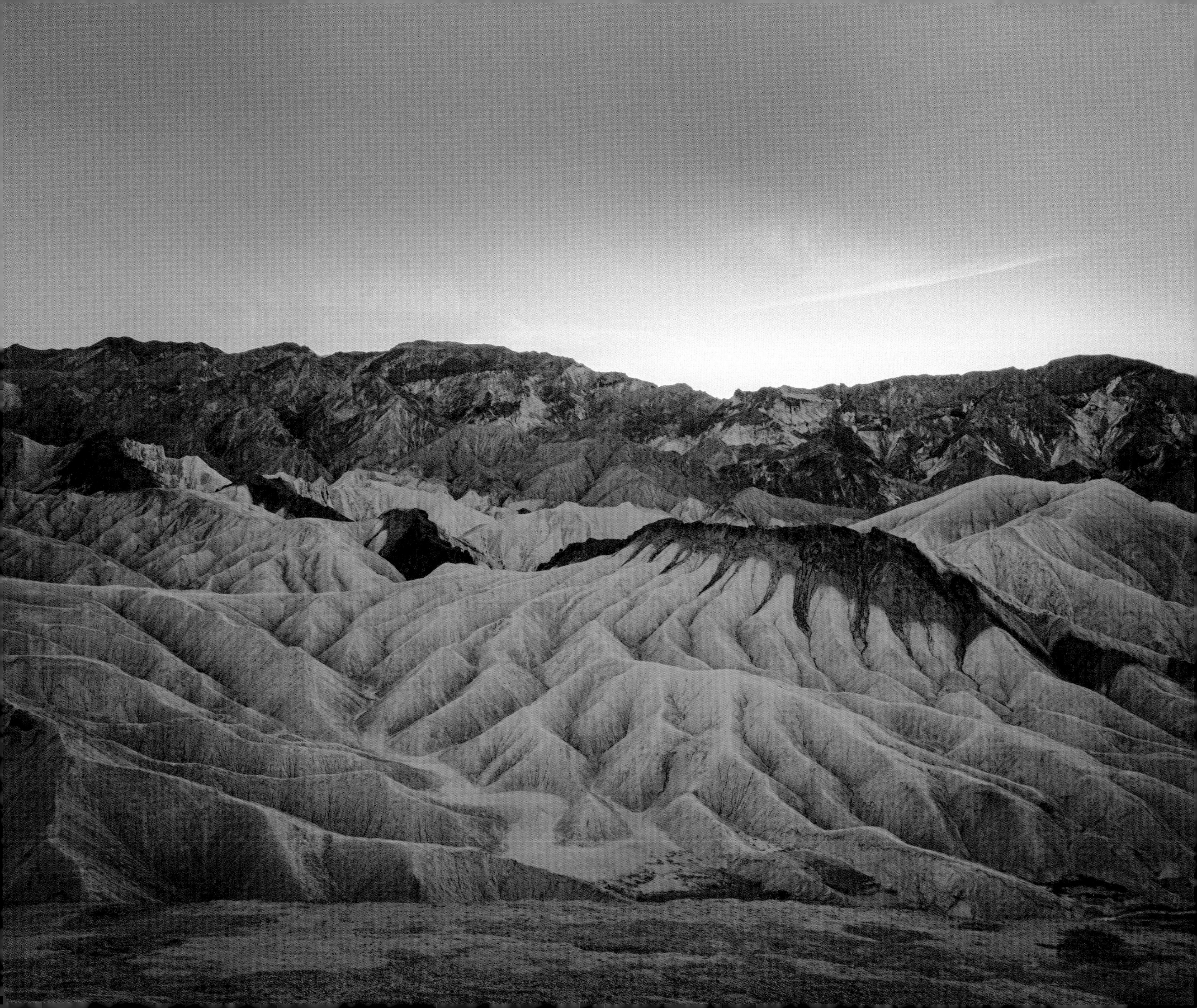

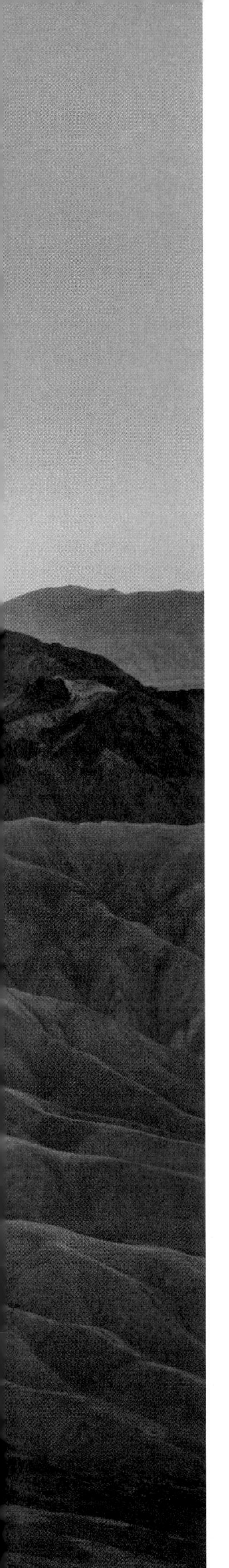

N 35° 41' 15.395" W 105° 56' 18.444"

SANTA FE, NEW MEXICO

“There are many different secrets and lessons hidden in every tree, every rock, and every leaf. They are our relatives who teach us things, just the way it used to be among the native people.”

[Sky Red Hawk]

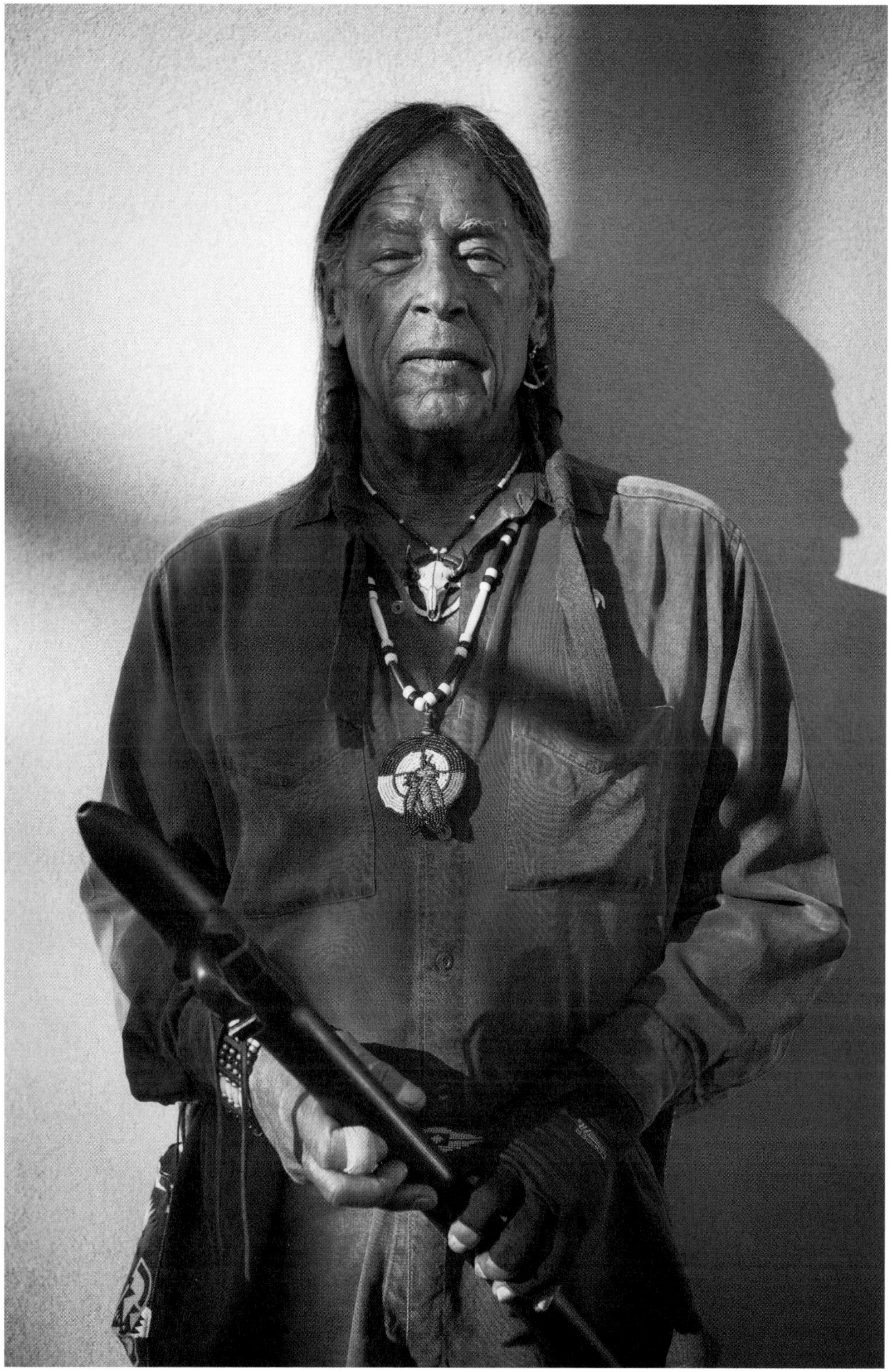

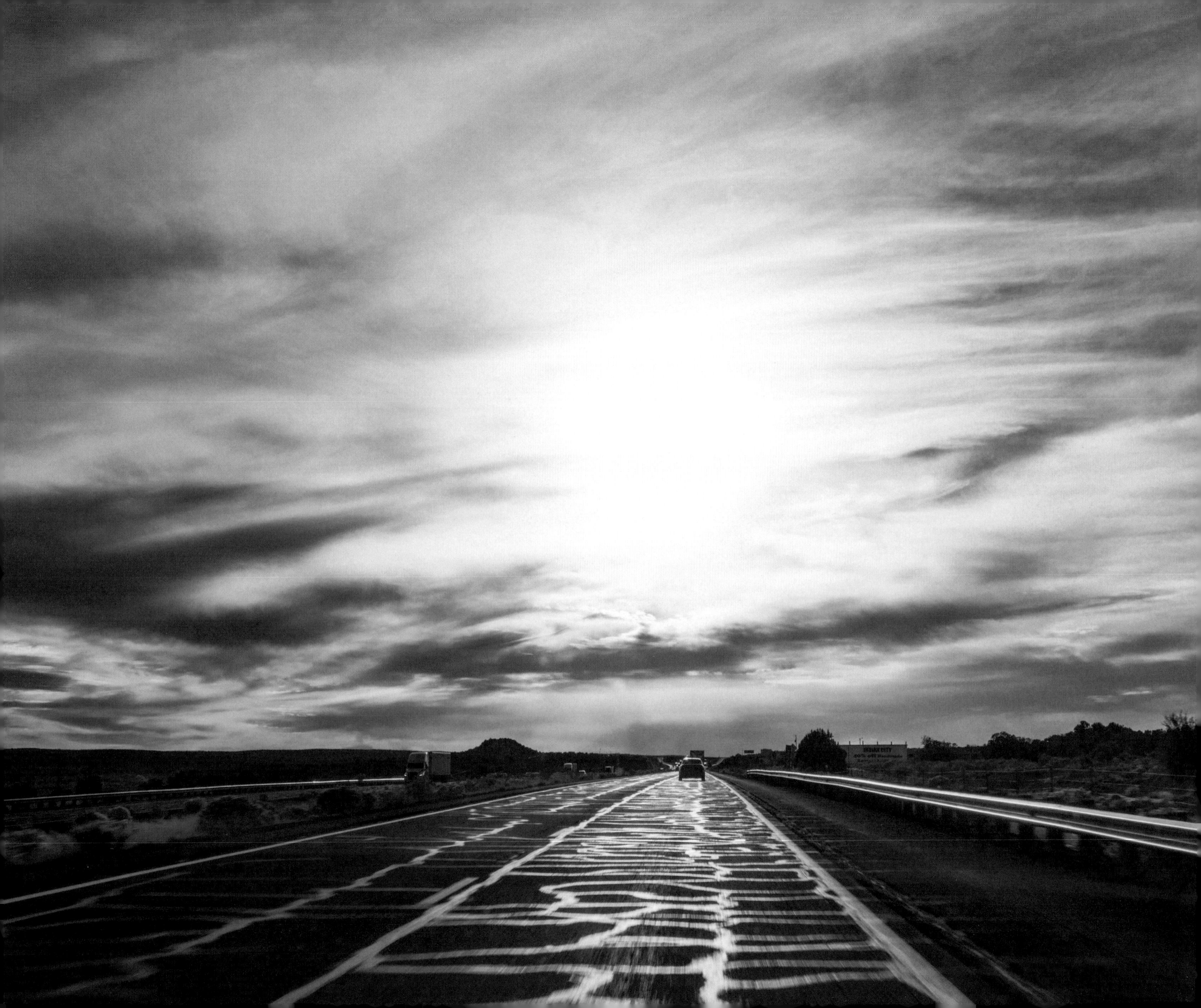

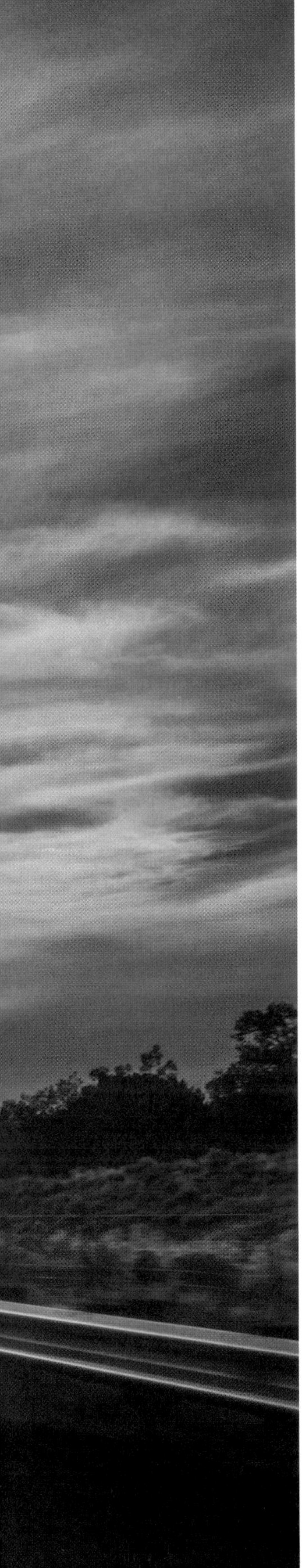

A radio voice crackling a sermon about the end of days keeps me company in the dark. On the side of the road, a discarded umbrella has been swindled out of its chance to serve during a rainstorm in Oklahoma, where people and trees alike bend in the wind.

I want to take a new look at the United States and capture the spirit of this era in all its complexities. Not only is the nation continuing to evolve as new people make it their home, but the landscape is also physically changing due to the climate crisis we are facing, with record-breaking temperatures and radical weather patterns regularly making headlines.

Like a throw of the dice, it was left up to chance whom I would encounter along my 7,000-mile round trip across the continent. On a route influenced by the 20th century's historic migration — one of hopes, dreams, and opportunities — I was certain my female immigrant perspective would influence the vision.

An electric vehicle doubled as my mobile studio, and the random locations of the charging stations enabled me to encounter and photograph people from all walks of life. I acted on opportunities as they appeared and treated everything as a sign that was directing me while the journey unfolded.

Against the backdrop of a uniform man-made landscape, with the repetition of strip malls, endless parking lots, and billboards urging people to consume more, I witnessed the economic difference between Americans who have and those who have not, many in survival mode and barely making ends meet. The forces of nature were on display, along with their almighty powers: a dark palette of landscapes with brooding skies in contrast to the portraits of people against a light canvas, vulnerable yet hopeful.

In New Jersey, I photographed two homeless young men, one of whom had been knifed after selling candy on the street. In Pennsylvania, I came across a beauty pageant, with girls as young as eight competing. In Missouri, members of a Christian charity offered clothing and furniture out of a container. In Oklahoma, I spoke with a Cheyenne and Arapaho social service officer working to find safe homes for Native foster children. In Nevada, a woman broke into tears when asked about her dreams. She and her mom had both been diagnosed with cancer recently, and their lives changed forever.

There is something radical about an encounter with a stranger. In the meeting between the eyes, all things external seem to fall away. The reveal: Each person standing against the same blank canvas illuminates how in the end, more connects us than divides us. This may be what helps prevent the intrinsic fabric of America from being ripped apart.

My headlights only reveal a small stretch of asphalt in the darkness that lies before me. The eye of the camera rises into the air, changing the focus from my narrow point of view to one that takes in the entire moonlit landscape. I see myself from above, a small fragment of light moving through the night.

Florence Montmare

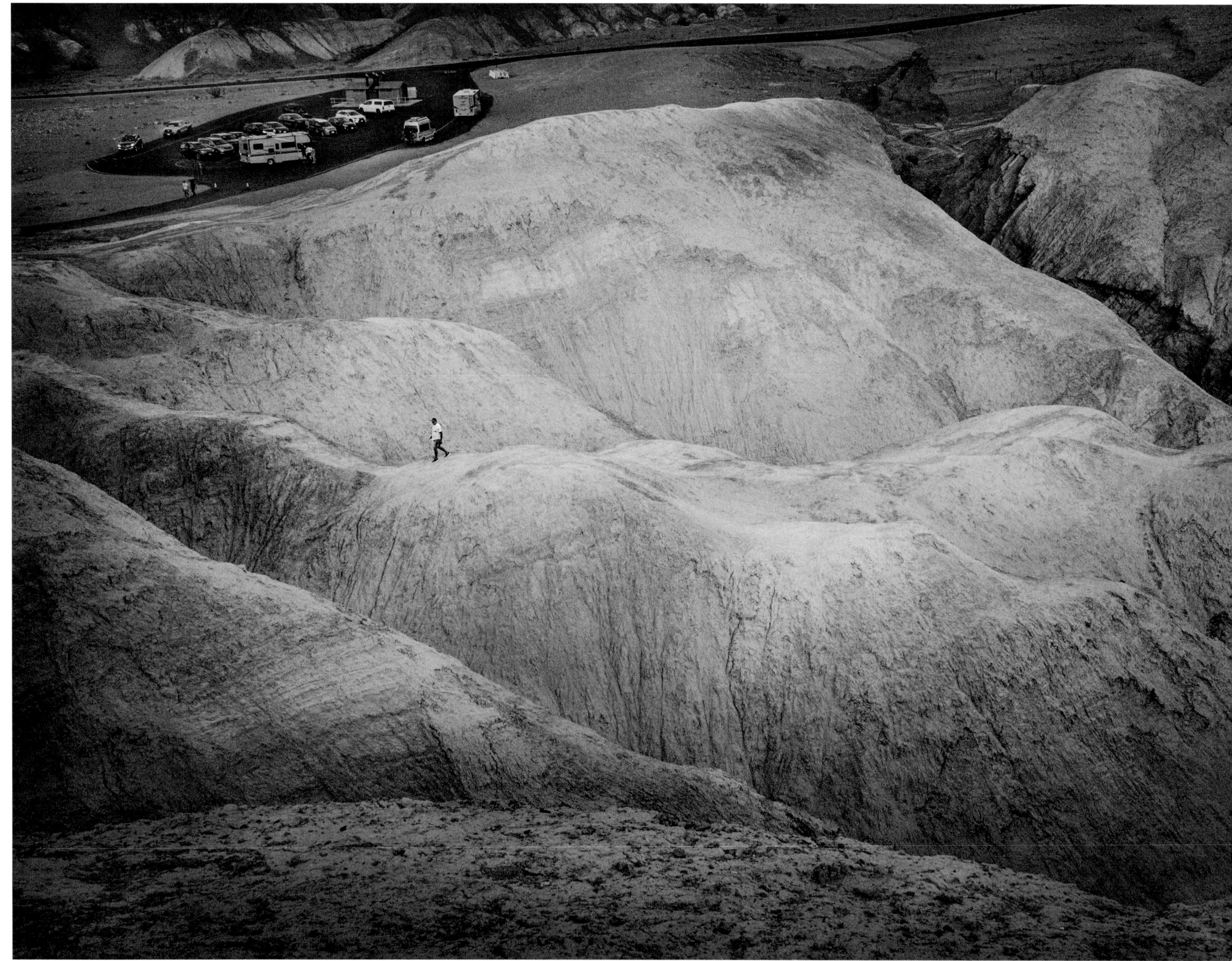

Death Valley, California

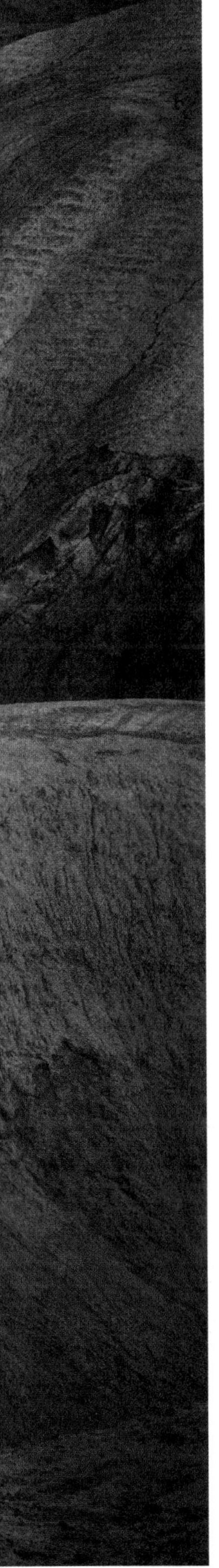

In her monumental pilgrimage, Florence Montmare has reimagined a brave new America: allegorical, stringent, and introspective. Poetry is expressed in the landscape and the people who occupy this sacred space. Sky Red Hawk, from the Lakota tribe, is the portal by which we enter Montmare's imaginary narrative — with a person native to this land and its unending panorama. We see his eyes in an extreme closeup, but how does he see the world?

The worldwide health nightmare and ongoing climate crisis have disrupted our social fabric, changing every aspect of life. Following months of isolation at the height of the pandemic, Montmare endeavored to explore the nation in the same tradition as male photographers in decades past — Evans, Frank, and Avedon — and shares her views of the country she calls home.

She includes herself in this unfolding — not as an outsider constructing a critique but as an active participant on the road to self-discovery. Her portraiture is performative. She is part of the piece even though unseen. In the tradition of Joseph Beuys and participatory art, interviews become the canvas on which her subjects paint a picture with their contemplations.

The artist sets up a doubling theme: landscape and portrait. Nature and humanity. Sometimes we see the scenery untrammeled, without traces of civilization's "circles of confusion." A few characters gaze upon the wildness with unflinching resolve. Is it about "consciousness itself?"

These pictures of America are "cinema paintings." Artists such as Albert Bierstadt and Georgia O'Keeffe showed us the mythology of the "virgin" landscape. At times, Montmare reveals this to us as well. But make no mistake — these are interior landscapes of the mind's eye. She meditates on a kaleidoscope of truths in worlds rapidly disappearing. Continuing the Modernist tradition, every pictorial detail is clearly articulated.

Montmare's exploration is haunted by spiritual forces and affected by characters straight out of a road movie. There are ghosts in these photographs. They are our collective unconscious. Her portraits perfume unique languages. The body never lies. Her panoply of characters aren't "sleepwalking." They maintain a distance and detachment, revealing only so much as they allow. Yet, via their postures, their souls begin to emerge the longer we stare at them.

There's a wide representation of different people, who for the most part stand — they are on display and cannot hide. The majority of the portraits are made outdoors with the subjects in casual attire, ordinary and unpretentious. What do the pictures say about these individuals? Do they represent a cross section of the United States? There's something about the shirtless male, the macho man, made vulnerable by the female gaze. She includes diverse gender identities who inhabit their selves securely.

Montmare traveled across the United States twice, traversing first on Route 66, the "Mother Road," from New York to California, then back again via Highway 10, gliding along the southern route through Arizona, Texas, up into Georgia, Virginia and finally back home.

She primarily depicts rural America: empty trailer parks, cheap motels, abandoned trucks, and telephone poles stretching across the horizon. Haggard trading posts. Lonely churches. A blaring casino. Like oases, these milieus are strewn across the land in a haphazard and abandoned way. Public spaces are sanctuaries for serenity and devotion. They're a way to find communion with others after the isolation of individualist vehicles floating down the river-rapid roads. There are a few nighttime views, and in these a film-noir mood is revealed.

In the midst of this, magical animals appear, floating reincarnations of our desire for the freedom of limitless emotional depth and longing for a meaningful world. A black feathered bird is juxtaposed with a man dressed in black — a crow's reincarnation? Or is it the other way around?

Despite the serious subject matter, Florence Montmare's pictures are celebratory. The individuals depicted in these searing portraits are all survivors, and the landscape will surely persevere, with or without us. In a final image, the artist casts her shadow upon the landscape — nature altered by humanity. This signifies the end.

Sam Samore

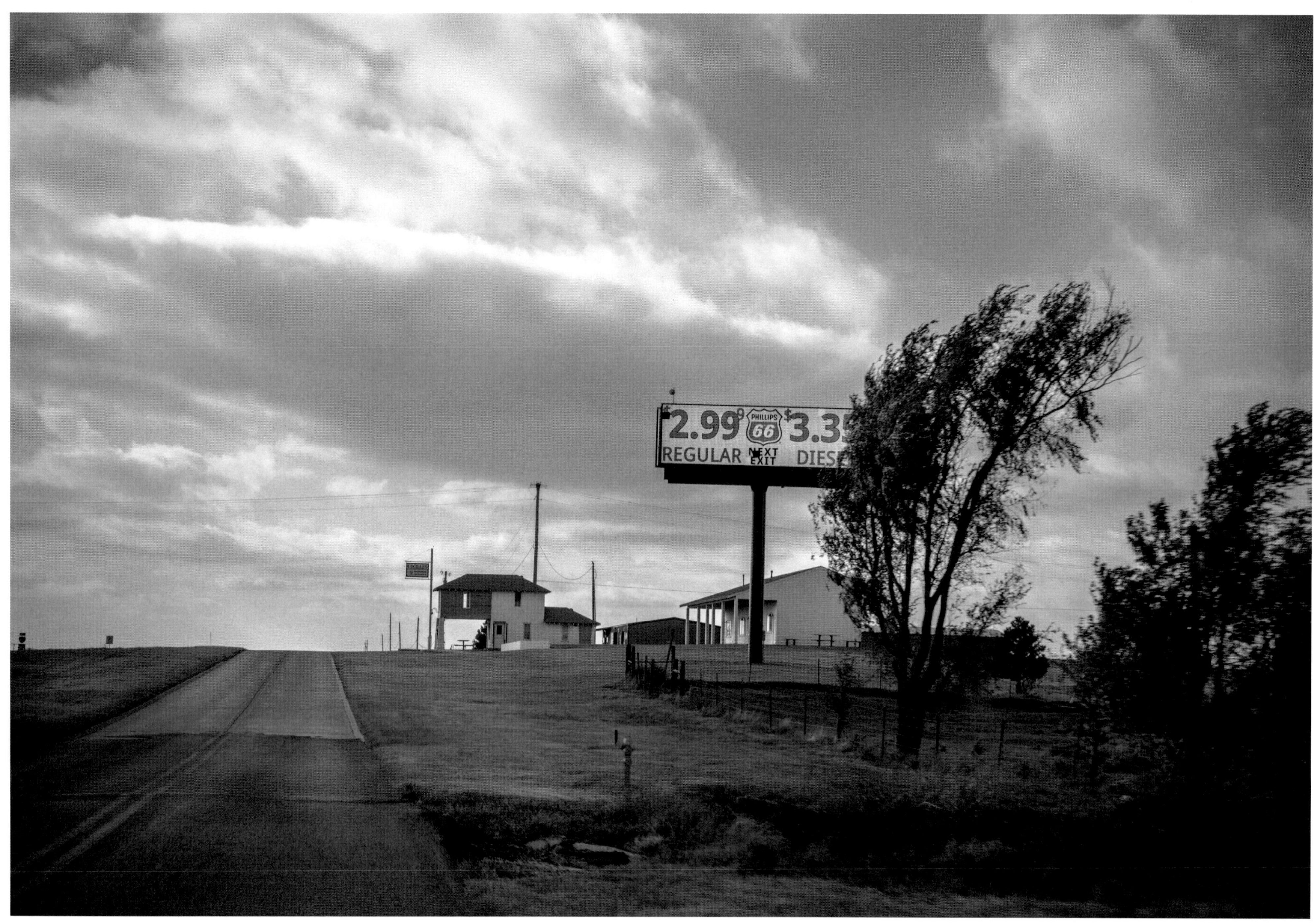

Diesel 3.35, Oklahoma

N 30° 28’ 16.1940” W 91° 8’ 50.5860”

BATON ROUGE, LOUISIANA

“The doctors say I will lose my hearing by the time I am 23. But I think by then I will have heard enough.”

[Remy]

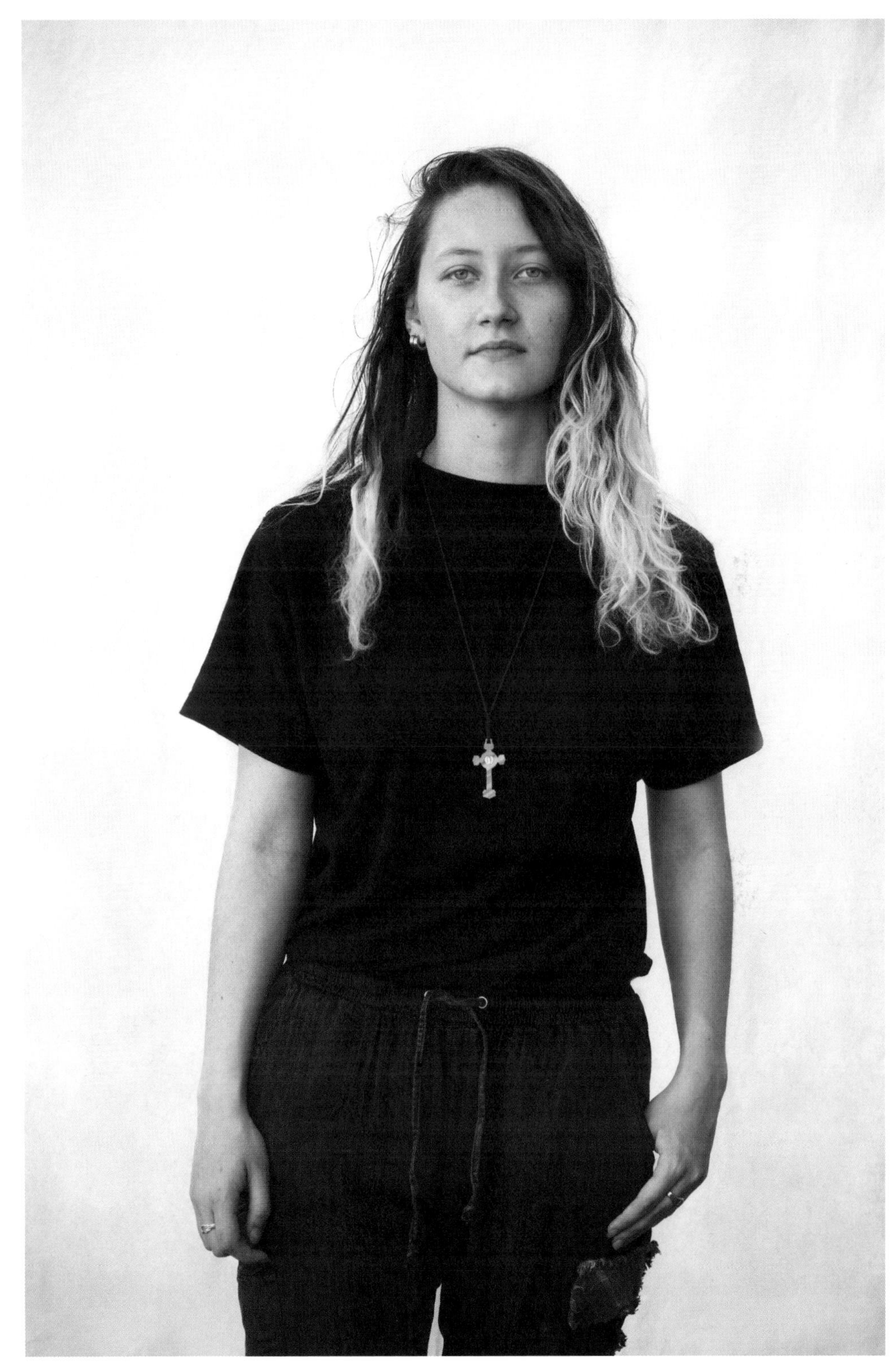

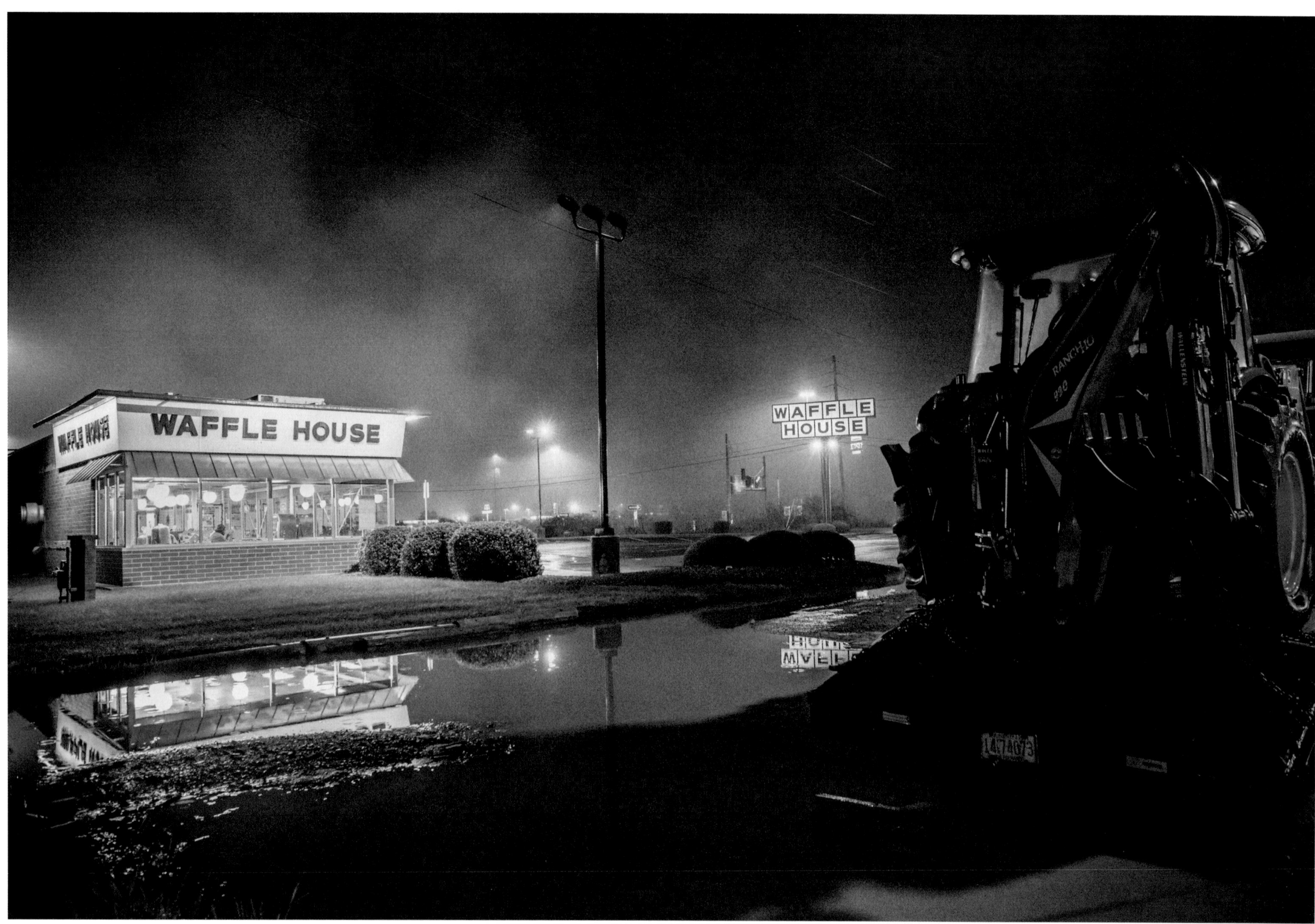

Waffle House, Pennsylvania

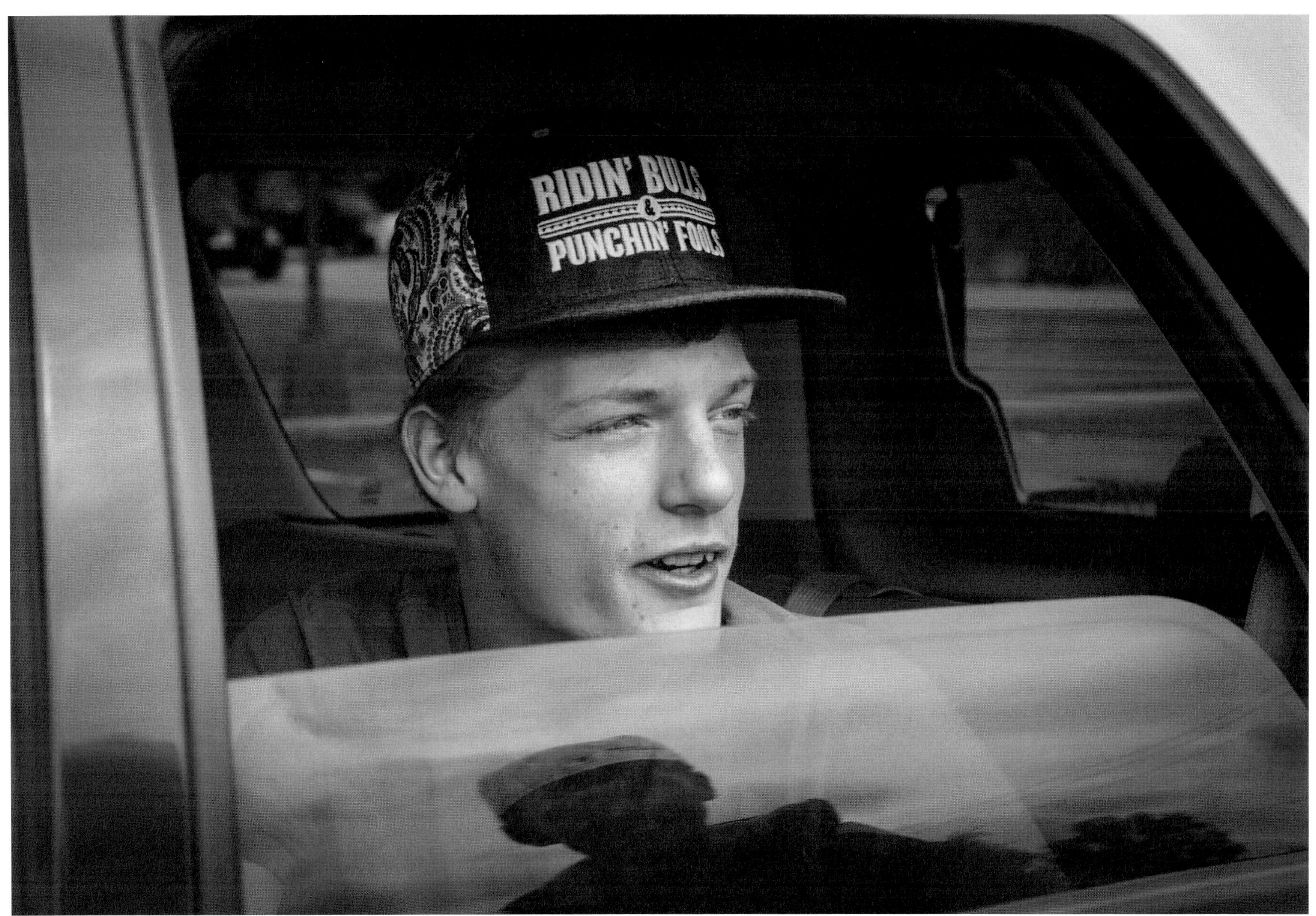

Ridin' Bulls Punchin' Fools, Oklahoma

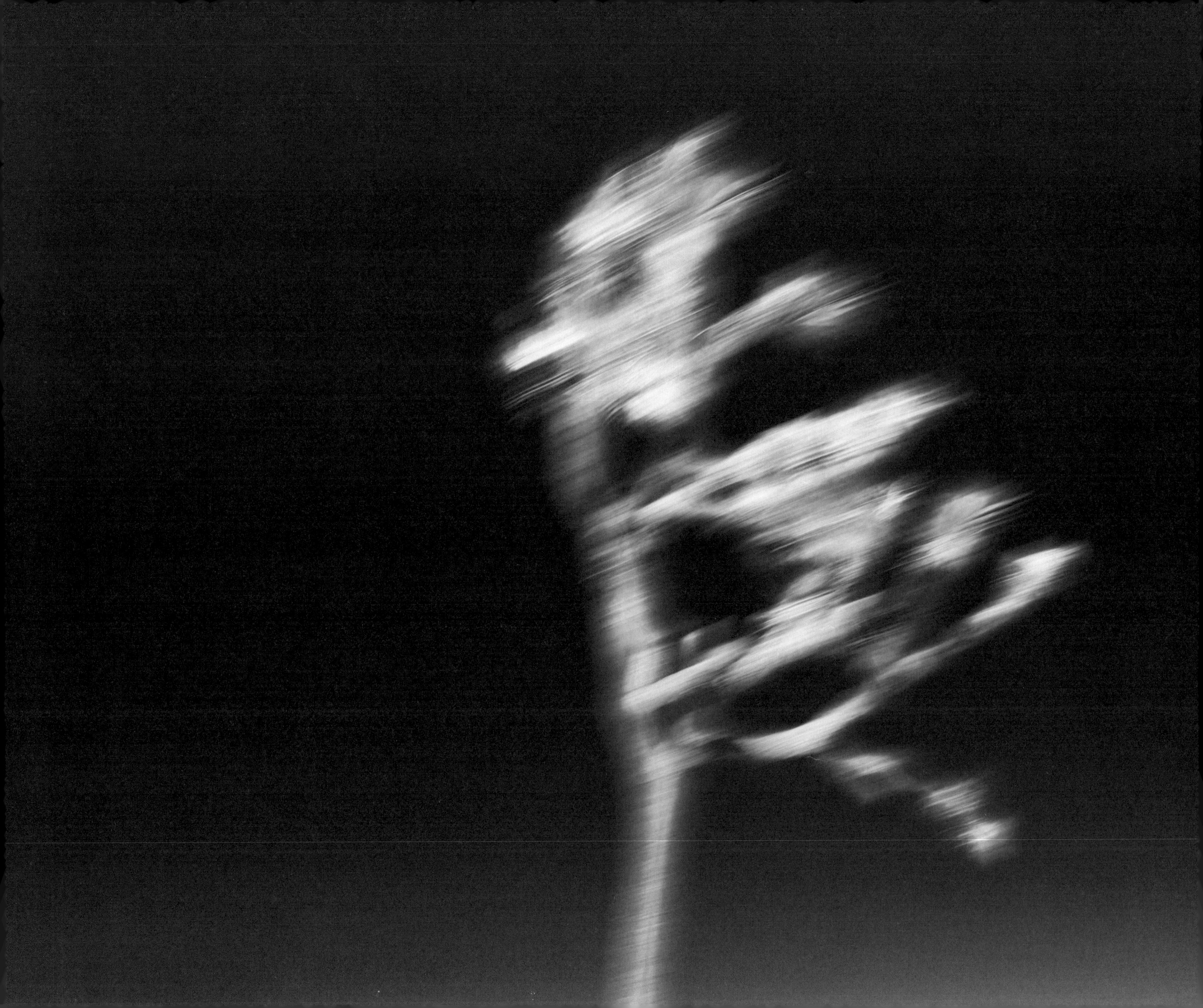

N 38° 19' 21.415" W 75° 13' 3.681"

BERLIN, MARYLAND

"My dream for humankind is to come together as people, to work together, and to see everybody for who they are."

[Akirra]

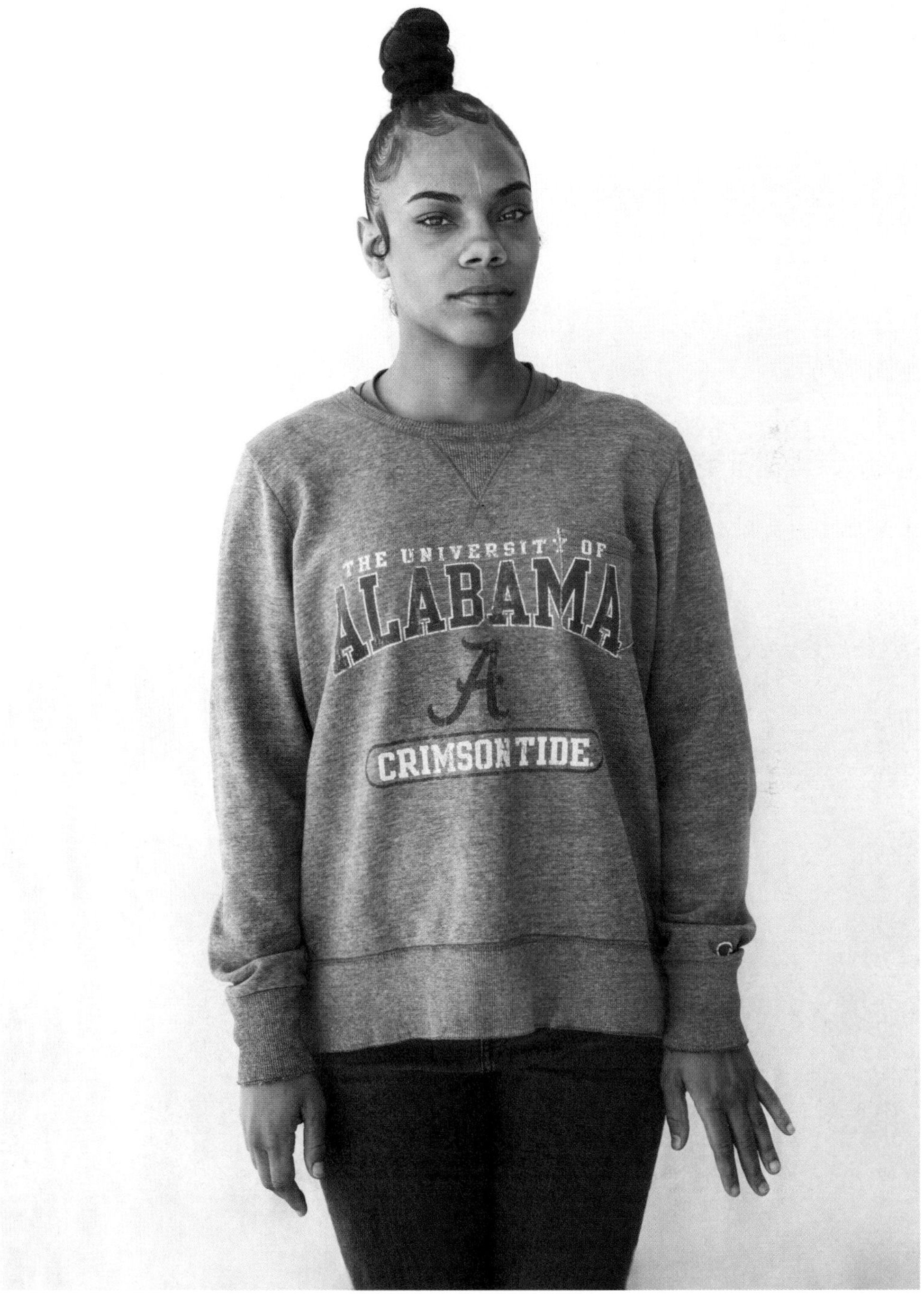

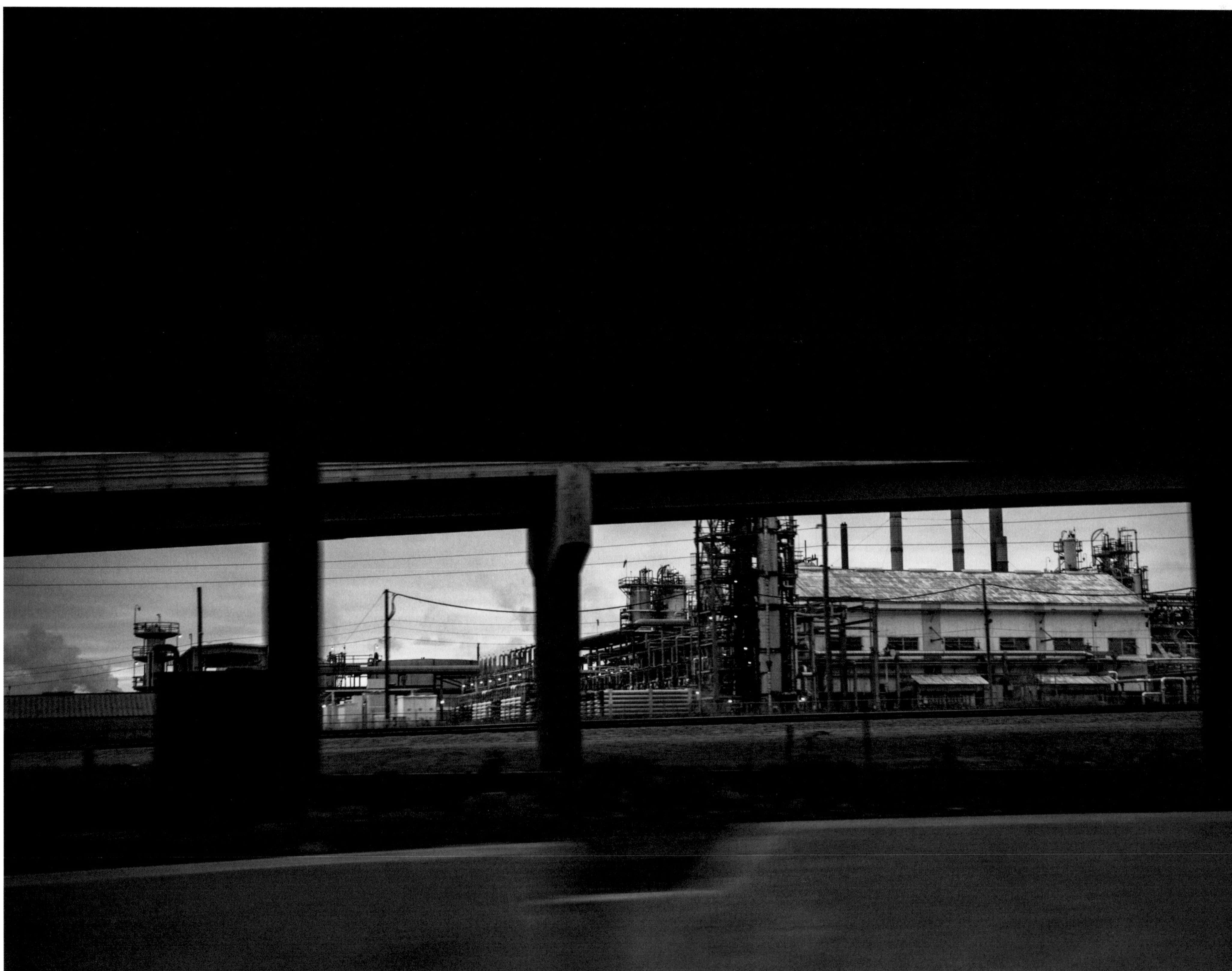

Underpass, Texas

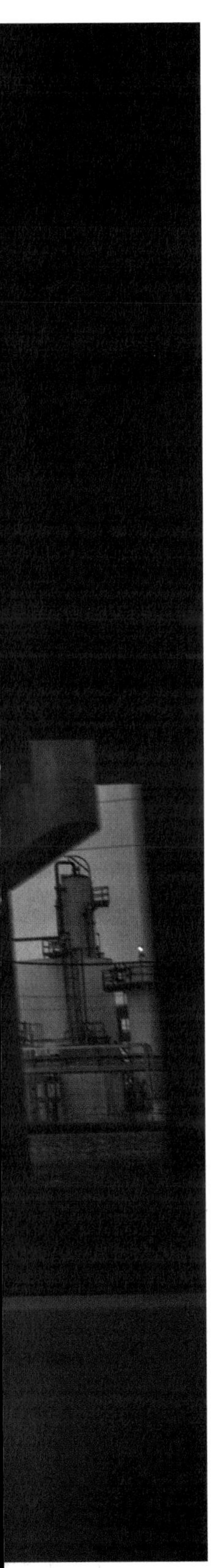

N 35° 41’ 15.395” W 105° 56’ 18.444”

SANTA FE, NEW MEXICO

“America represents freedom, and my dream is to live and let live. I long for equality for everyone. The future is vague and unsure.”

[Paul]

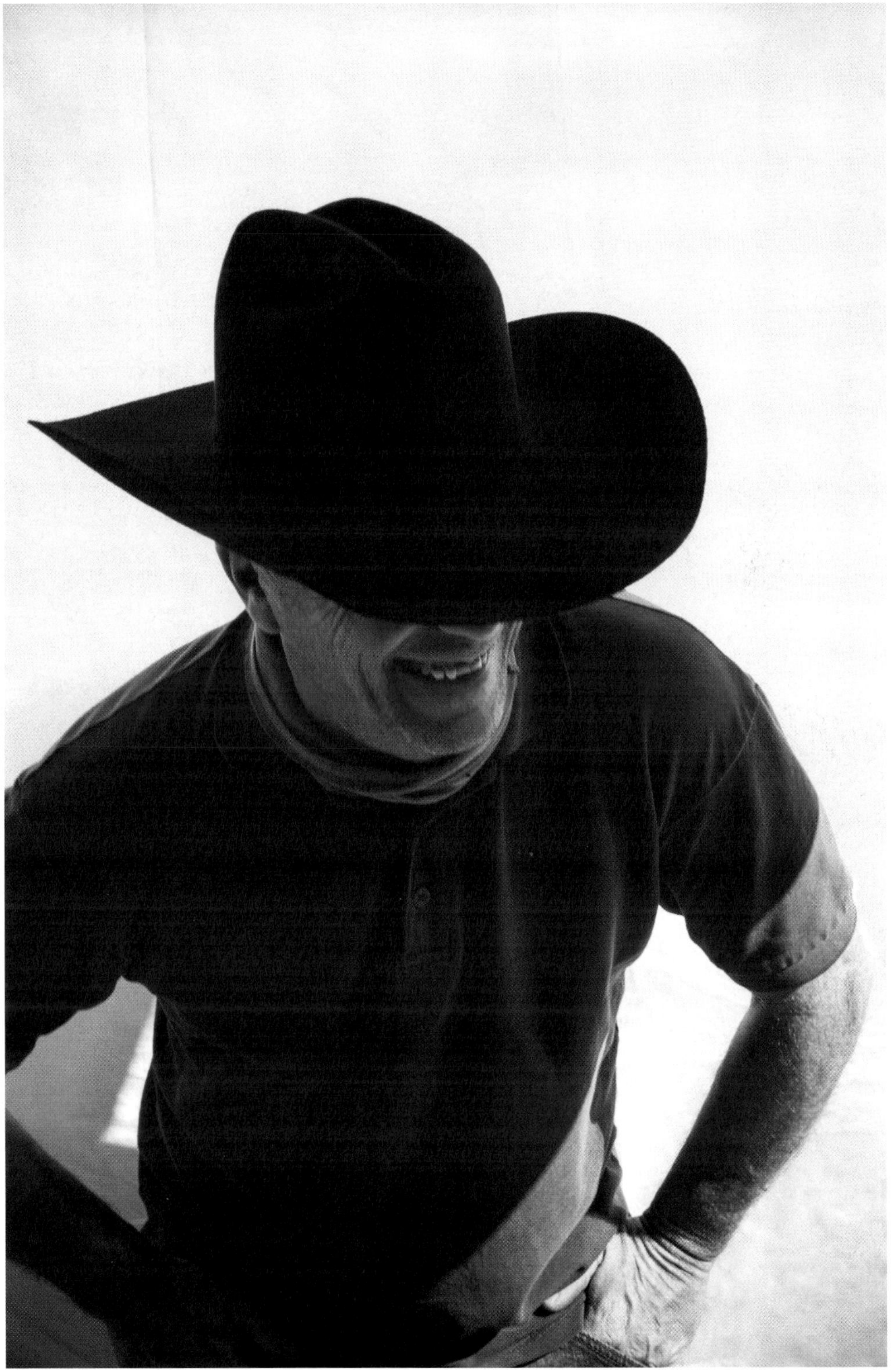

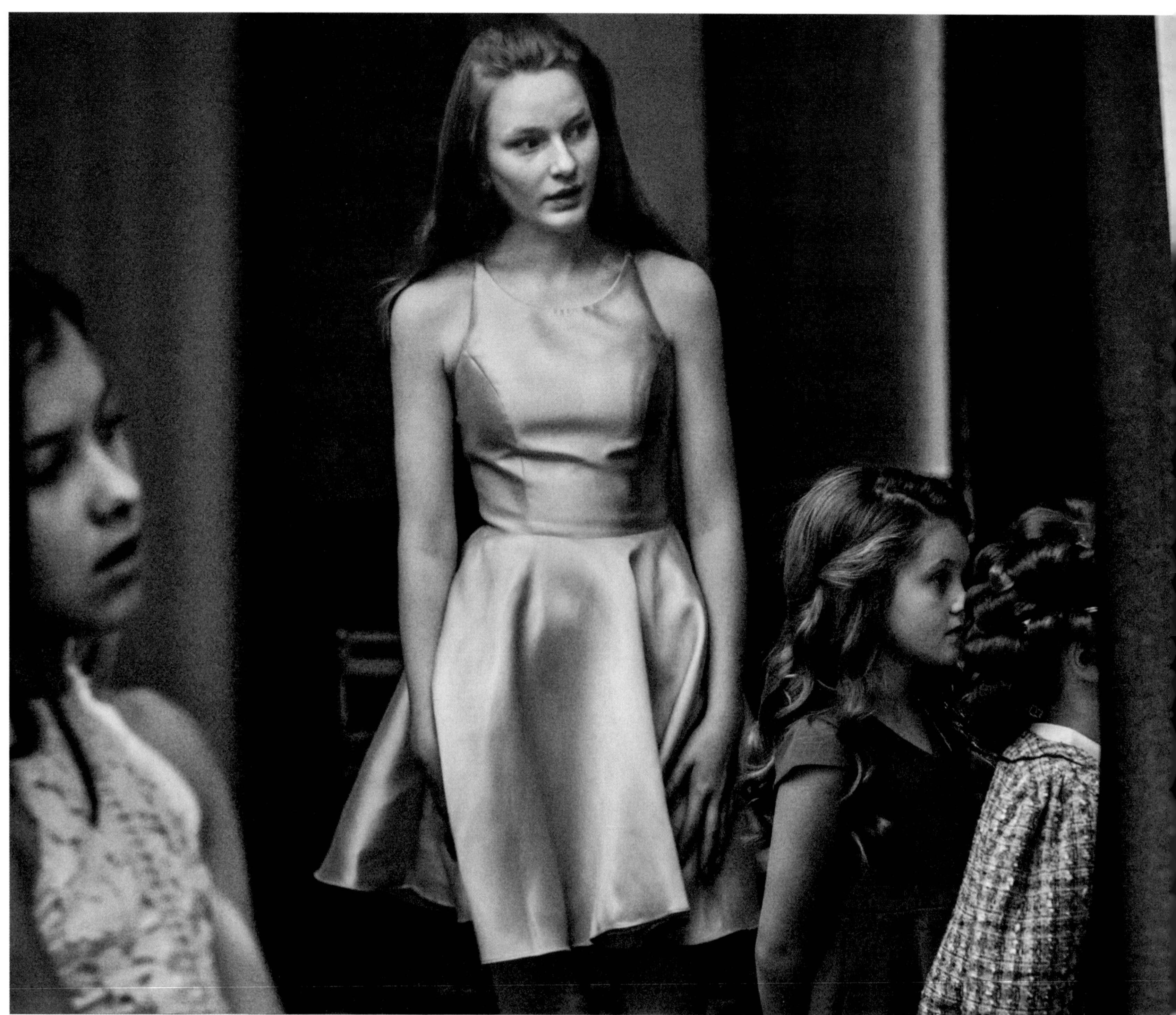

Beauty pageant trophies, Pennsylvania

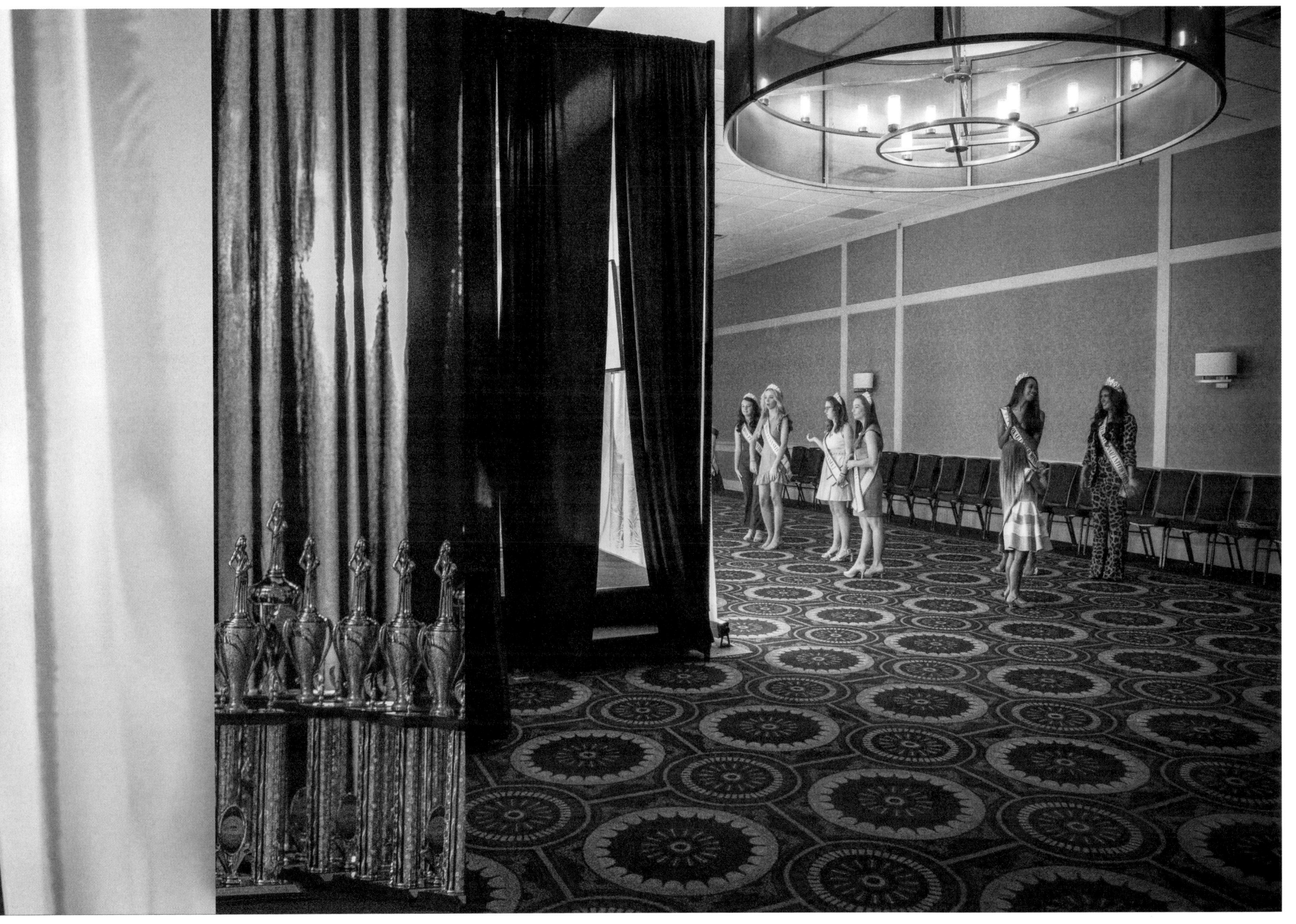

"So come up this way ... you in blue... I try to think of the littlest ones ... perfect, so we can see you. So can we start from where we left off?"

[Beauty pageant announcer, Pennsylvania]

White box, Arizona

N 32° 58’ 40.2204” W 111° 31’ 3.43”

COOLIDGE, ARIZONA

“When I went through breast cancer treatment with all that hair loss, everything disappeared … you know how that goes. It came back a lot different.”

[Eva]

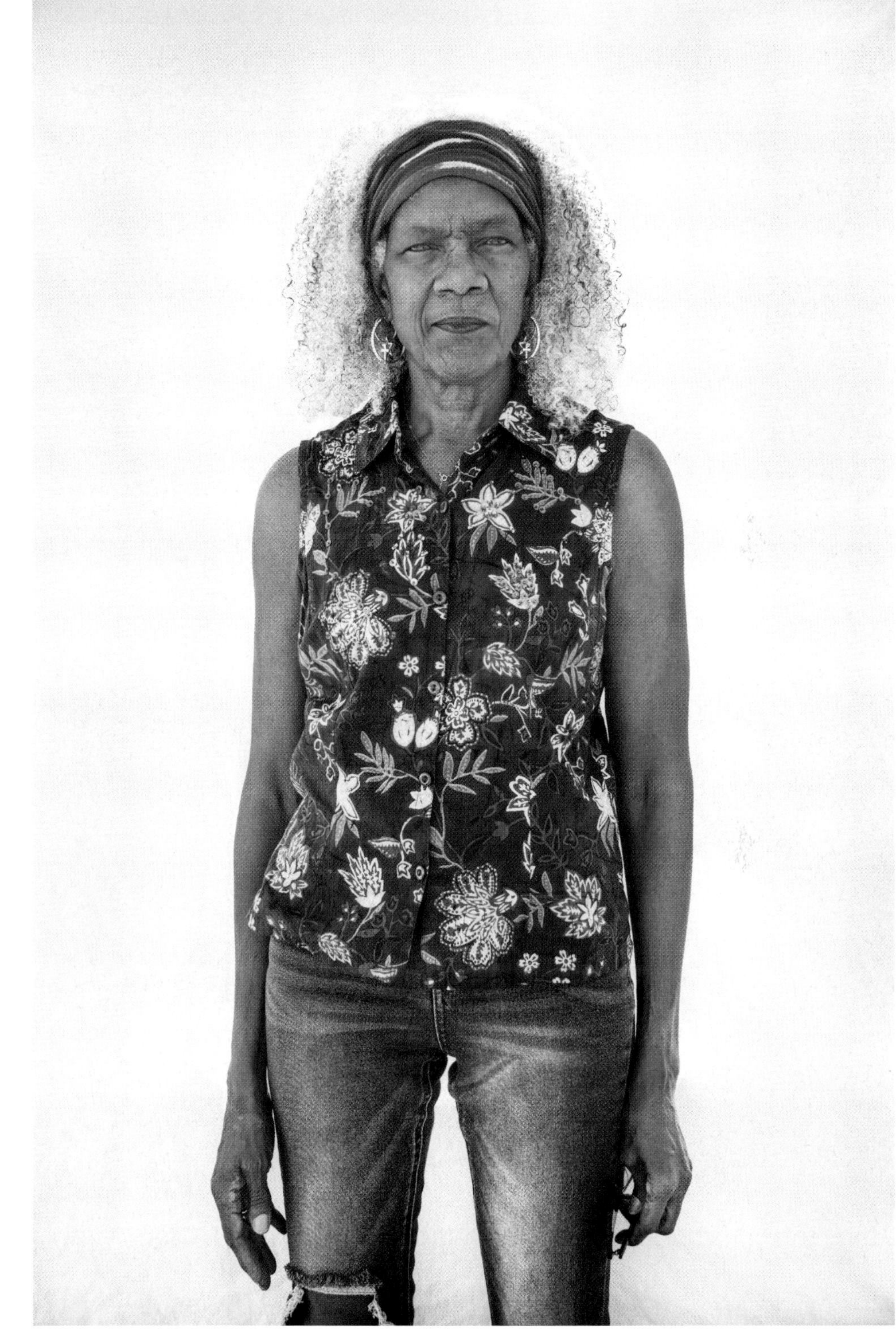

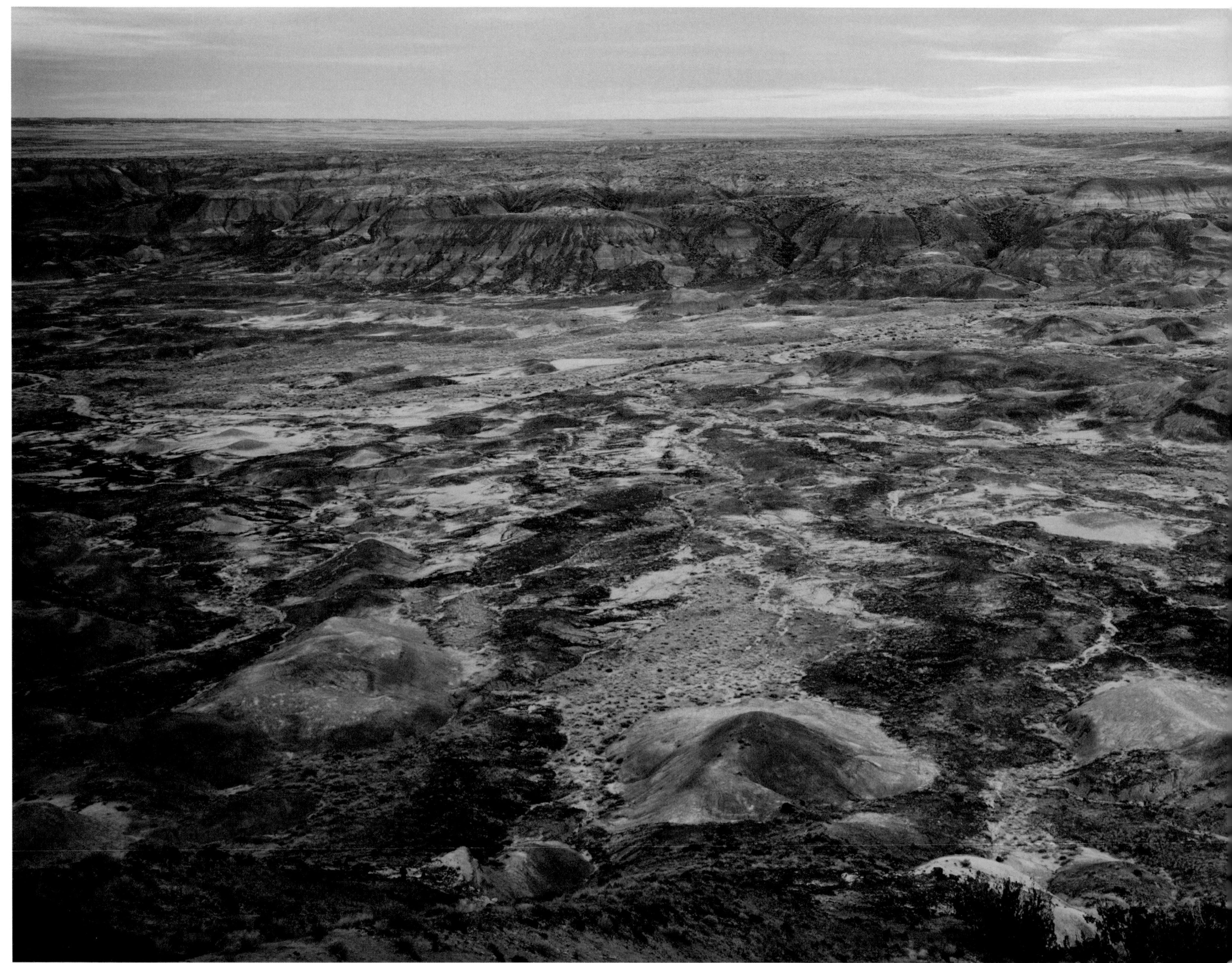

Painted Desert, Arizona

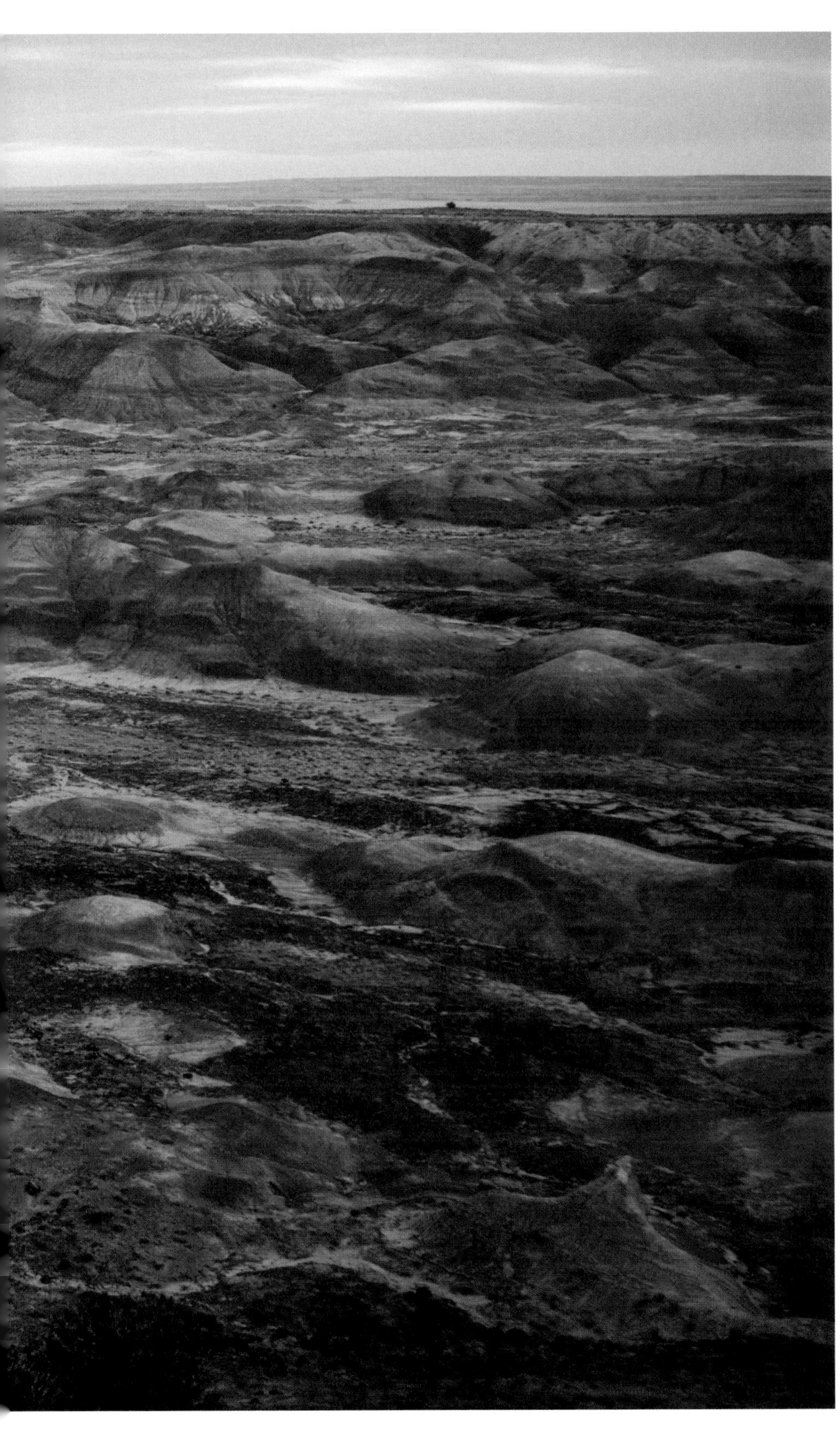

N 36° 8' 12.8616" W 111° 14' 24.6228"

TUBA CITY, ARIZONA

"We call it Mother Earth, Father Sky. Mother Earth is taking care of us on the ground and the surrounding areas. Father Sky is providing the light and the night and the day. In our Navajo tradition, we have four different worlds. The First World was when the animals and the plants came. The Second World was when humans came. The Third World is where we all evolve. In the Third World, a lot of harm was caused because there was so much negativity that we had to escape to the Fourth World to balance out. Now we're in the Fourth World. We're all together equally and we're all talking and being good with one another: humans, animals, plants and nature."

[Francine]

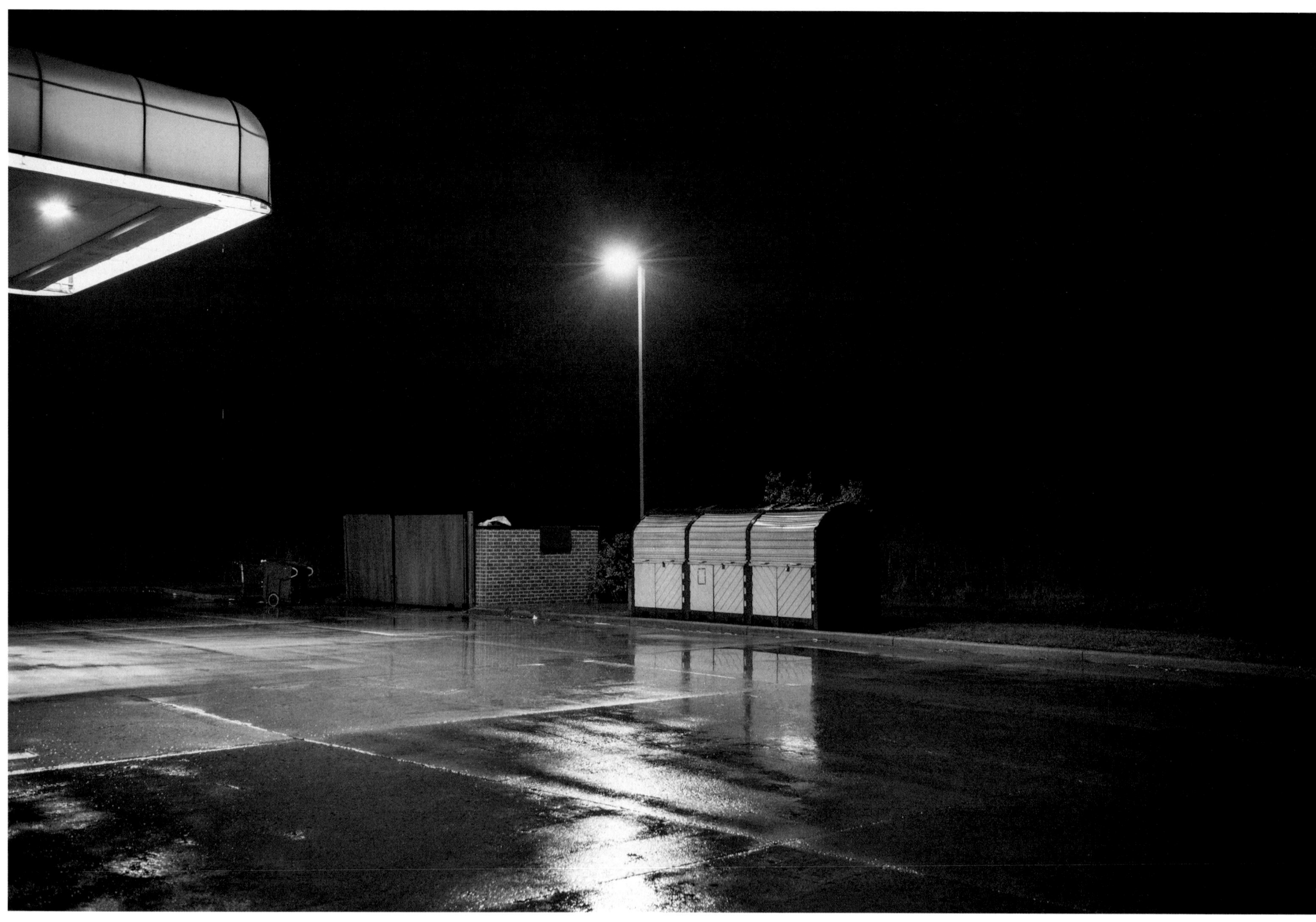

Trash bins, Pennsylvania

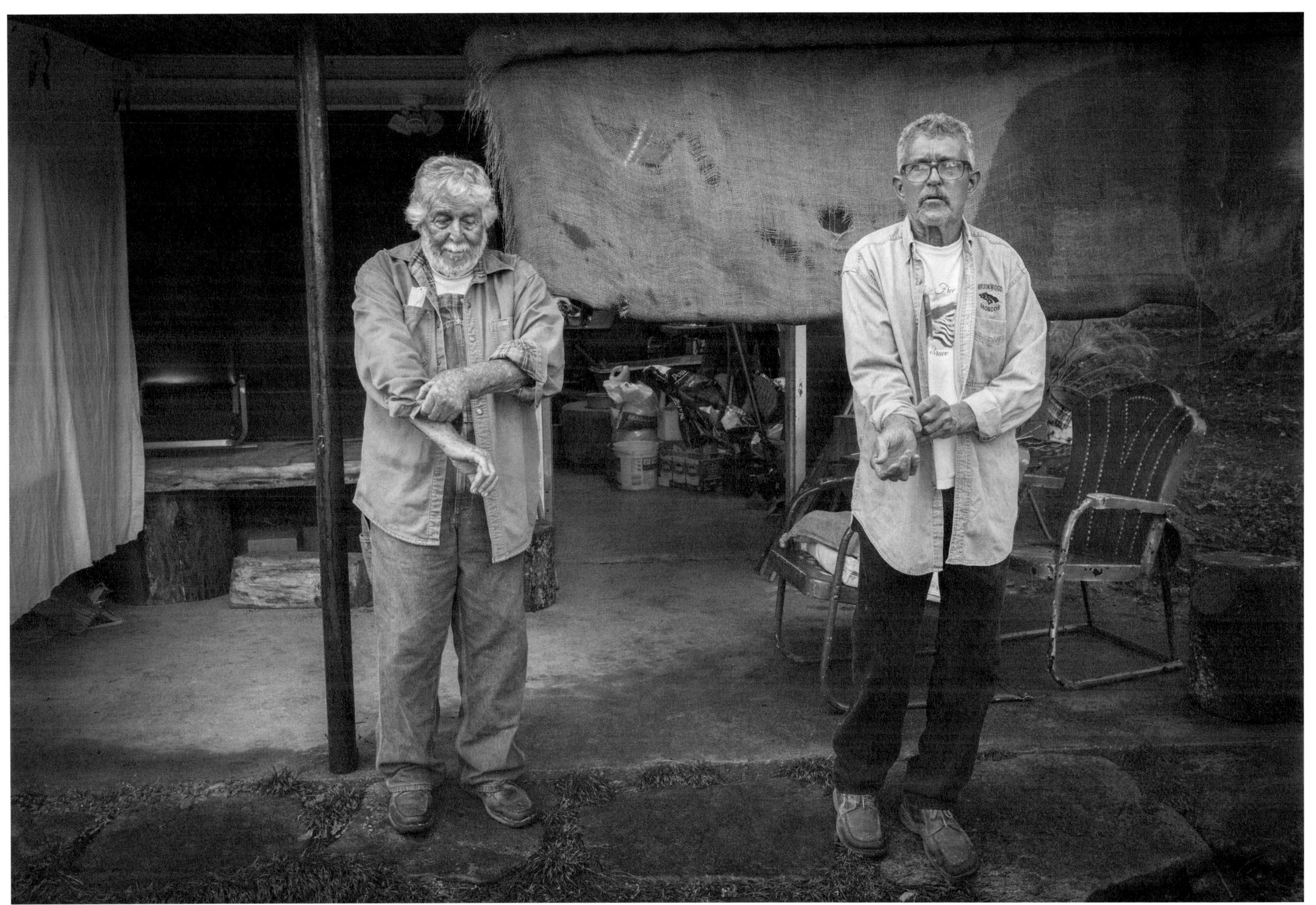

Mickey and Jerry, Georgia

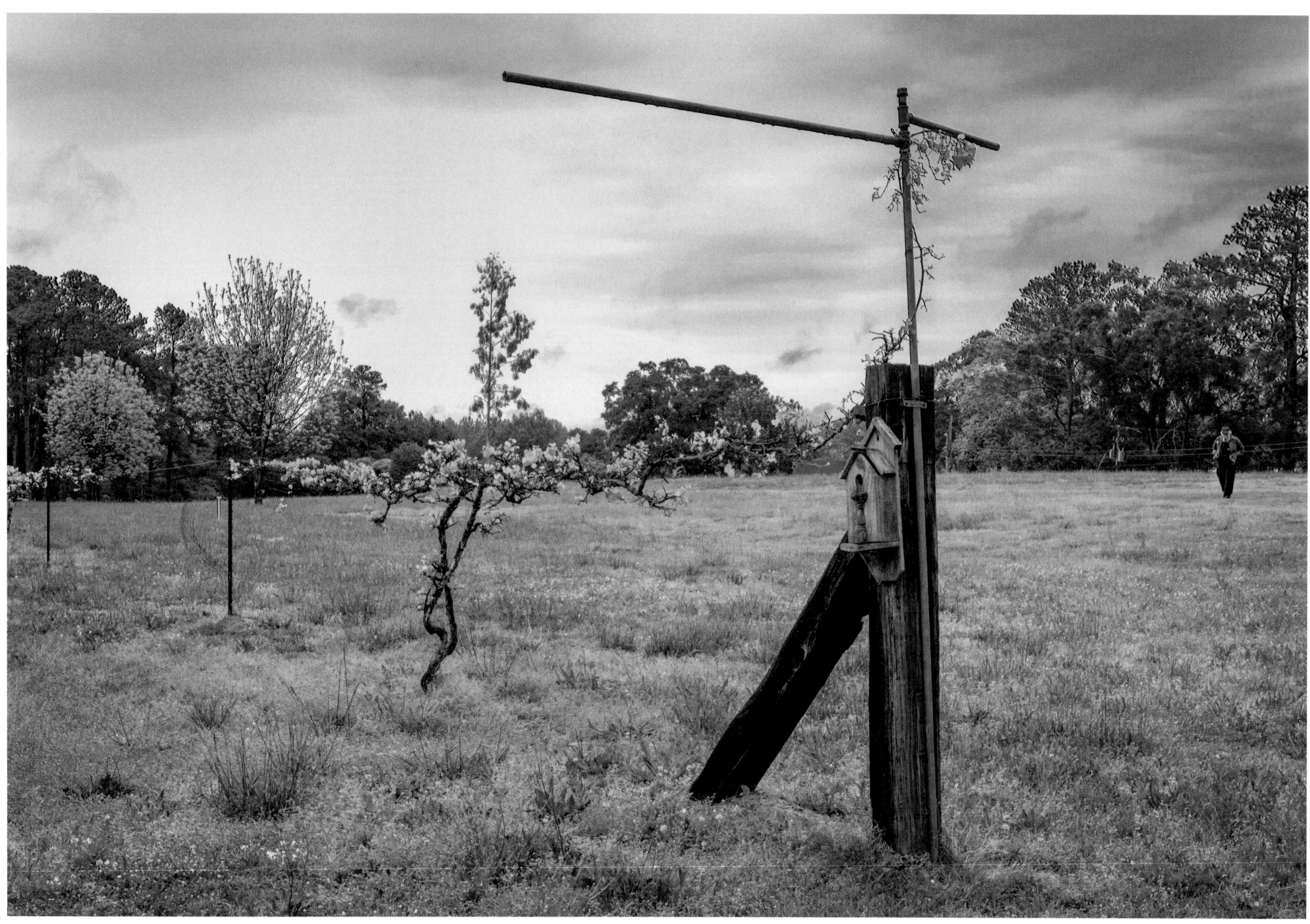

Bird house, Georgia

N 33° 35' 31.3944" W 84° 16' 11.792"

REX, GEORGIA

"When my brother and I came to Rex, we were the only Jewish people around. We started a nursery together."

[Mickey]

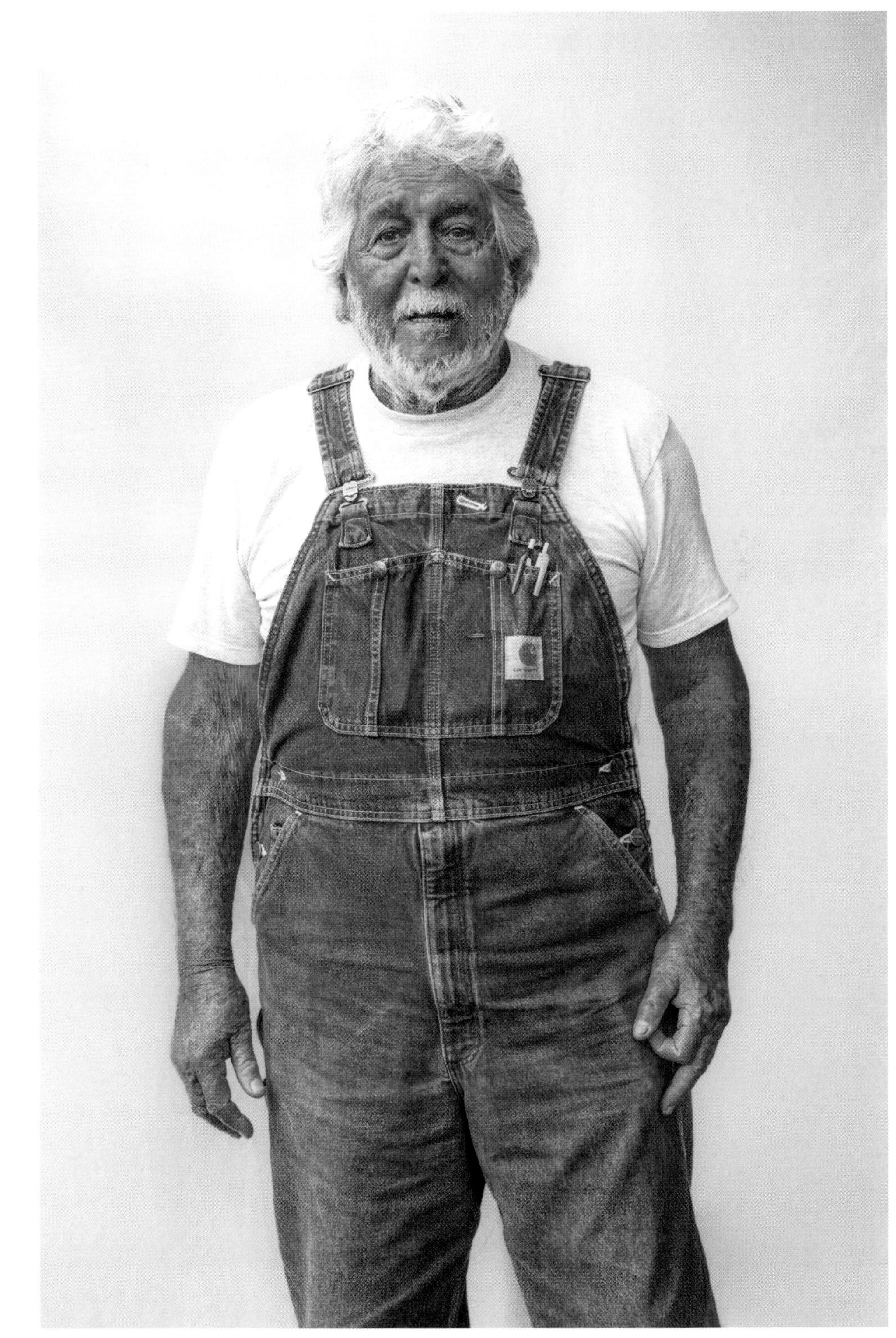

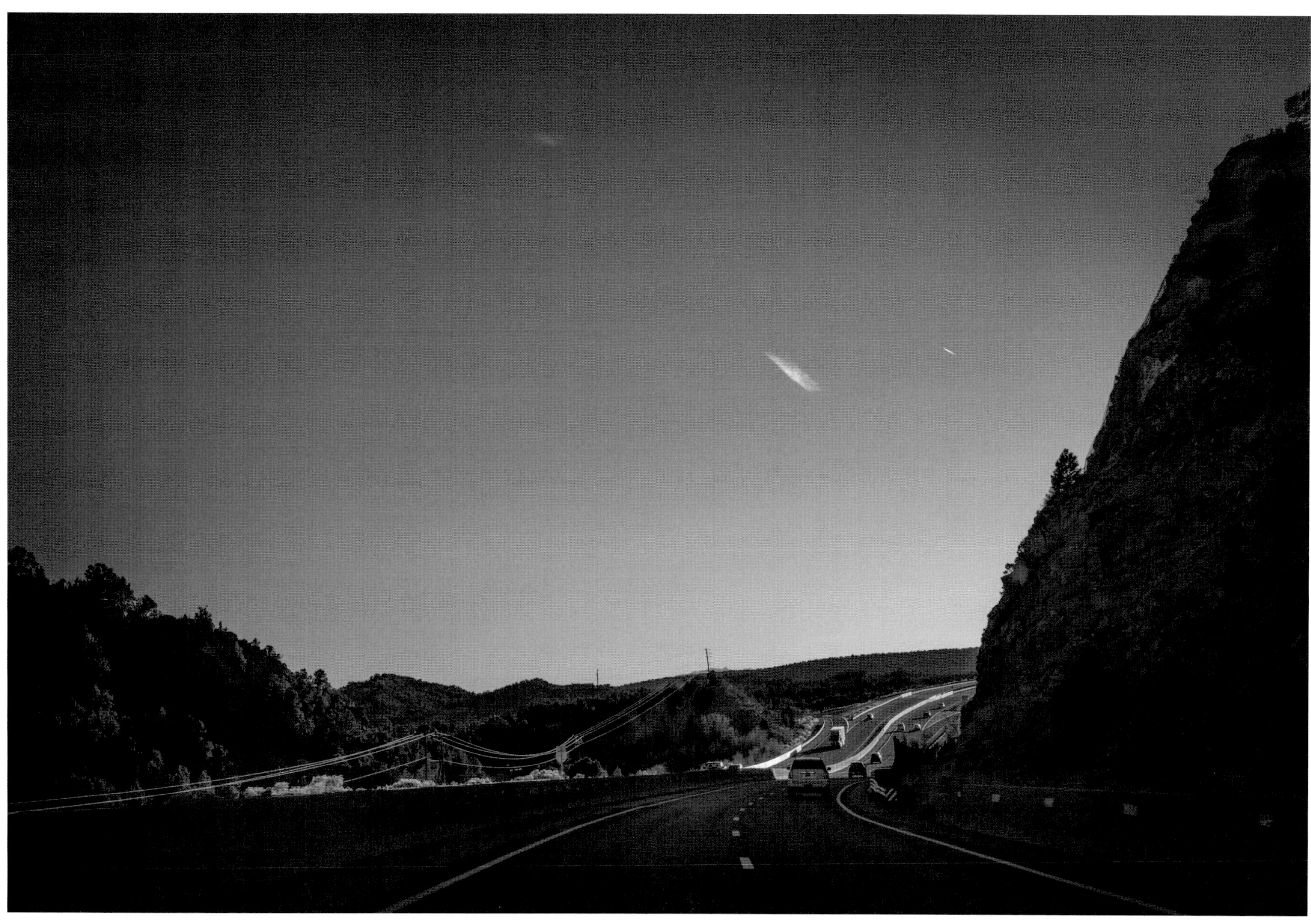

Highway afternoon, New Mexico

N 30° 15’ 9.342” W 93° 0’ 49.568”

IOWA, LOUISIANA

“Right now, all I wanna do is truck driving.”

[Kadan]

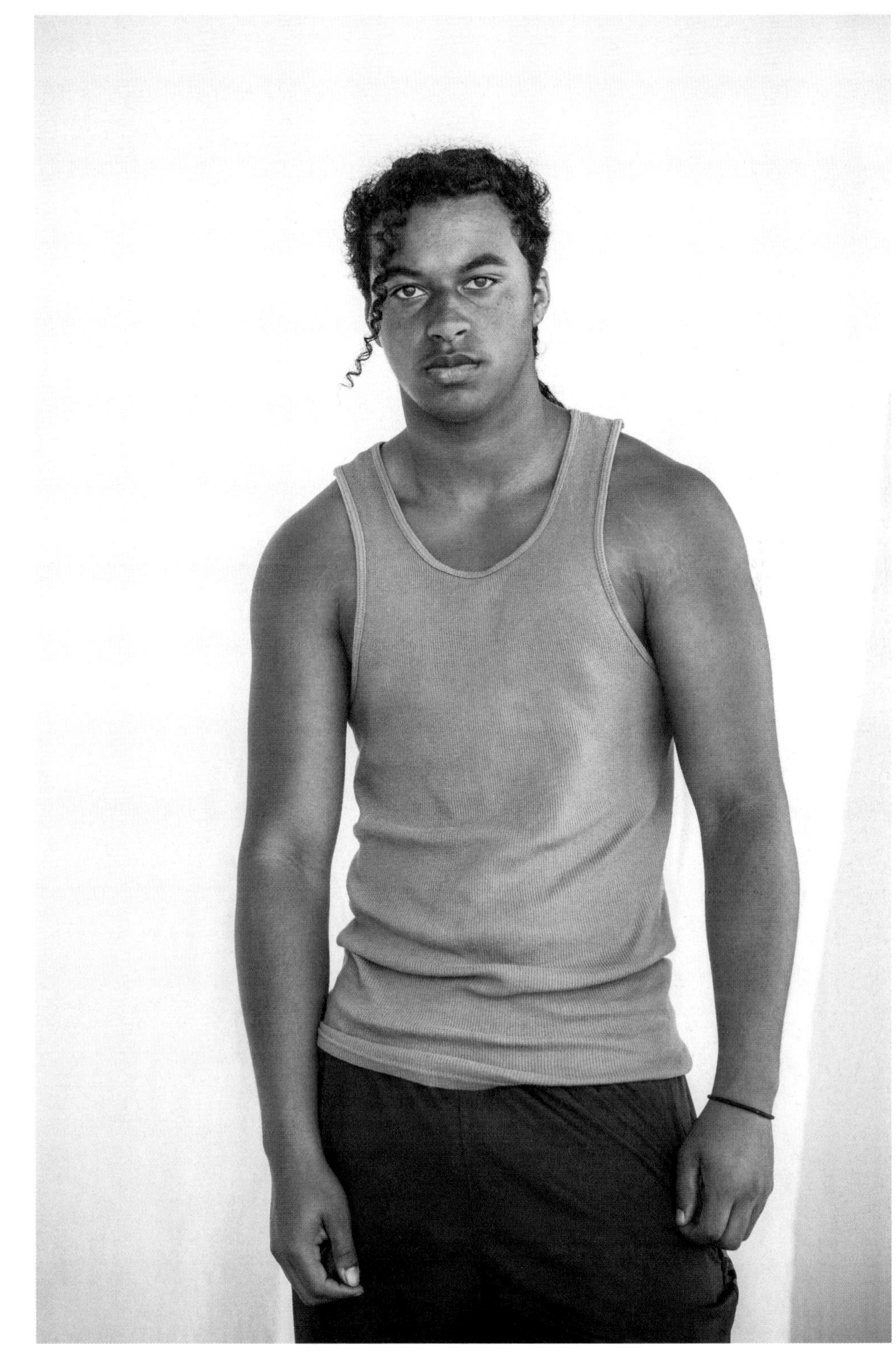

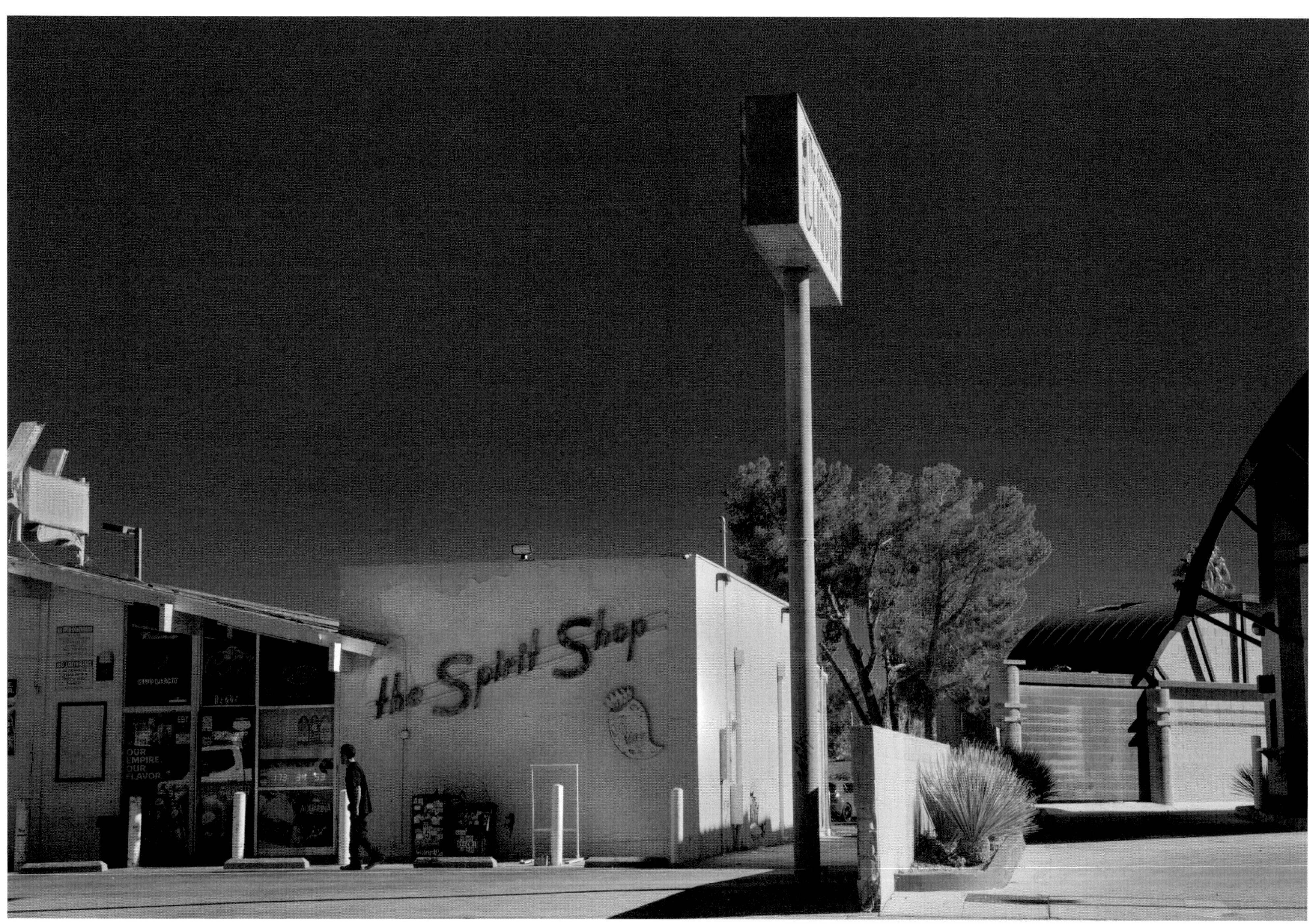

The Spirit Shop, California

N 30° 15’ 59.9976” W 97° 43’ 59.9880”

AUSTIN, TEXAS

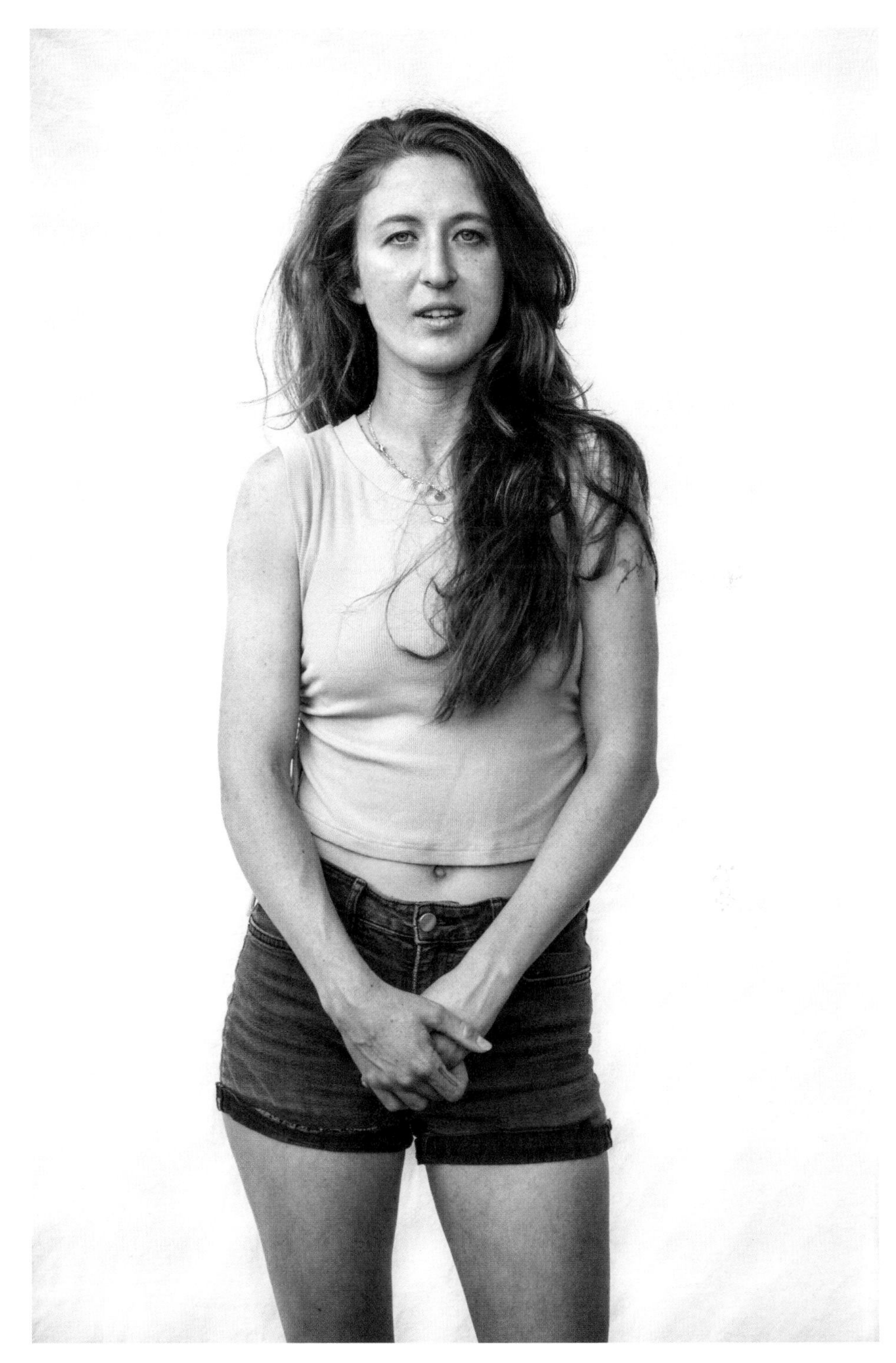

Rain, Texas

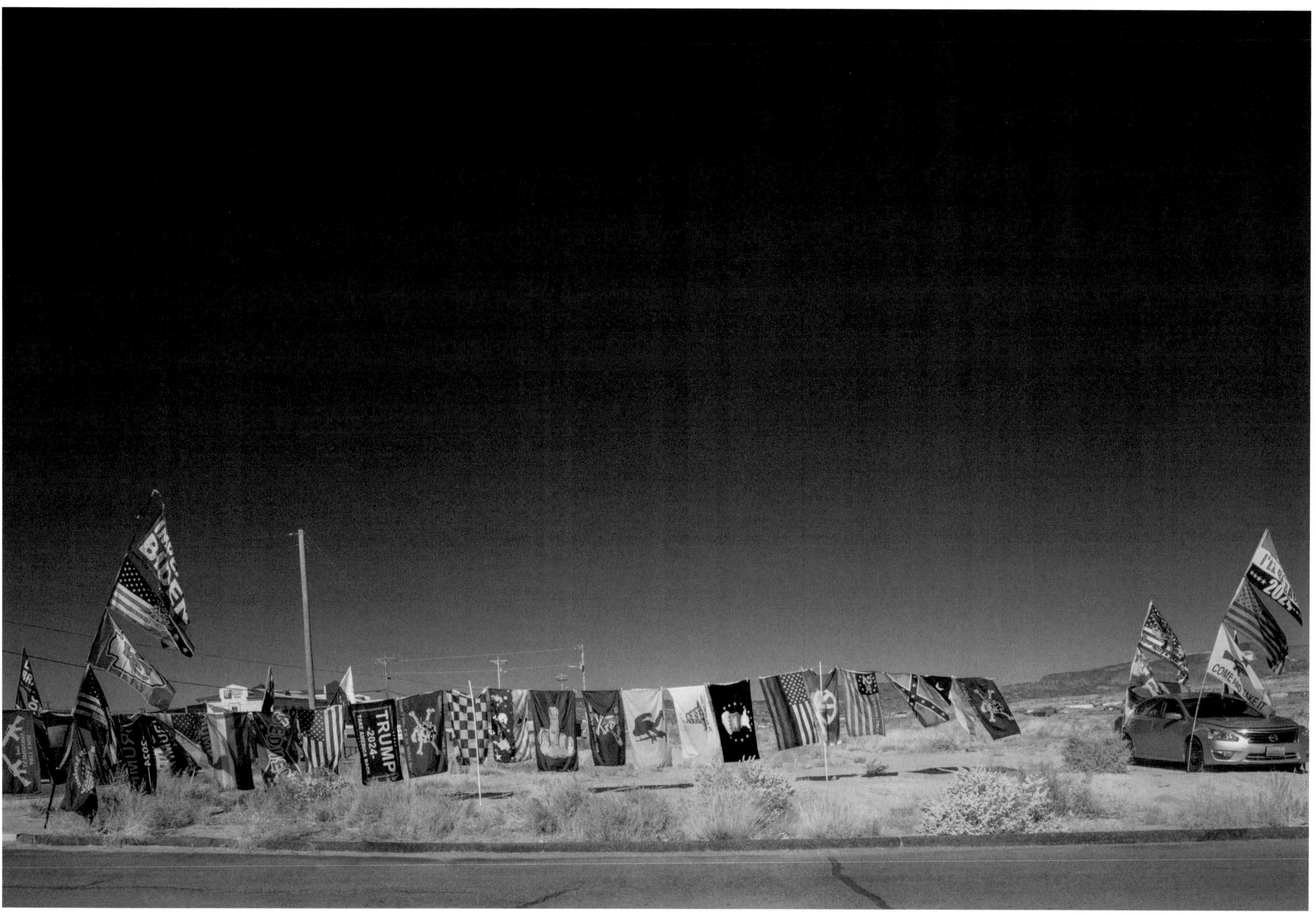

Flag sale, Arizona

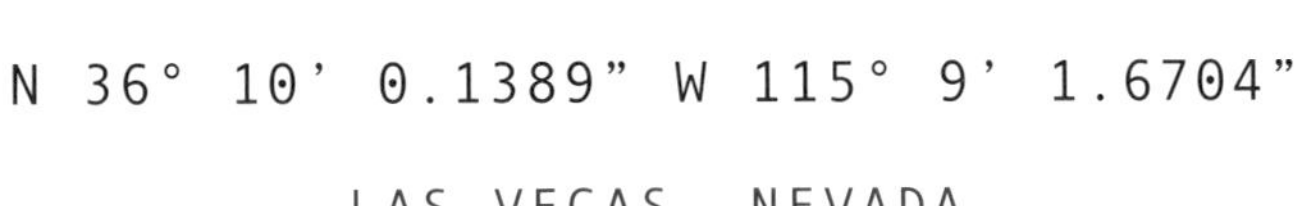

N 36° 10’ 0.1389” W 115° 9’ 1.6704”

LAS VEGAS, NEVADA

“Any time I meet a new person, my priority is to learn about them and see how our worlds relate. I dream about a world where I can provide for all the people I love. Love is free, so it’s not limited to how much you can put into the world.”

[Katriel]

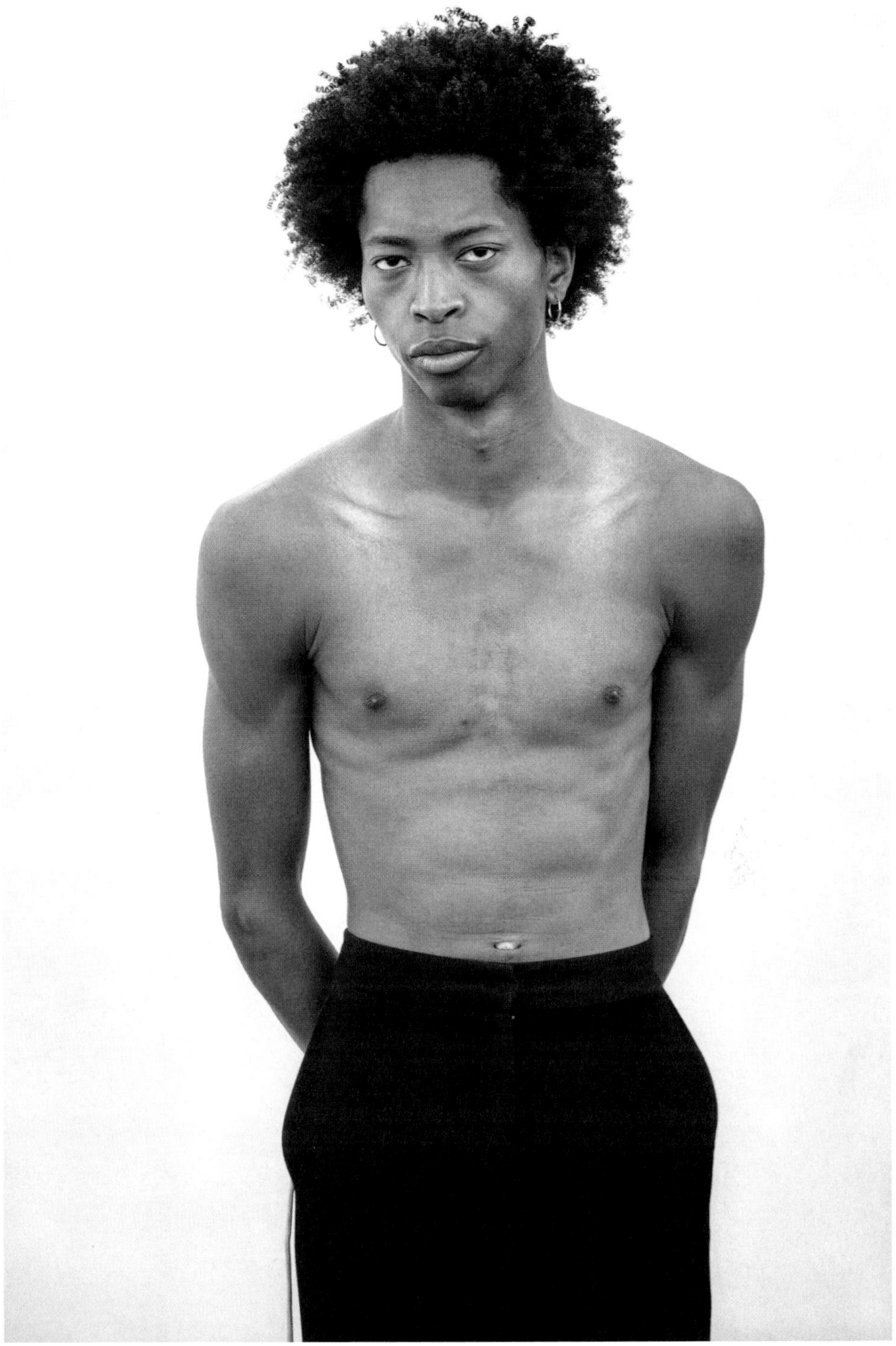

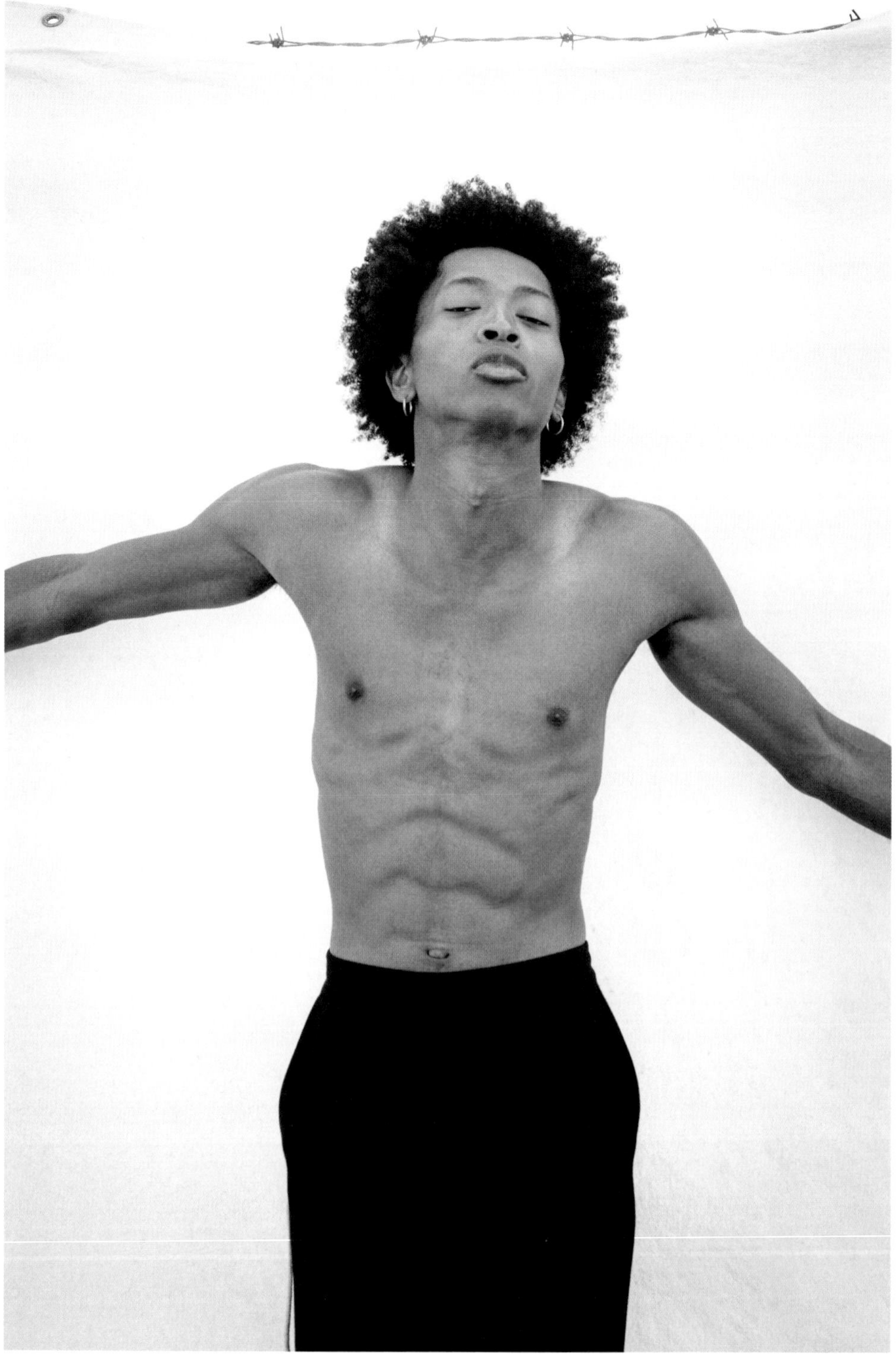

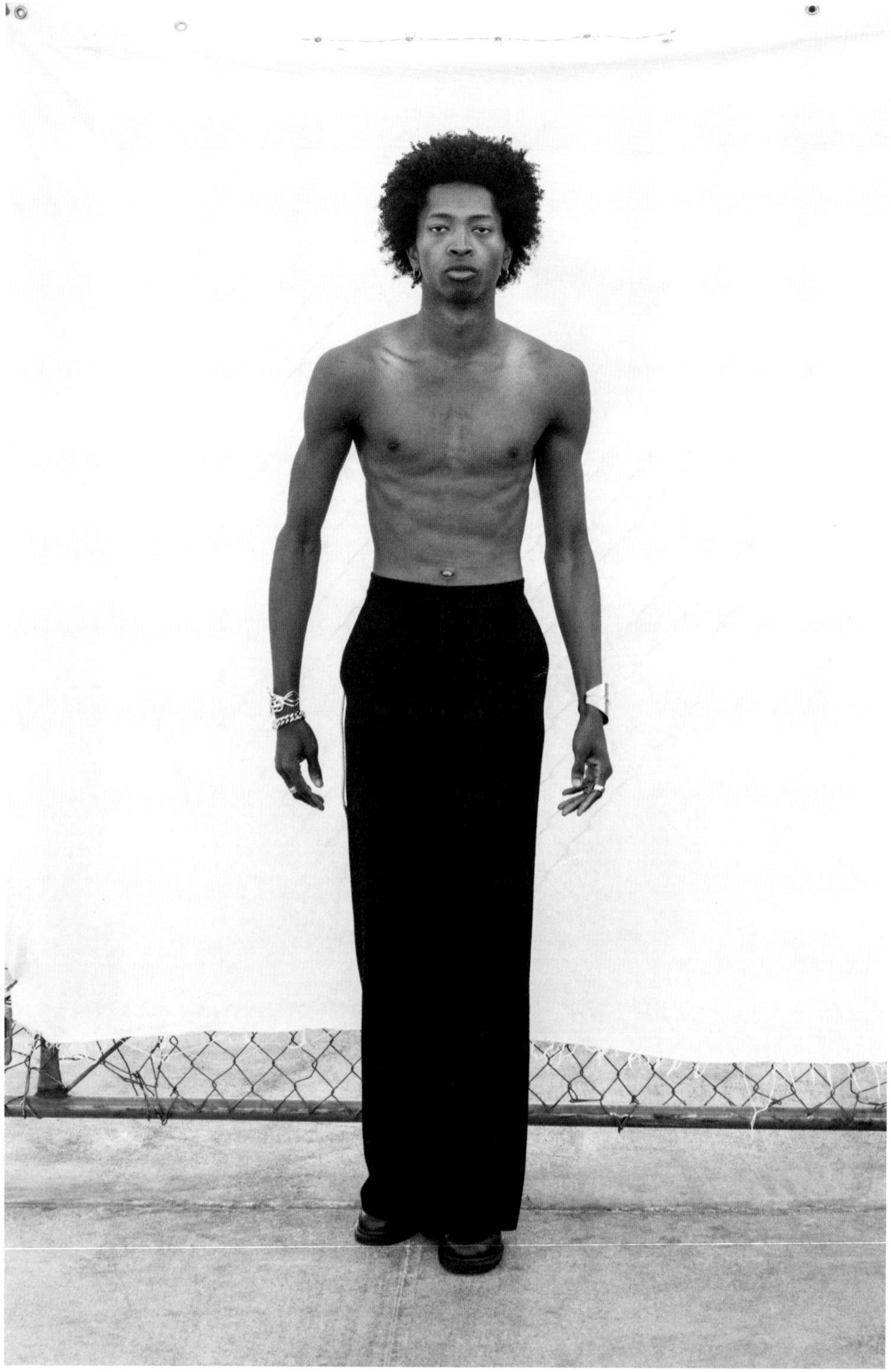

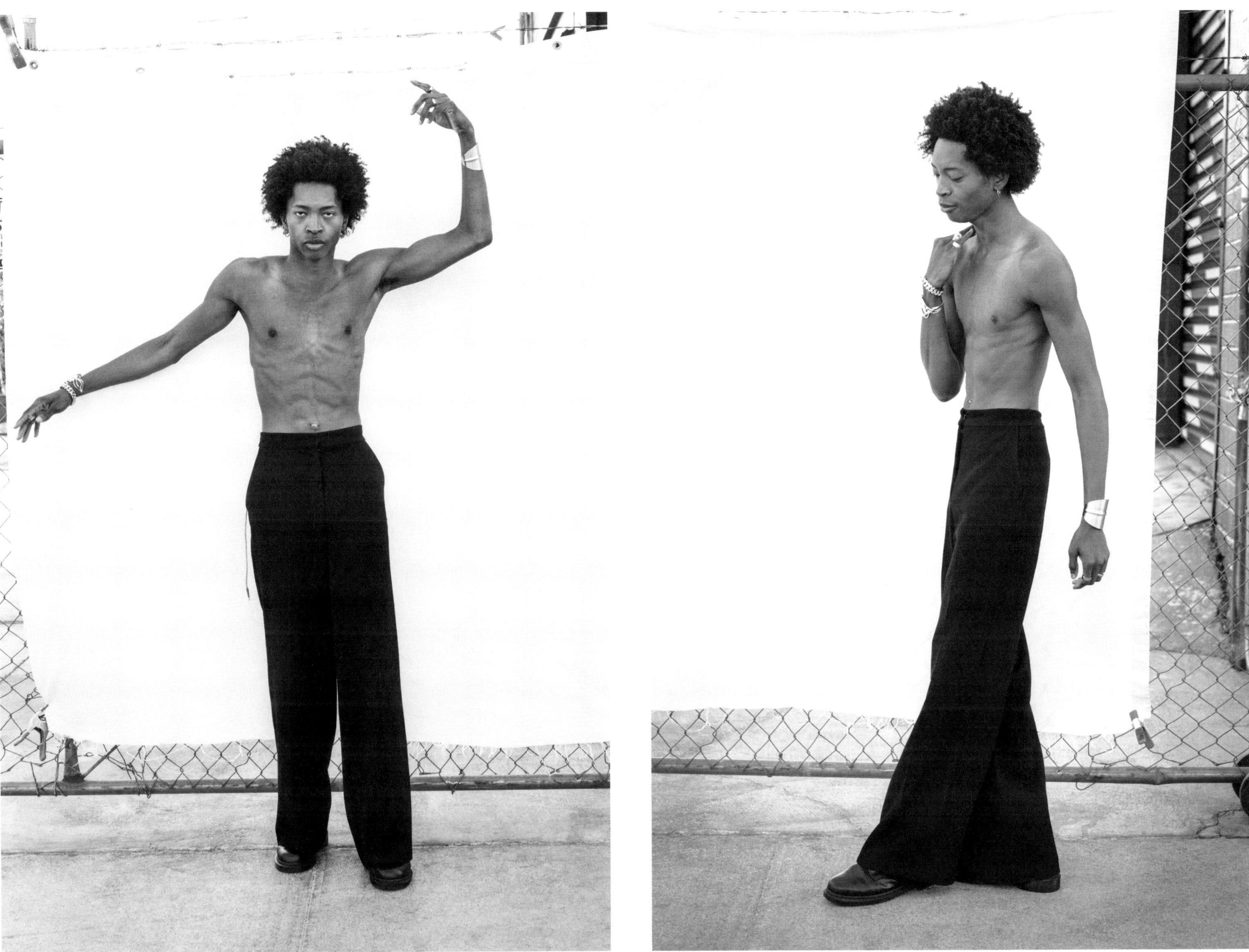

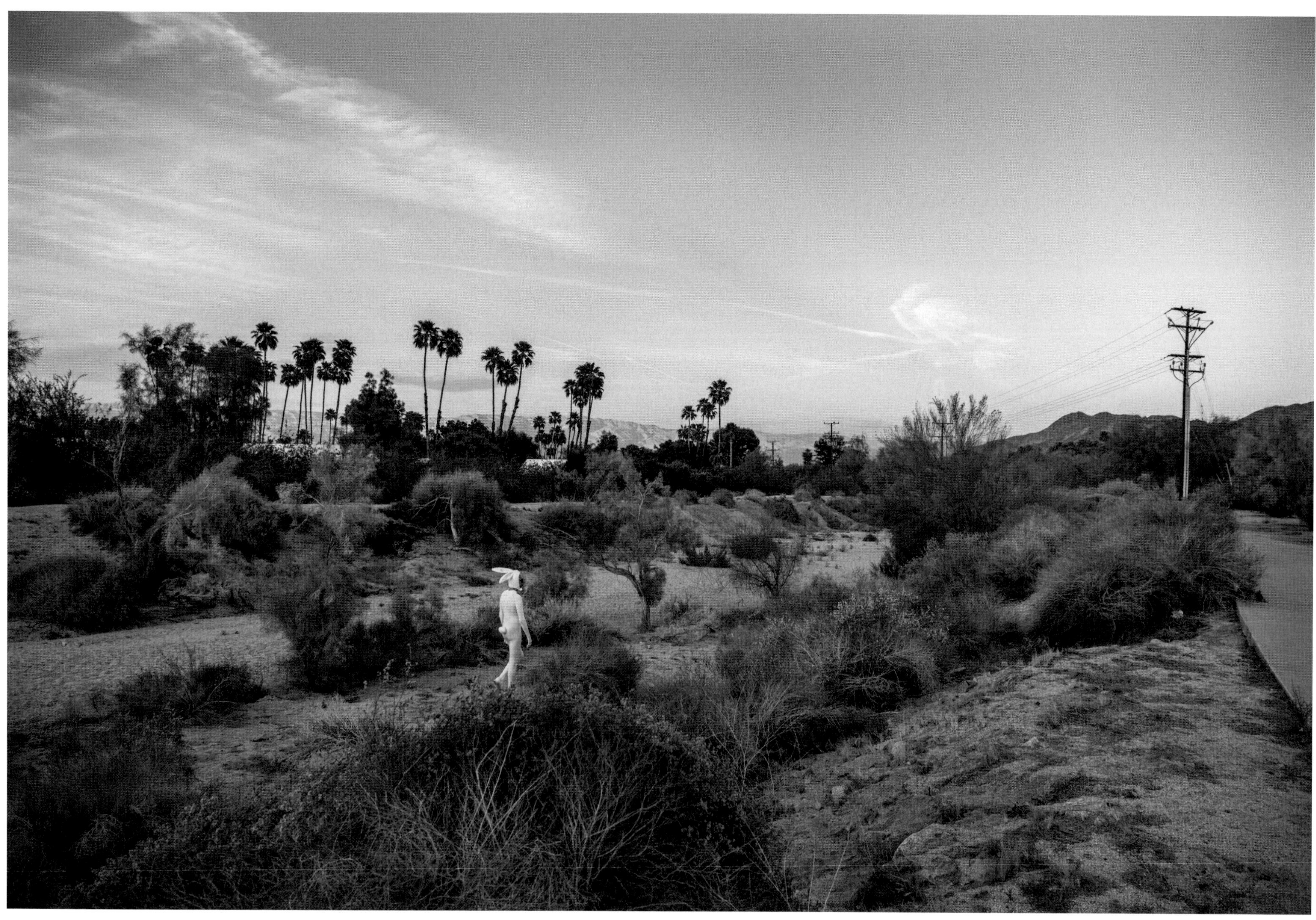

Rabbit, California

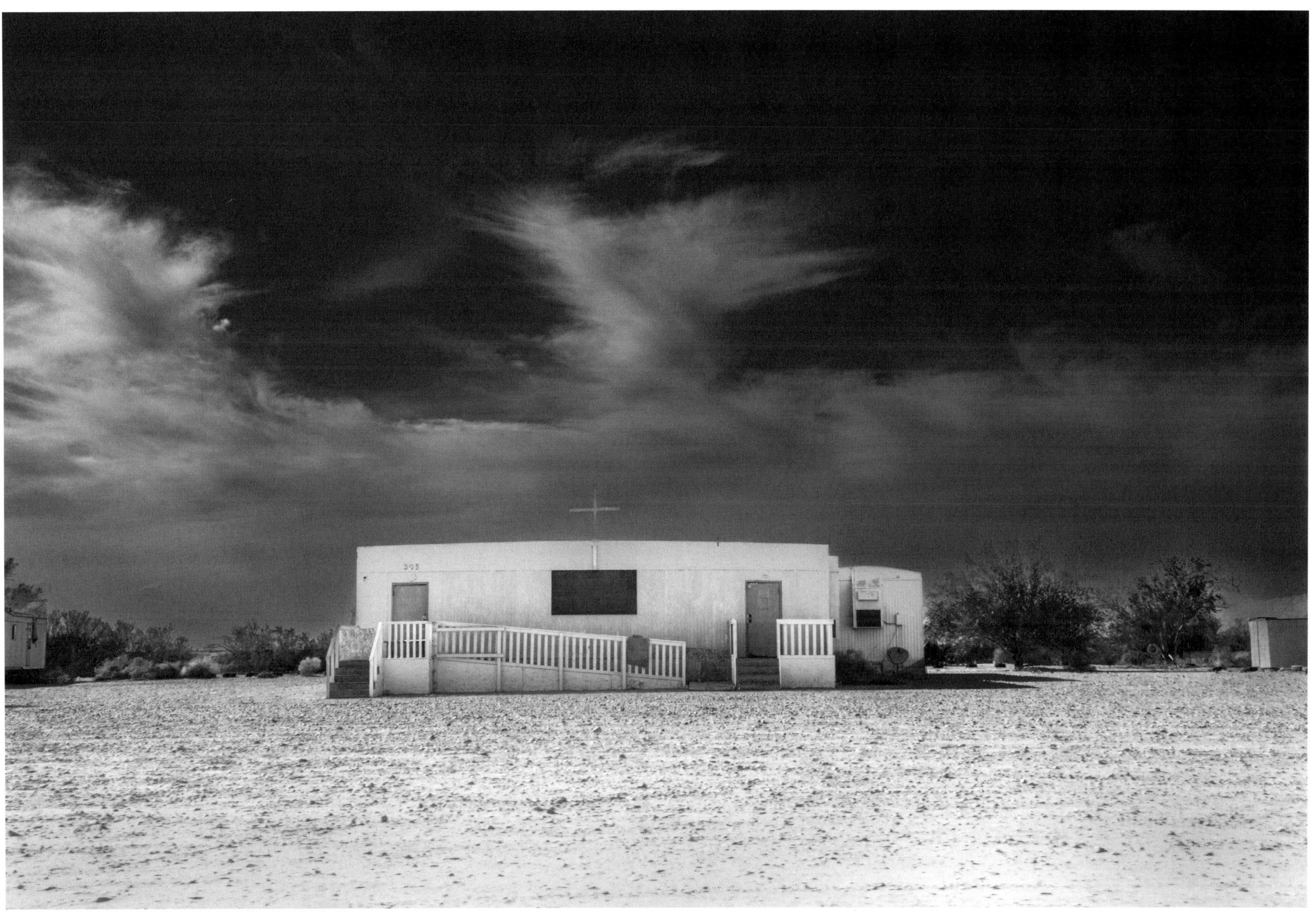

Devotion trailer, California

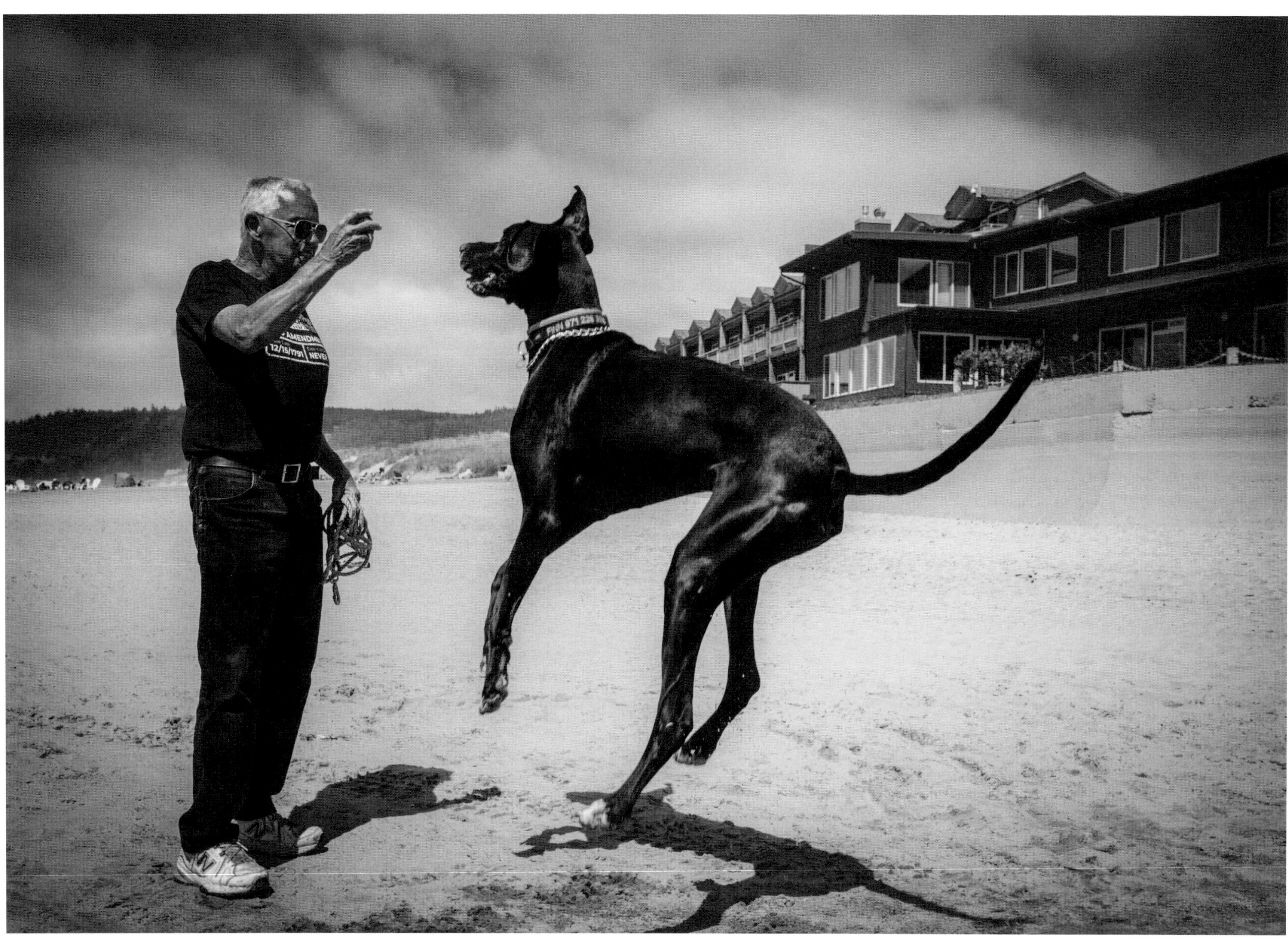

Great Dane jumping, Oregon

N 45° 53' 30.3864" W 123° 57' 41.4972"

CANNON BEACH, OREGON

"This is my gun permit.
Name: 2nd Amendment
Issue Date: 12/15/1791
Expiration Date: Never"

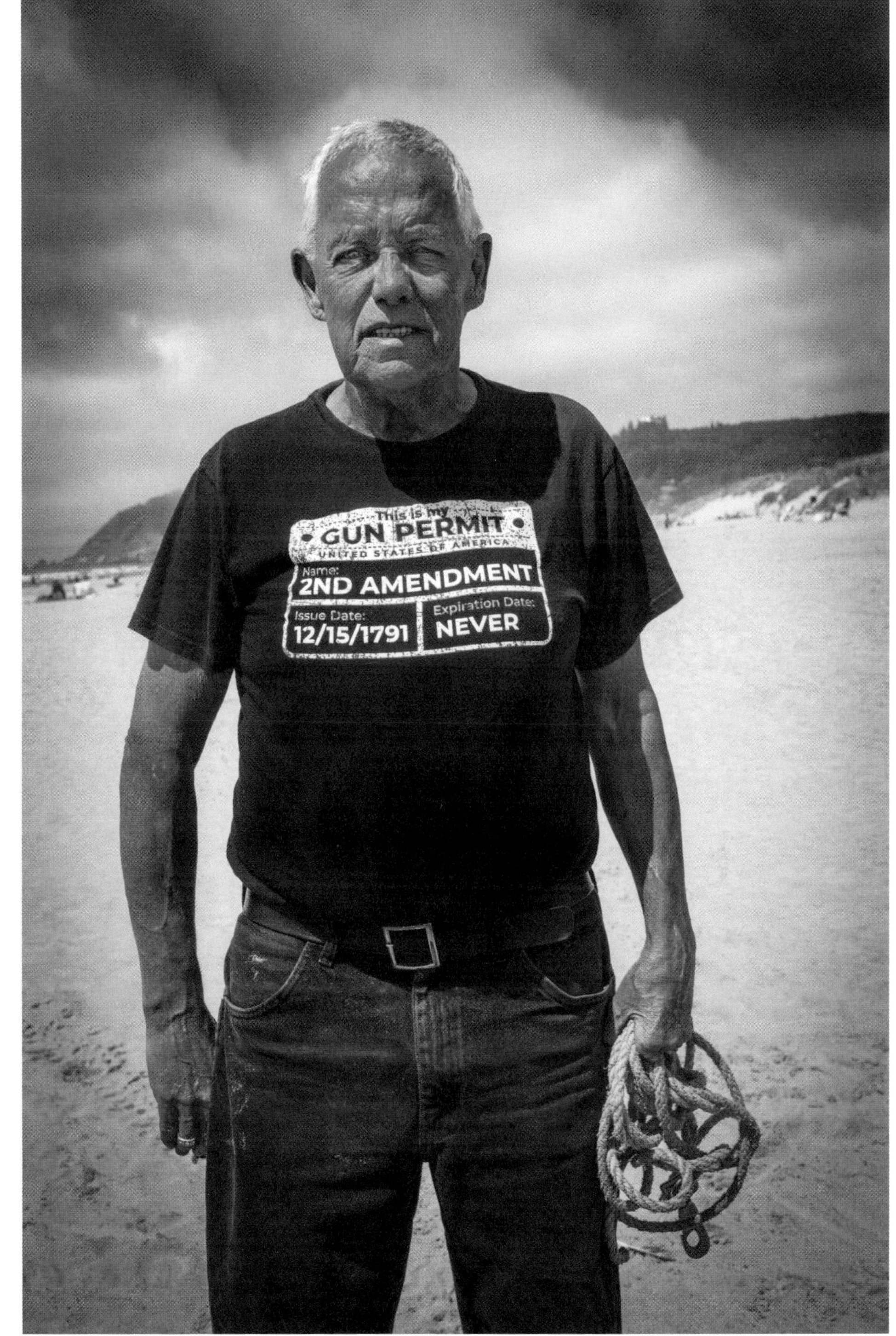

Cannon Beach gun permit, Oregon

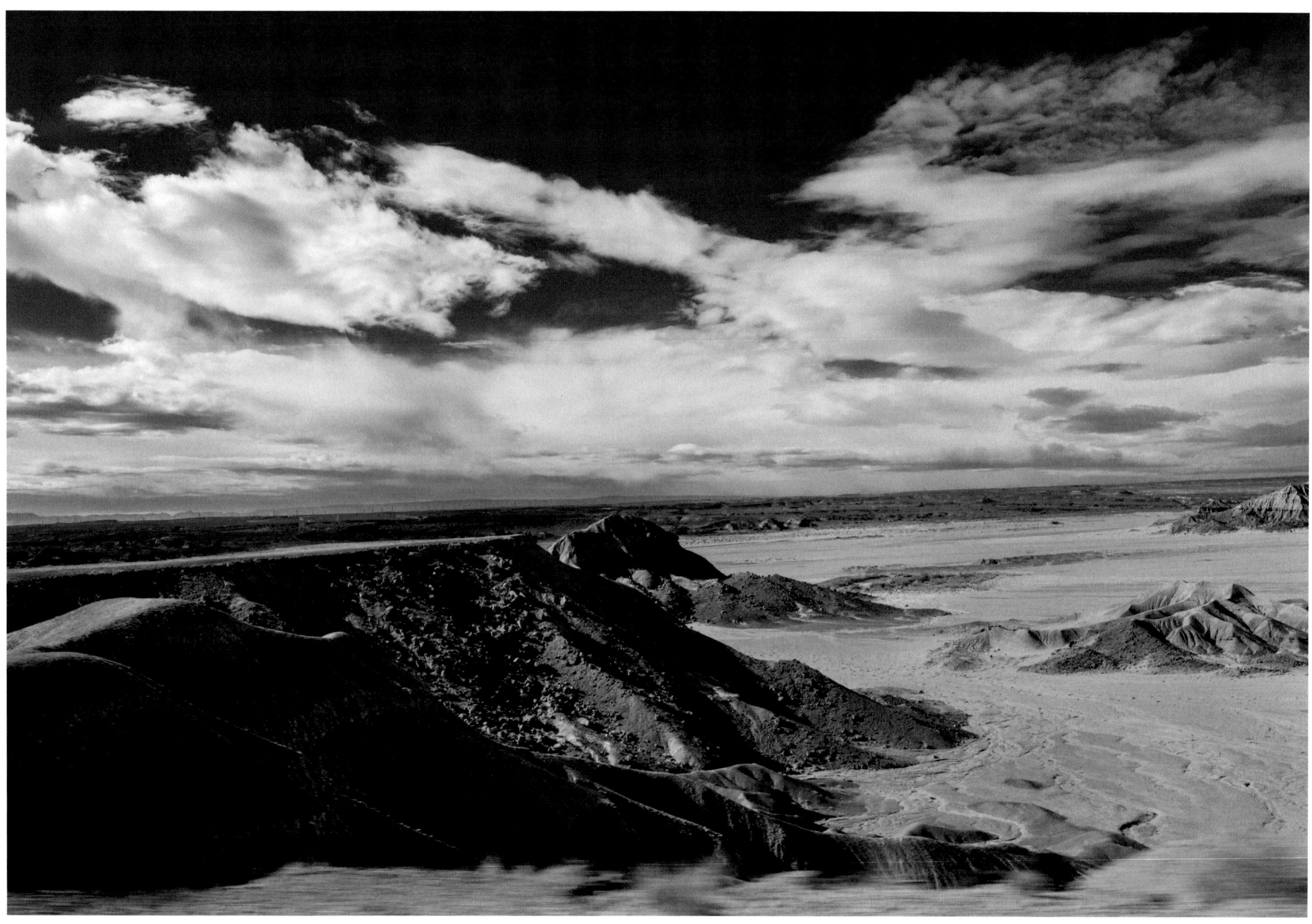

Dunes, Arizona

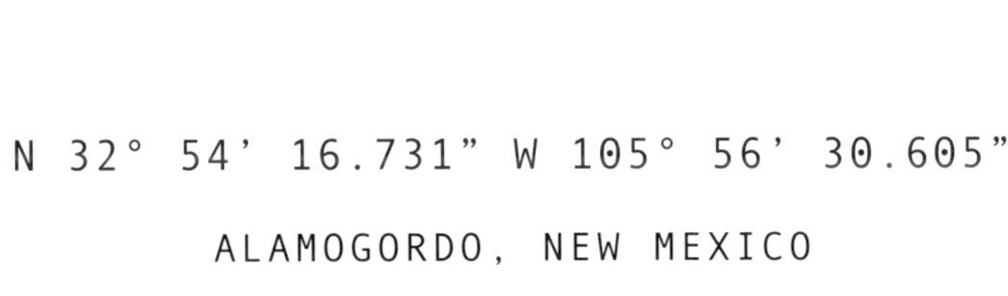

N 32° 54’ 16.731” W 105° 56’ 30.605”

ALAMOGORDO, NEW MEXICO

“My great uncle was born in 1922 on the Mescalero Apache Reservation. He was the first white child to be born on the reservation and helped to keep New Mexico as New Mexico, and not give it to Mexico. I have Native American cousins, because my family married into the tribe. People who come into the restaurant ask ‘You’re calling them cousins?’ Well, they are my cousins!”

[Sunny]

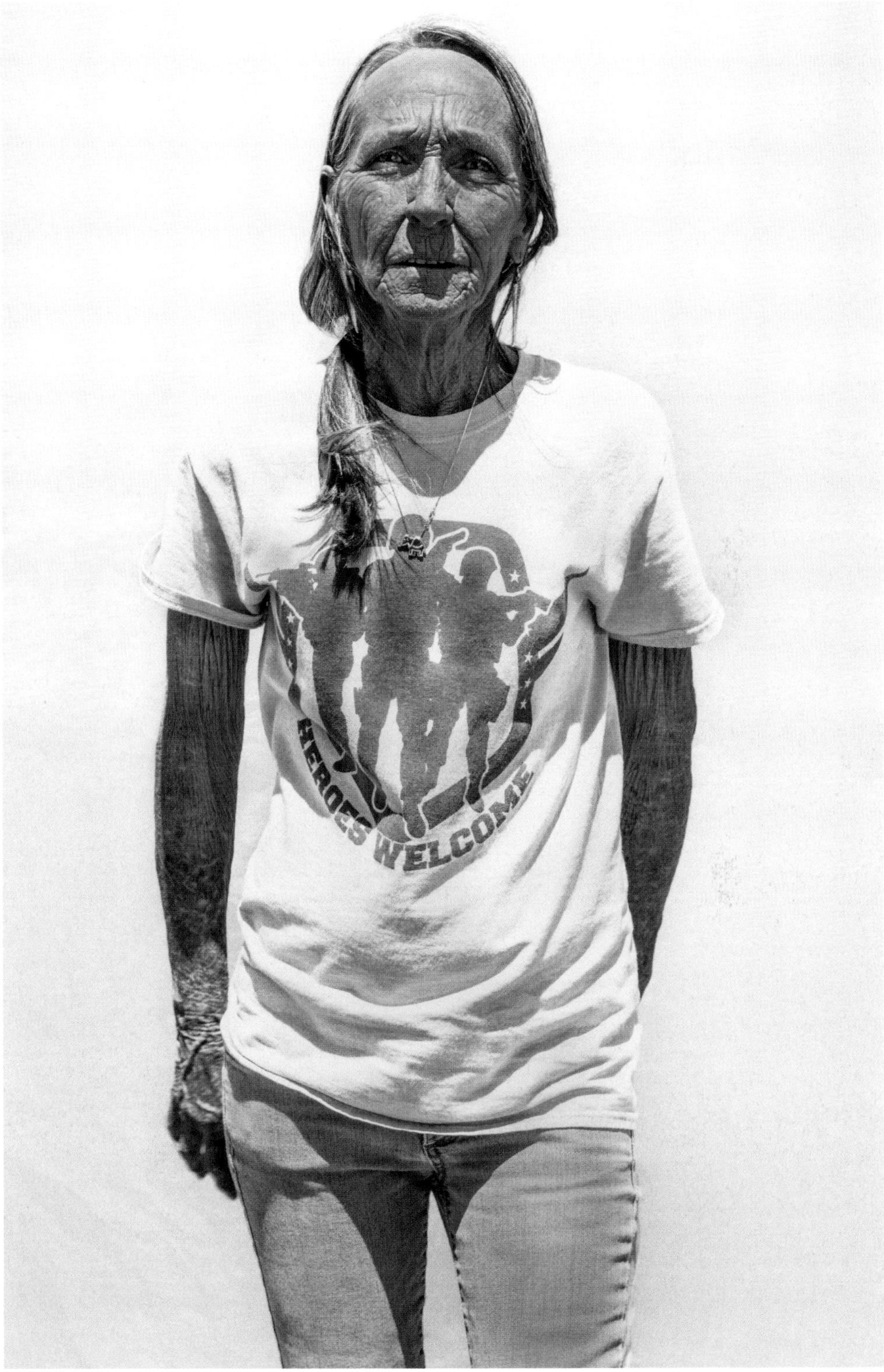

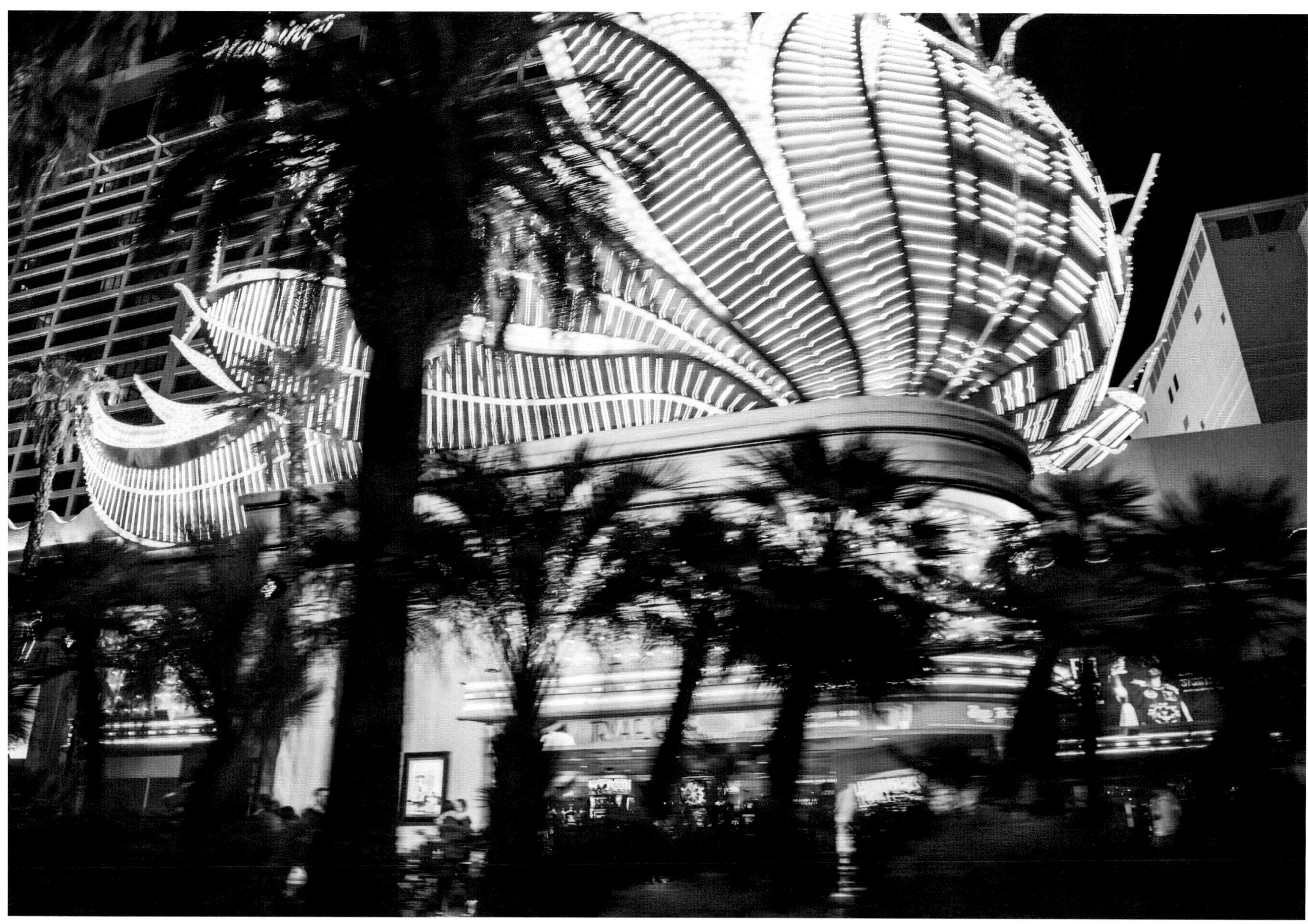

New York Las Vegas, Nevada

N 35° 38’26.0016” W 120° 40’ 48.0288”

PASO ROBLES, CALIFORNIA

“During the time of slavery, the police in this country were formed to catch slaves, and that has continued. When you say systemic racism, that’s part of it. It’s ingrained in the fabric of how the country was built. I was traveling [in Texas] with another African American person in my car and got pulled over, even though I was going the speed limit. The officer had me step out of the car and said: ‘That’s a pretty nice car you have.’ I answered: ‘I worked hard to buy that car. I’m on the road with Cirque du Soleil.’ The officer put us on the side of the road for no reason, besides the color of our skin. That’s the harsh reality. To navigate as a person of color in this country, you learn how to survive. Do I say something? Or do I just move on and try to fight this some other way? With George Floyd, we’re having some shifts happen — the amount of people that hit the streets across the world was more than ever. It sparked the ‘great awakening,’ as I’d like to call it. It woke white people in this country up.”

[Michelle]

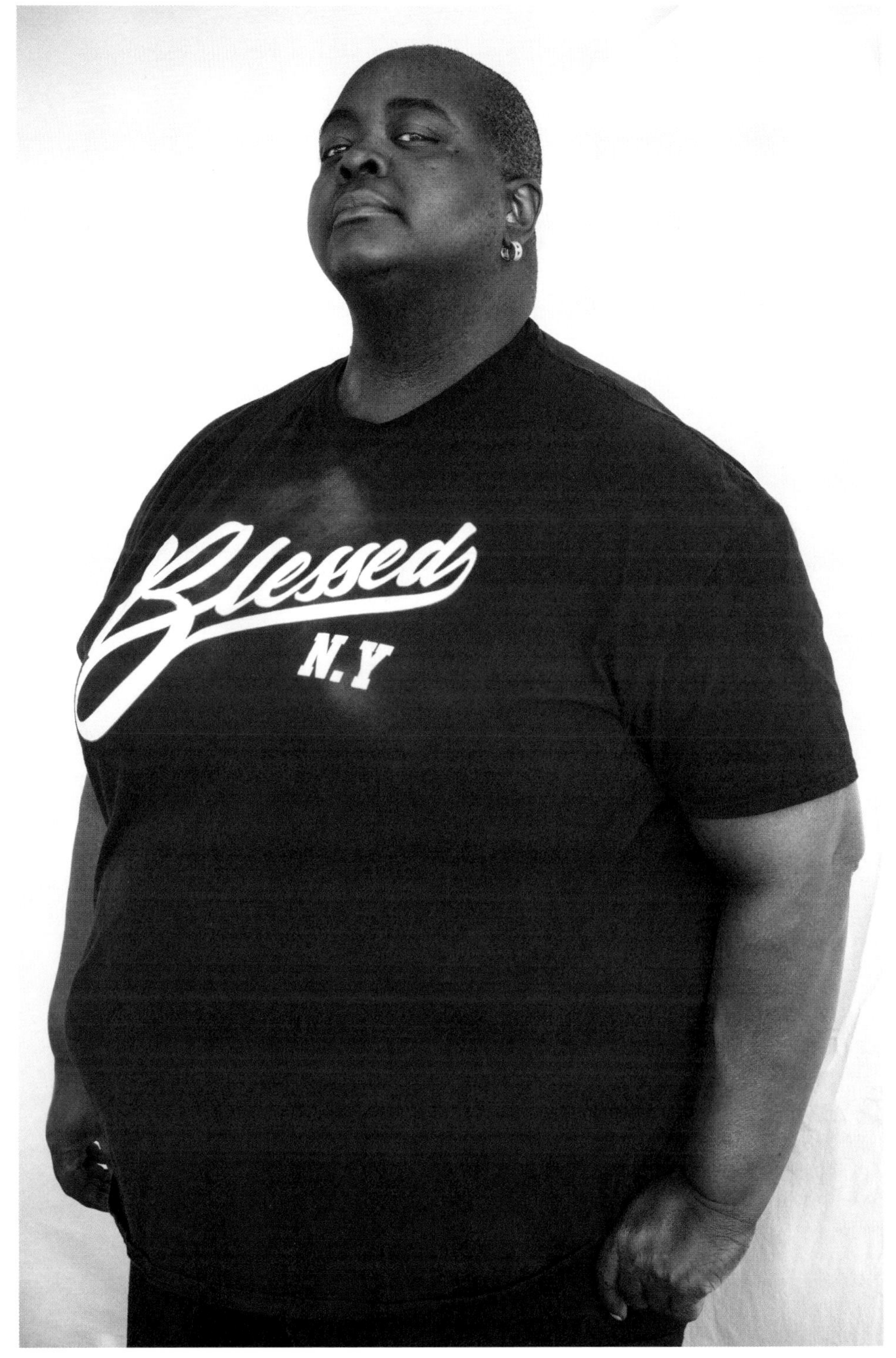

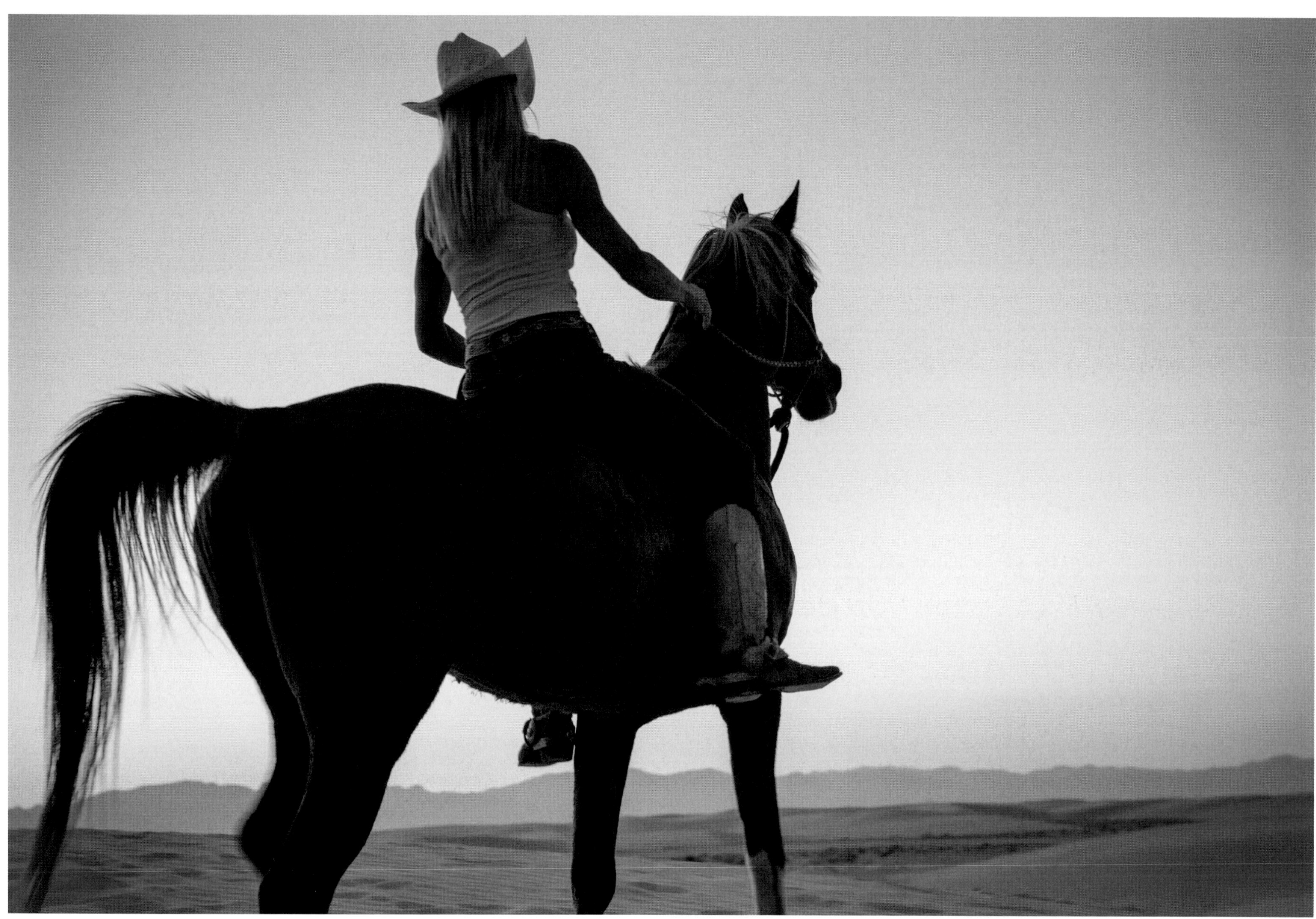

Jill, New Mexico

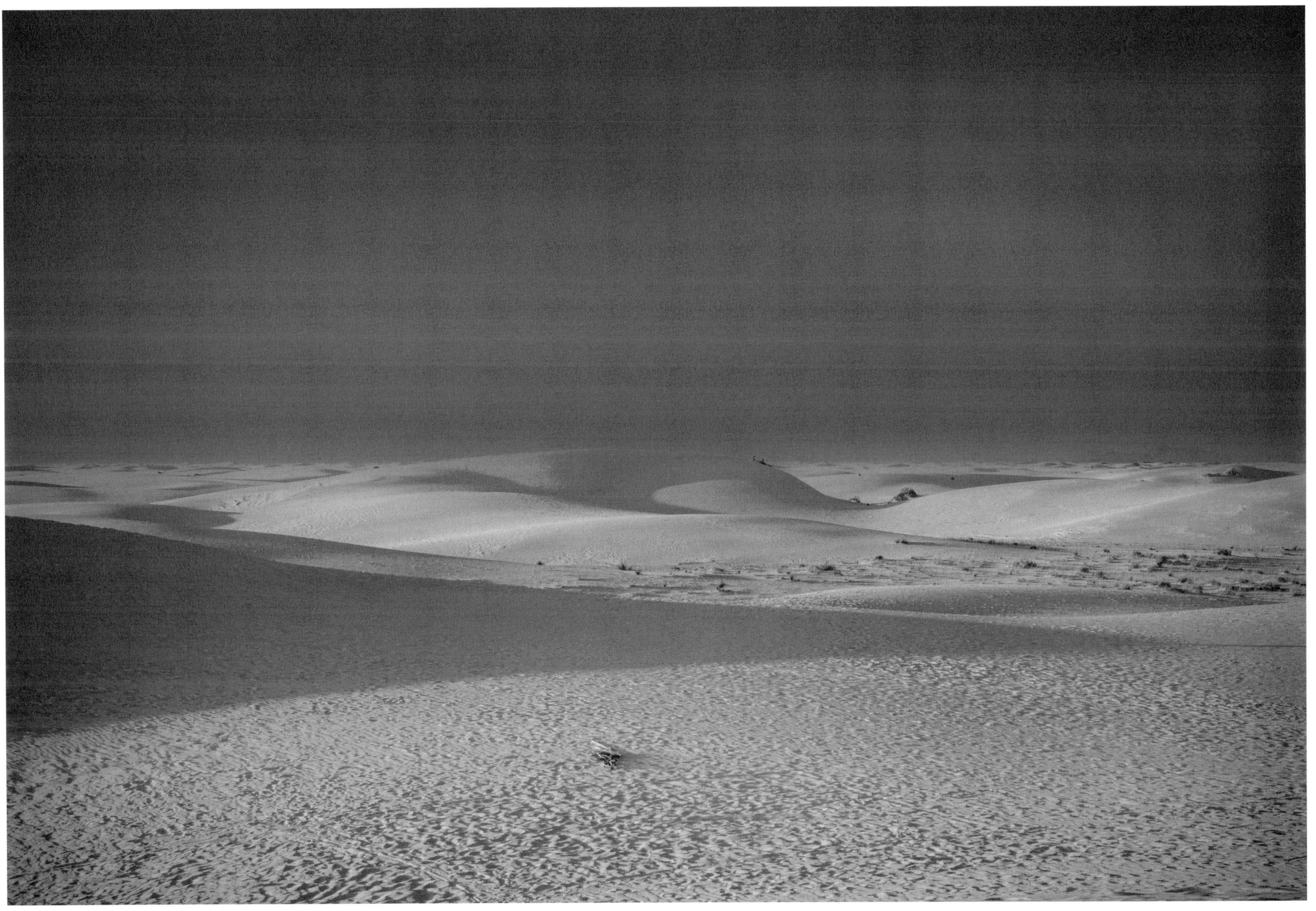

White Sands, New Mexico

N 36° 13’ 46.866” W 116° 46’ 4.5084”

BADWATER BASIN, CALIFORNIA

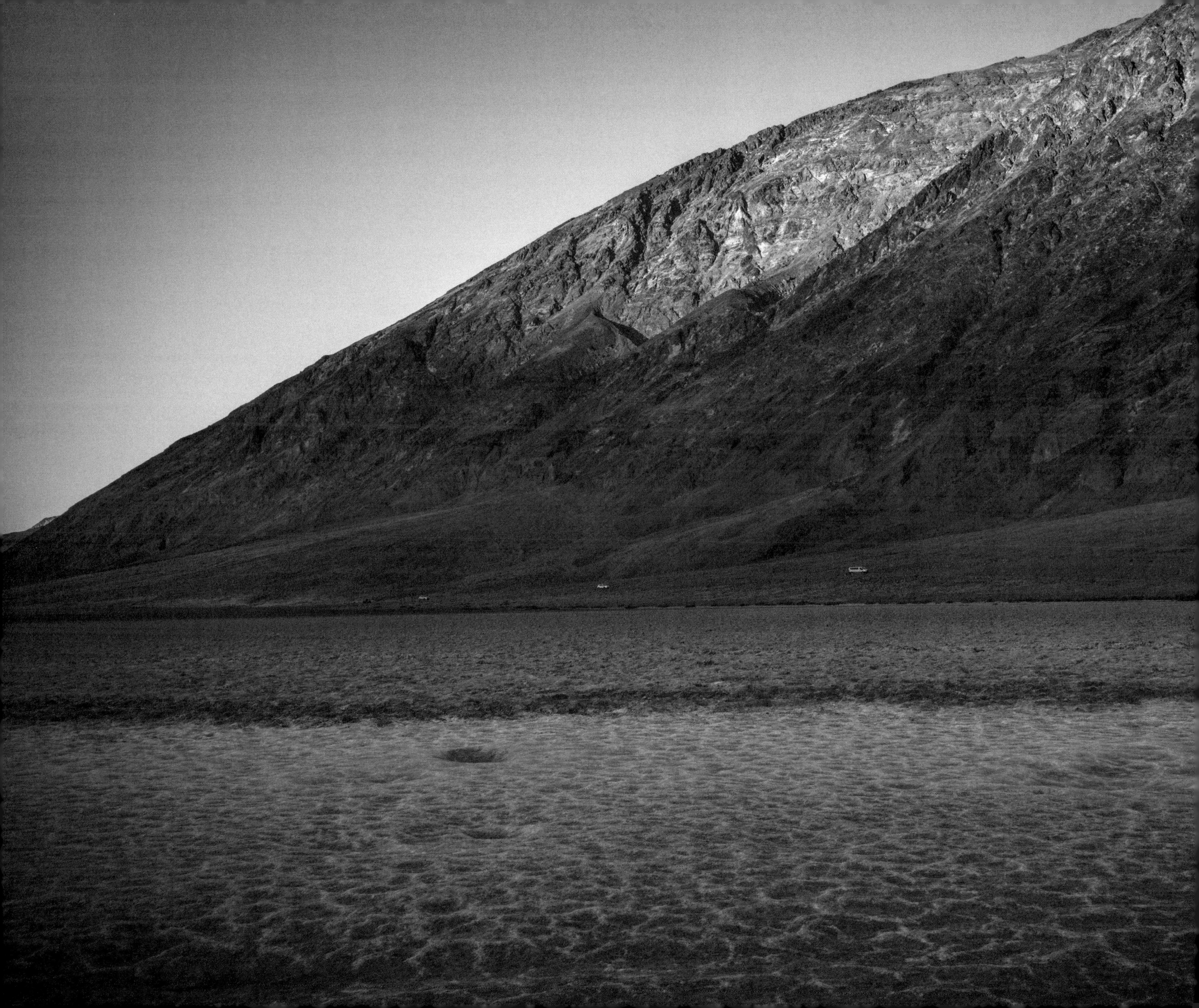

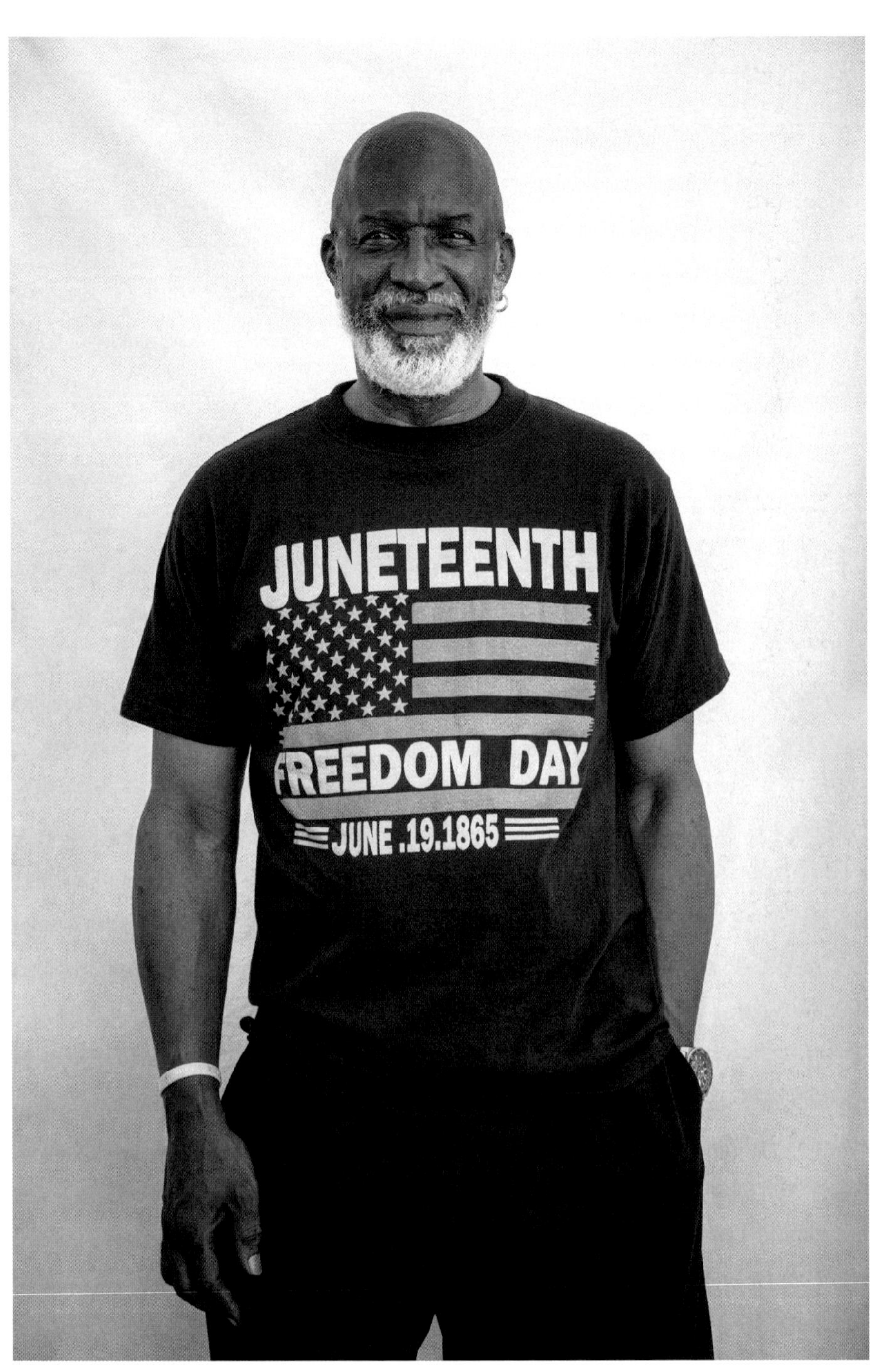

N 33° 23' 13.4088" W 84° 16' 58.7208"

HAMPTON, GEORGIA

"The 1965 Voting Rights Act did not give African Americans the right to vote, but it eliminated all obstacles that kept us from registering. I taught soldiers how to absentee vote, as a voting assistance officer for the government. I experienced something that made me cry. It was when Obama became president and they played this song by Sam Cooke, 'A Change Is Gonna Come.' I wept because my parents weren't there to witness this. When you come from nothing, not much is expected of you."

[Alvin]

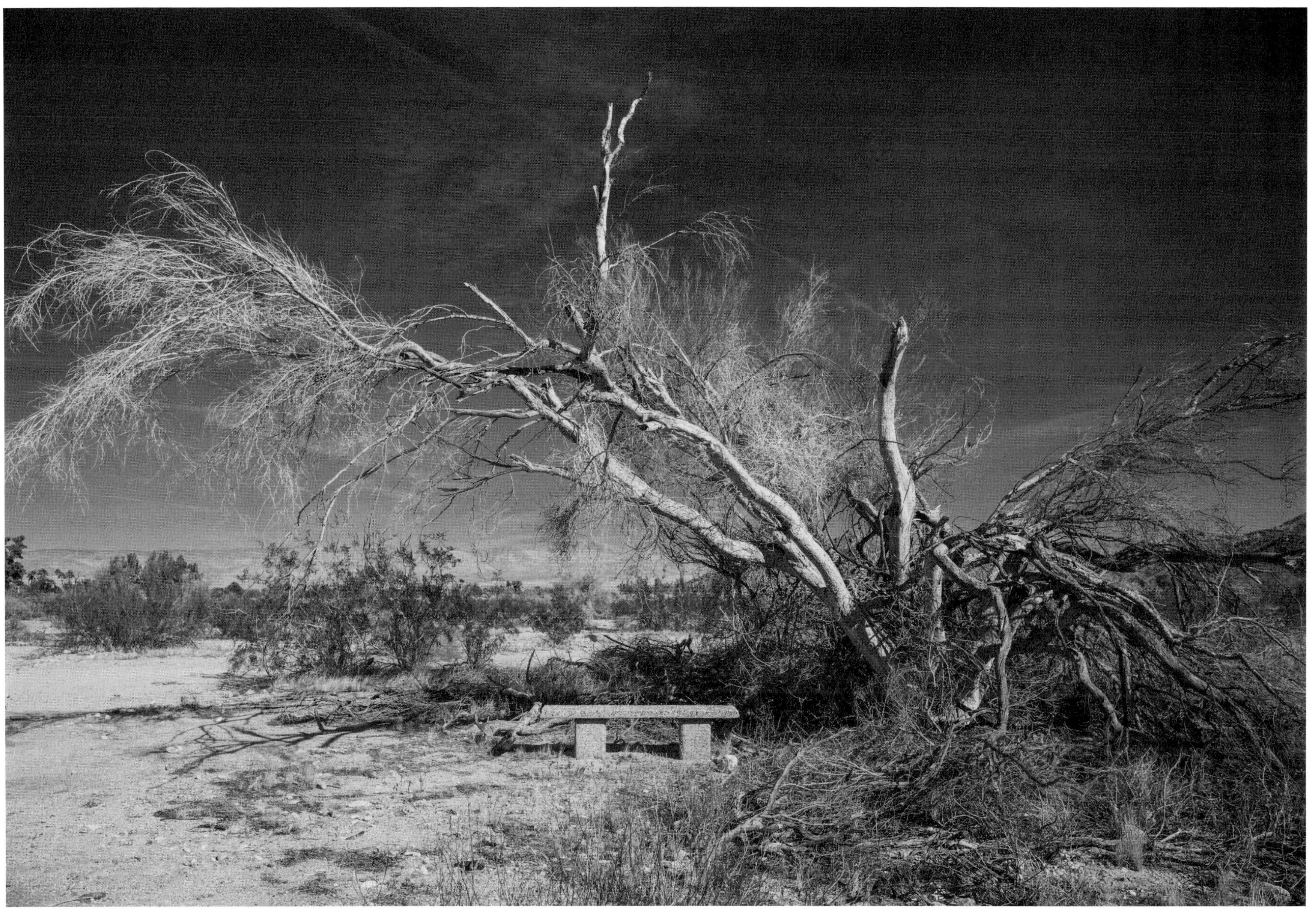

Thinking tree, California

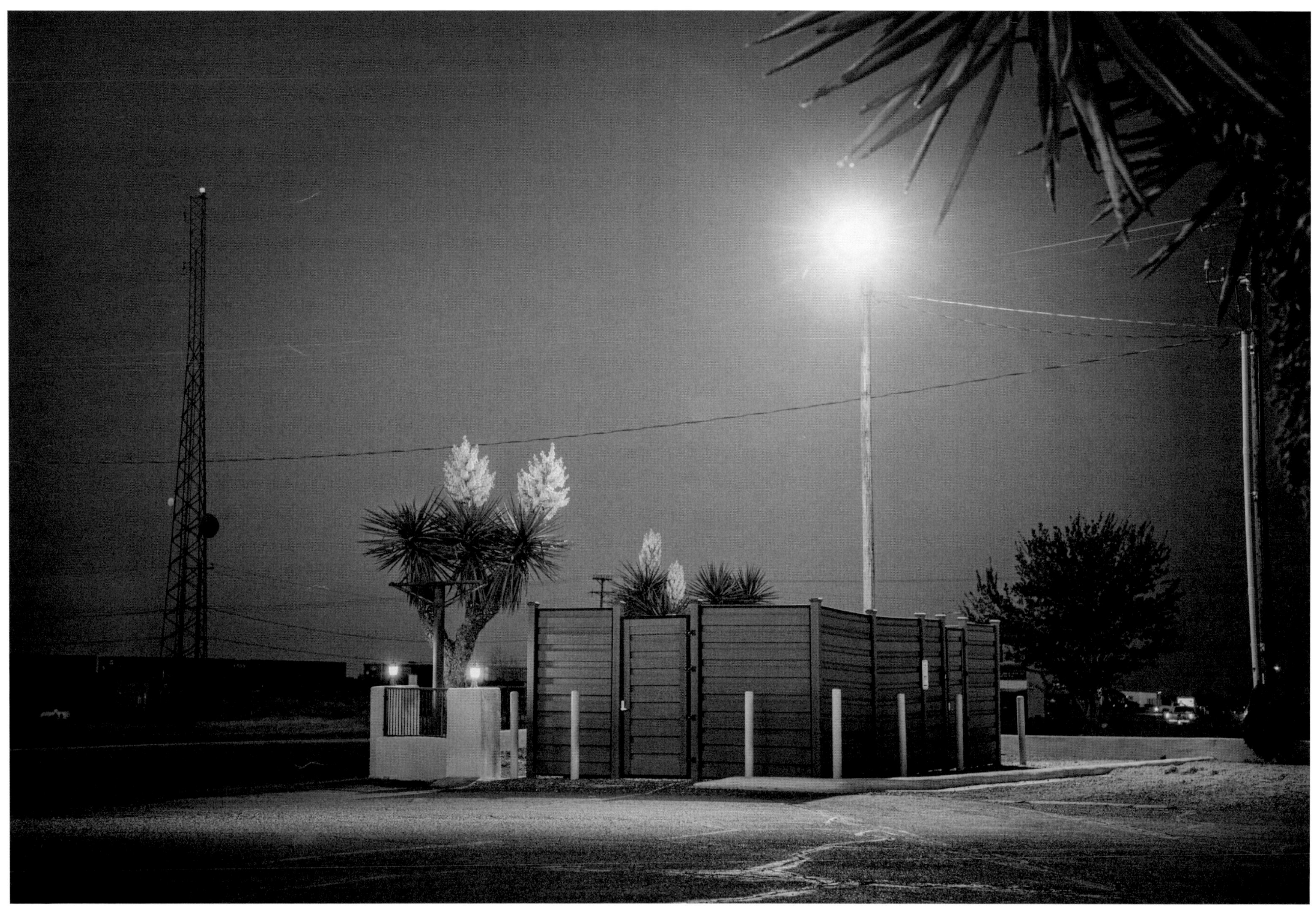

Charging station, New Mexico

N 37° 40’ 30.583” W 92° 39’ 34.453”

LEBANON, MISSOURI

“It’s messed up how insurance will only pay for a top set of teeth and not the bottom. What good is it just having teeth on the top jaw?”

[Charity volunteer]

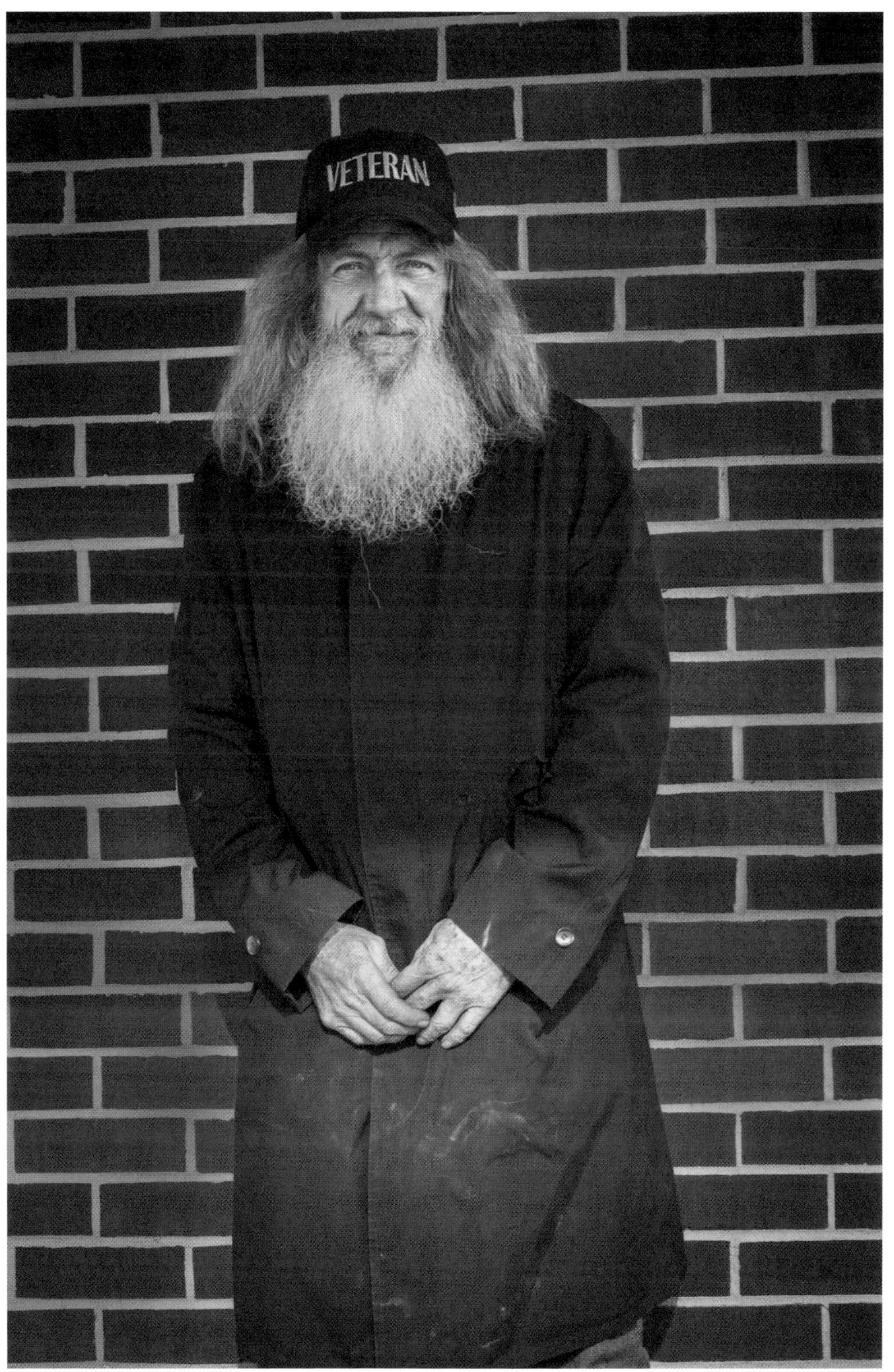

Brock’s hands, Missouri

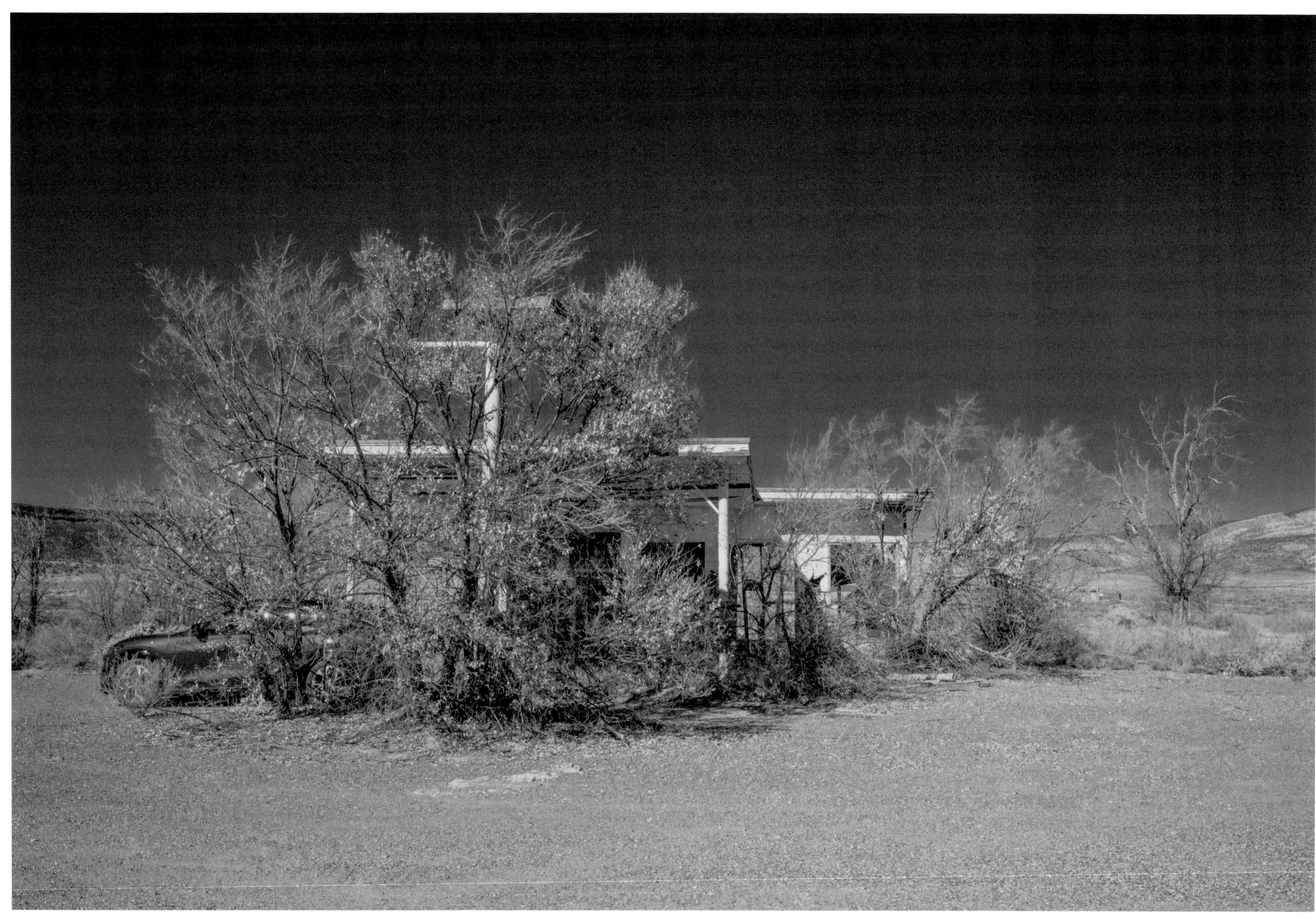

Abandoned gas station, Oklahoma

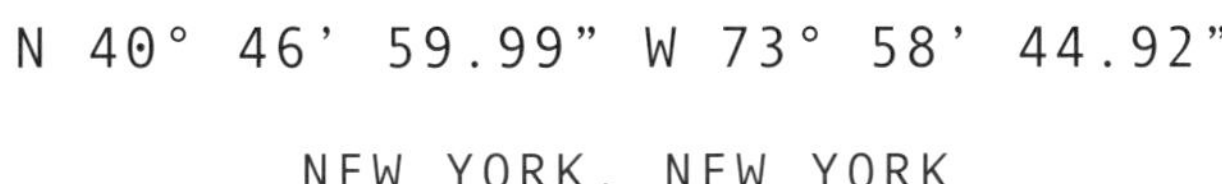

N 40° 46’ 59.99” W 73° 58’ 44.92”

NEW YORK, NEW YORK

“I have two motherlands, the Dominican Republic and the U.S. You have to protect it and take care of it, and that’s what I’ve done for 26 years in the military: caretaking, to help our nation. My son also spent six years in the military. We are both Navy men. We’re going through troubled times in the U.S., but it will get better because there is that kind-heartedness to Americans. We are just confused now. Hopefully, we’ll reach a point where we understand that we have to protect the earth. There has to be a balance. It’s the same system.
We’re all connected.”

[Ozzie]

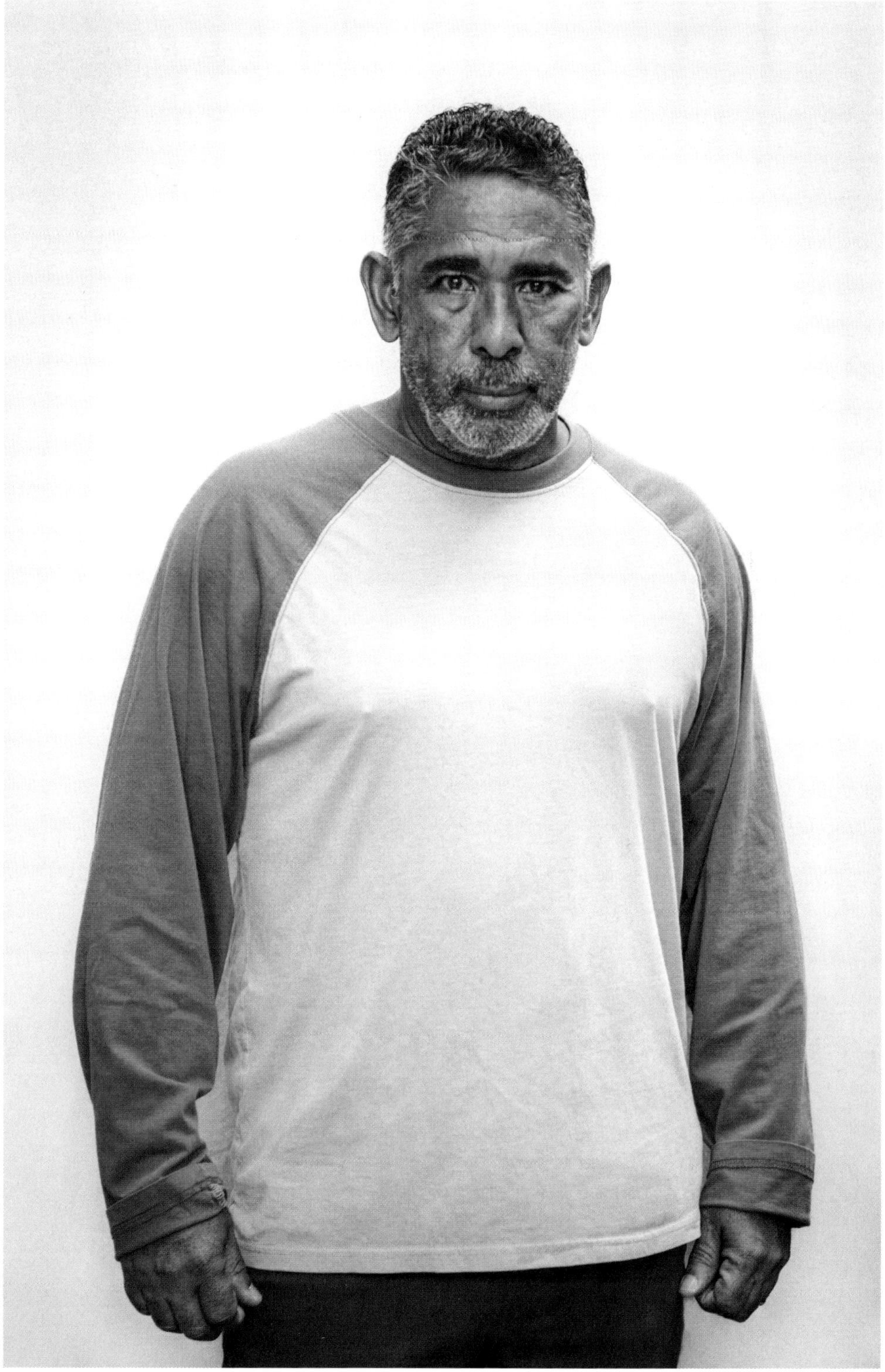

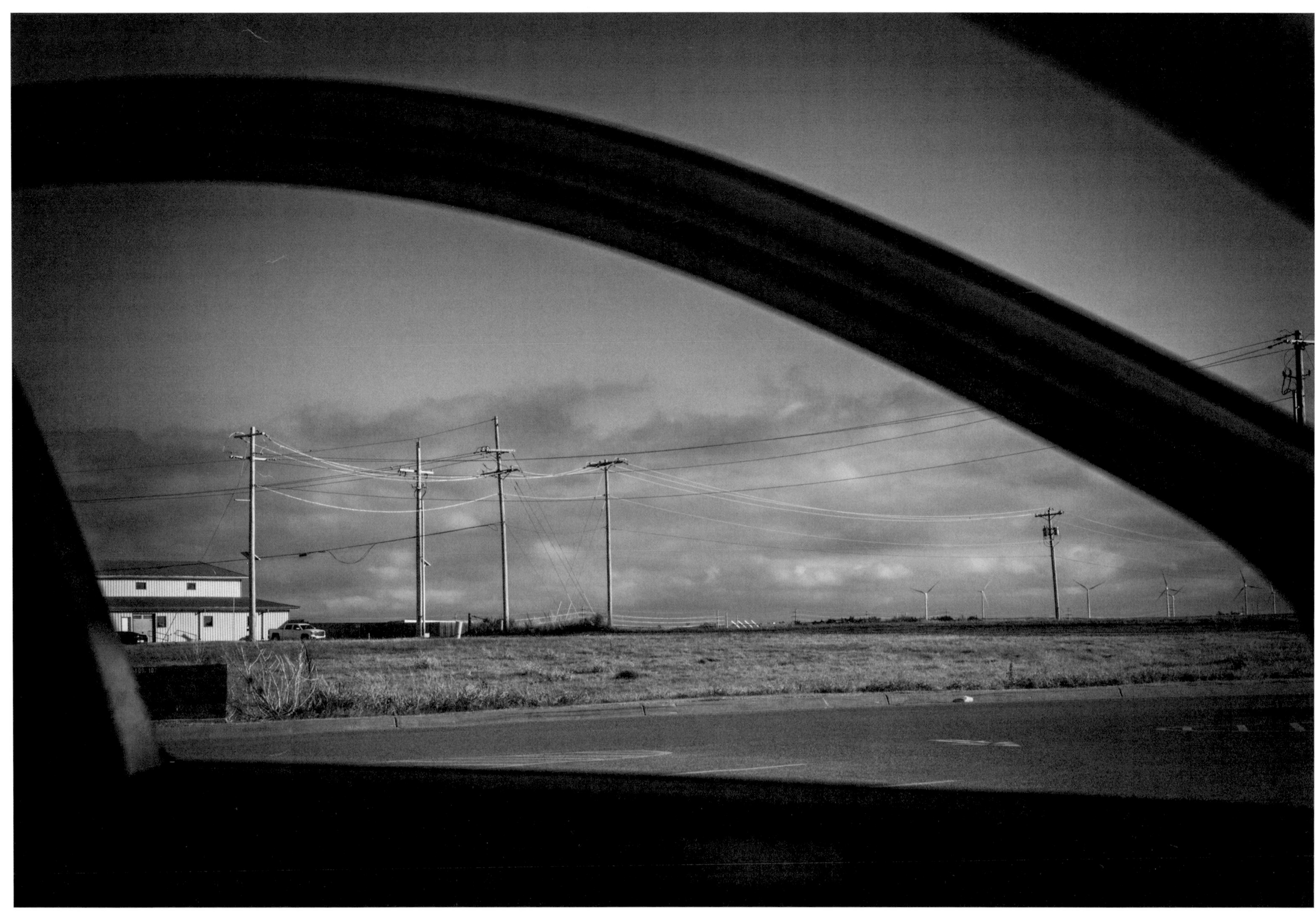

Power grid, California

N 42° 19’ 53.1372” W 83° 2’ 44.7144”

DETROIT, MICHIGAN

“I long for safety and beauty to return to the world. My dream is for everybody do their part to keep this Earth for future generations. Now I’m working on the next electric vehicle.”

[Sue]

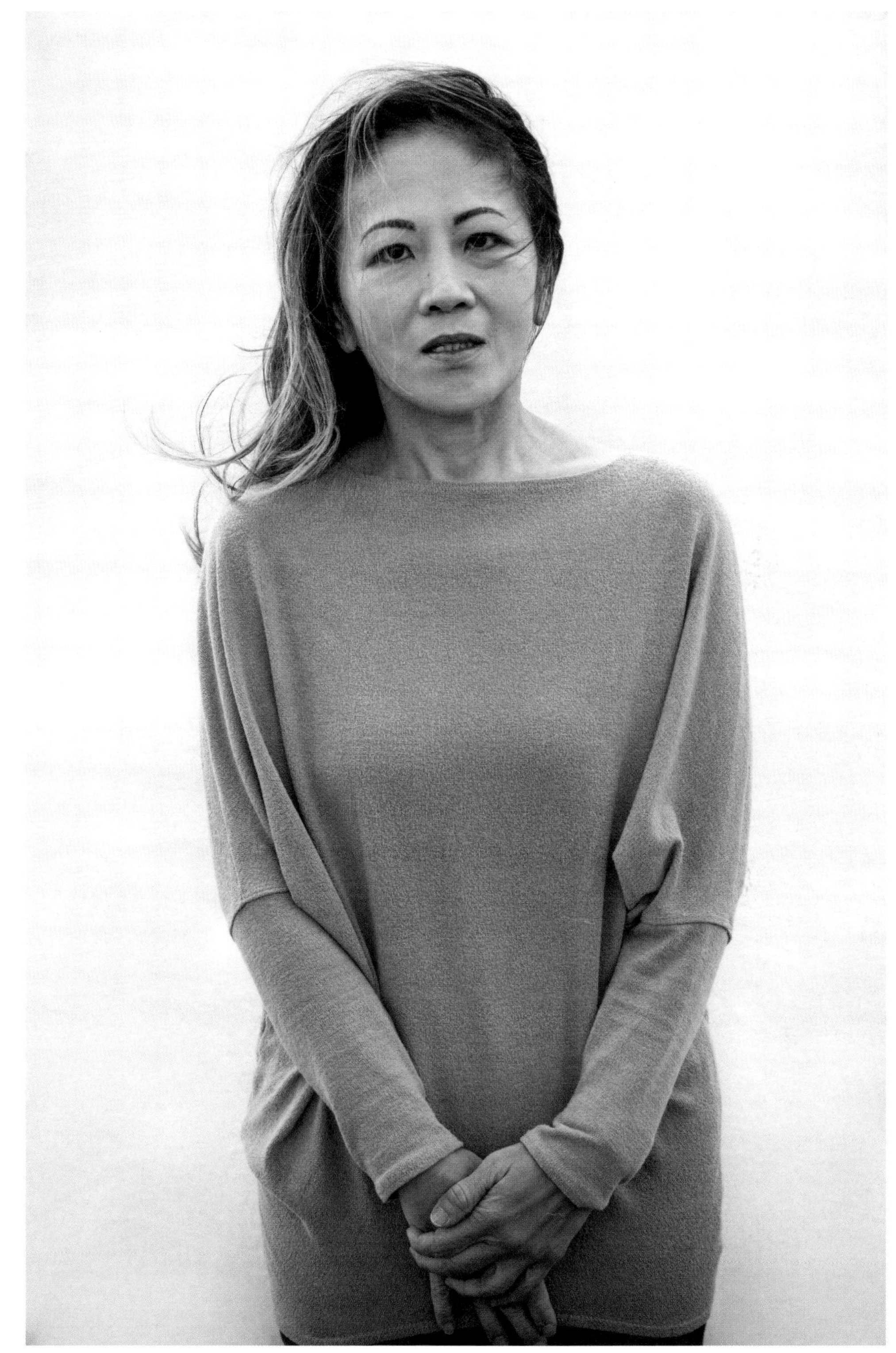

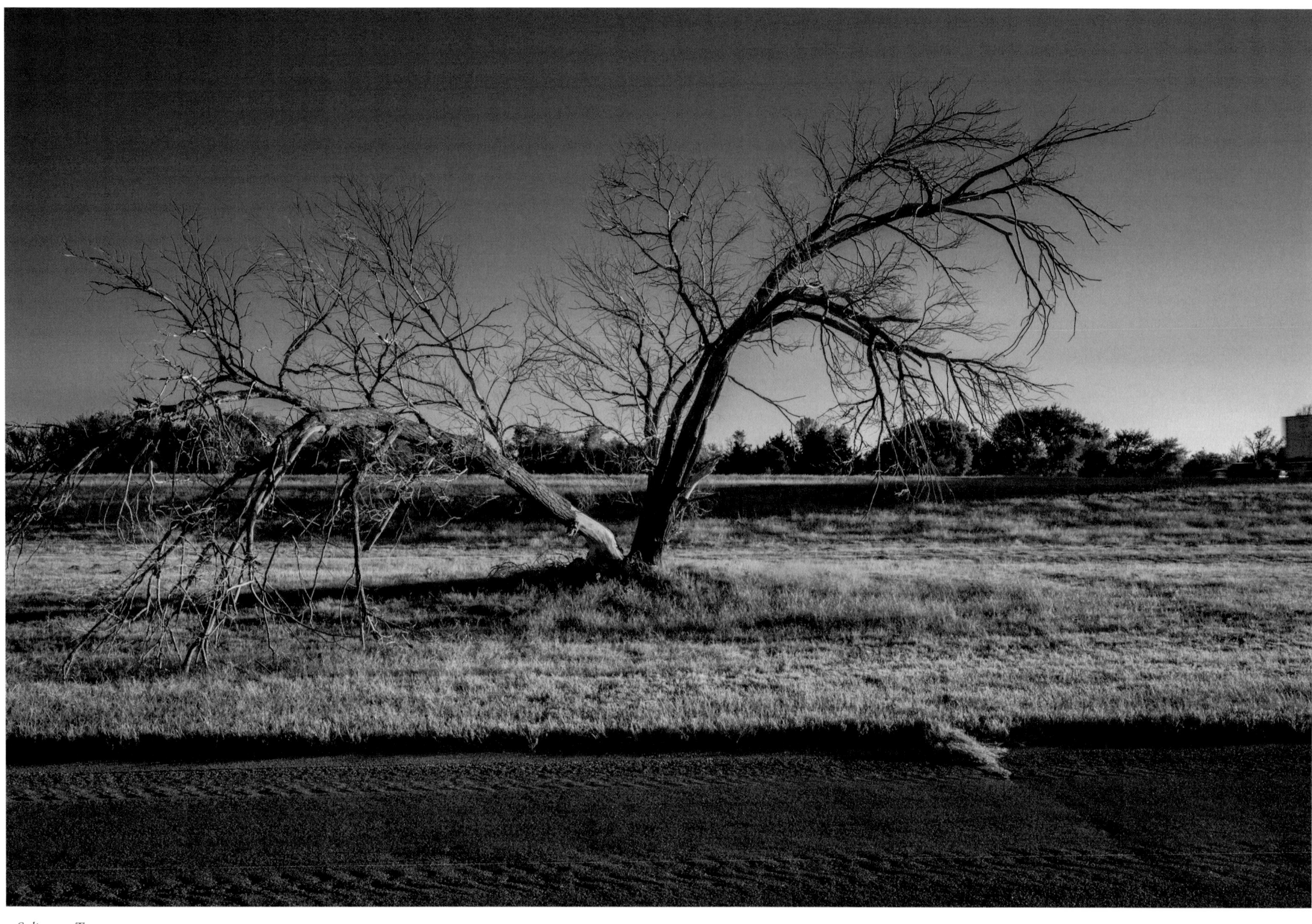

Split tree, Texas

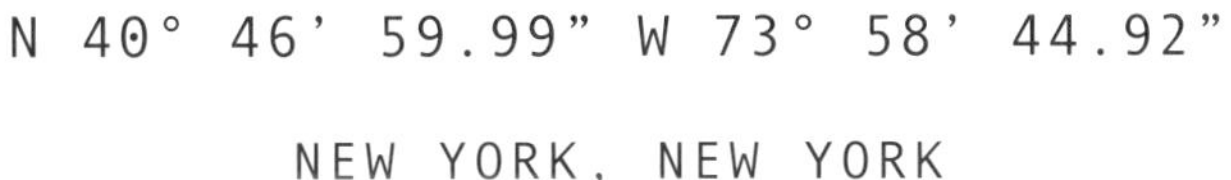

N 40° 46’ 59.99” W 73° 58’ 44.92”

NEW YORK, NEW YORK

“When I was 18, I came out as queer. My family had a real struggle with that because they had a really neoconservative ideology. At that point, I realized I could never return home. I empowered myself to live my own authentic truth. Then I realized I had shifted them. I had shifted their ideologies with my presence. There was no more space for them to hold that in front of me because I was in front of them and it was my being there.... So I chose to start returning.”

[Osun]

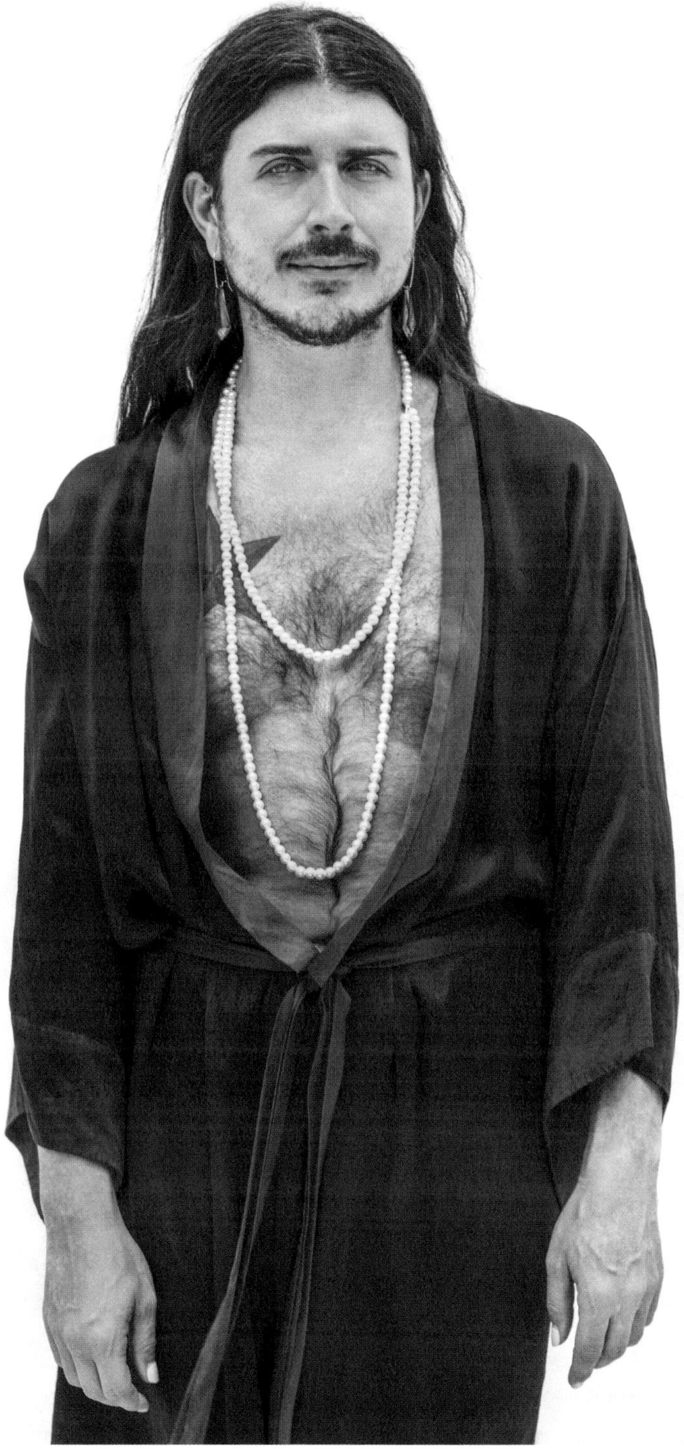

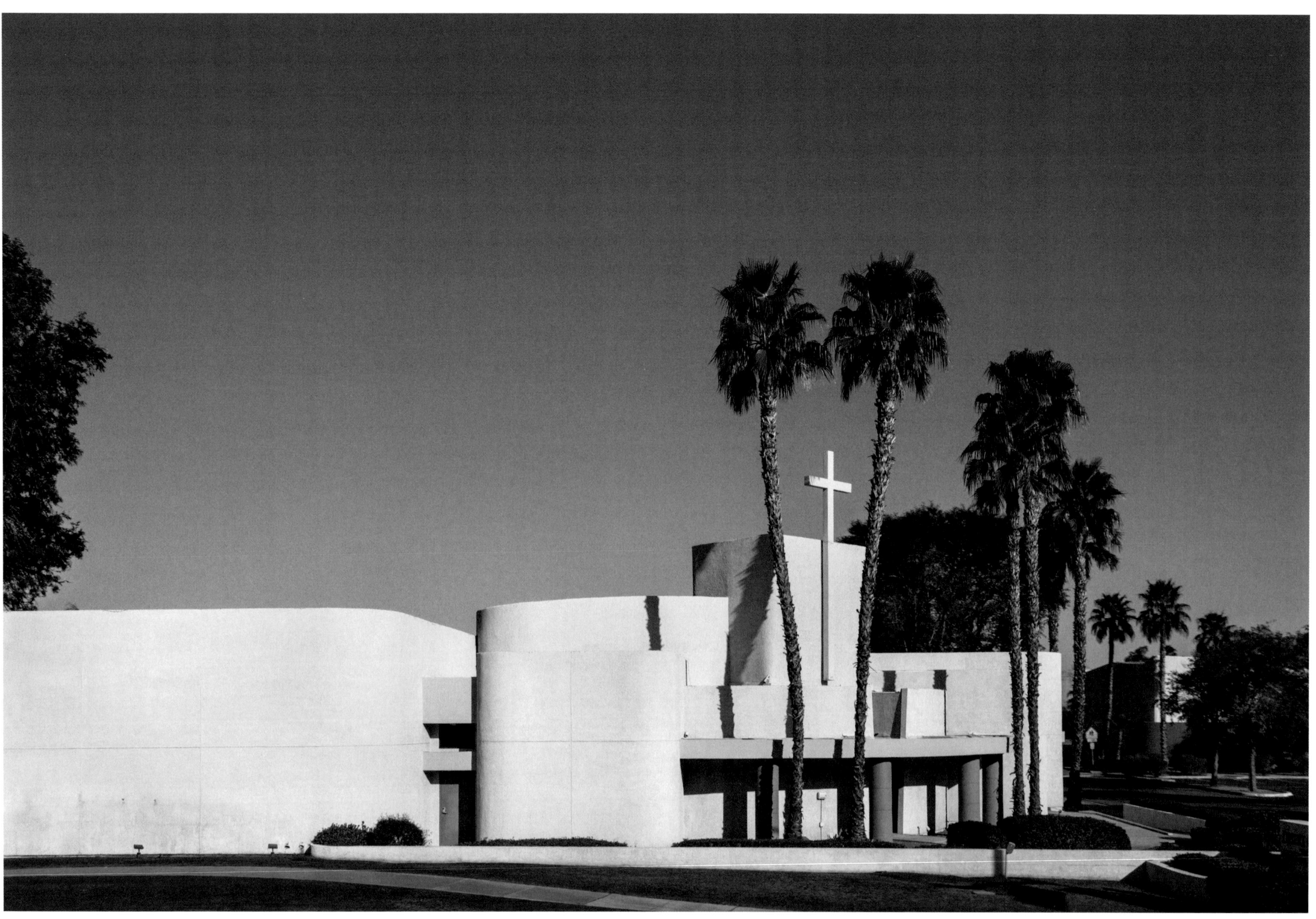

Desert church, California

N 26° 22’ 5.9016” W 80° 7’ 44.1552”

BOCA RATON, FLORIDA

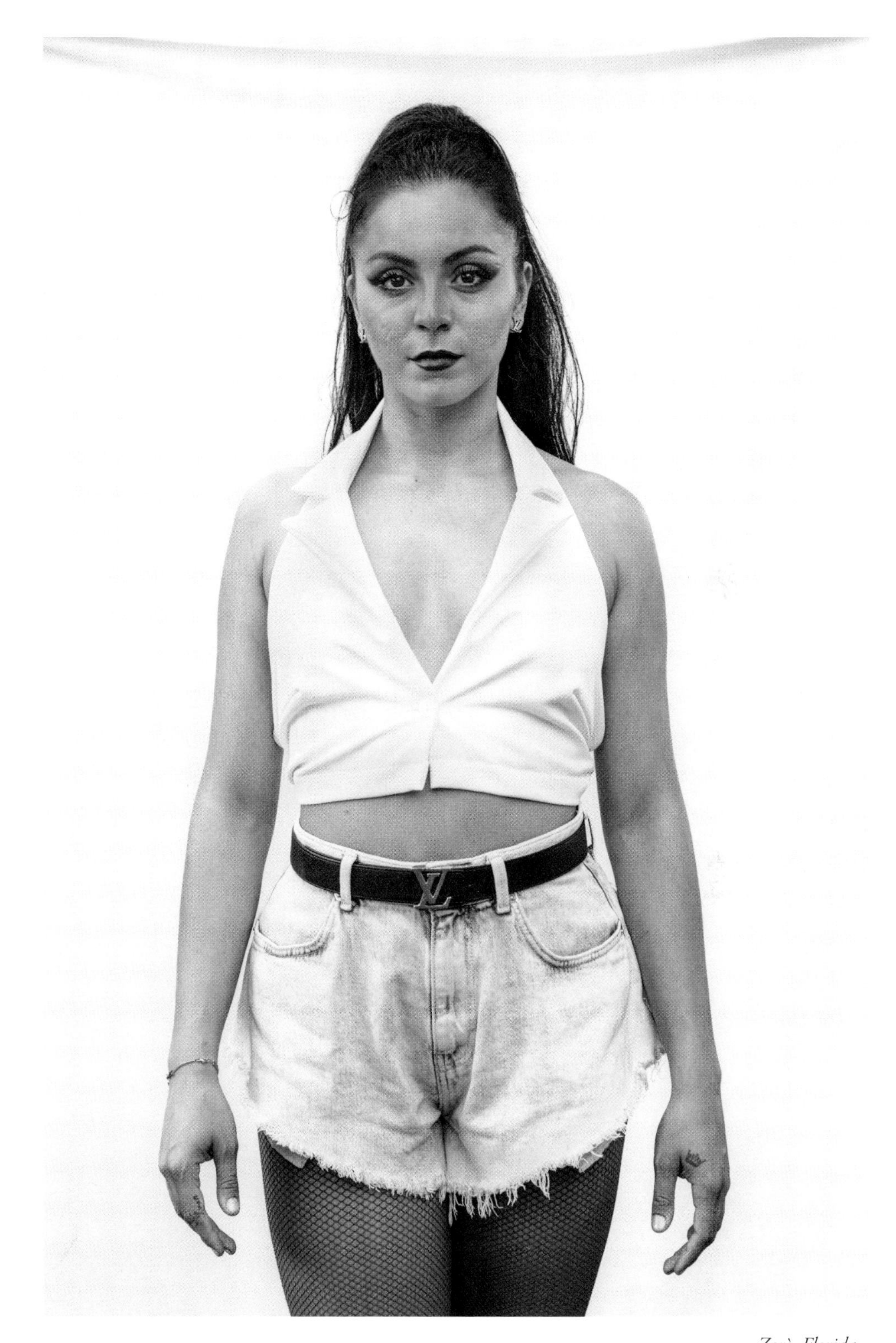

Zorè, Florida

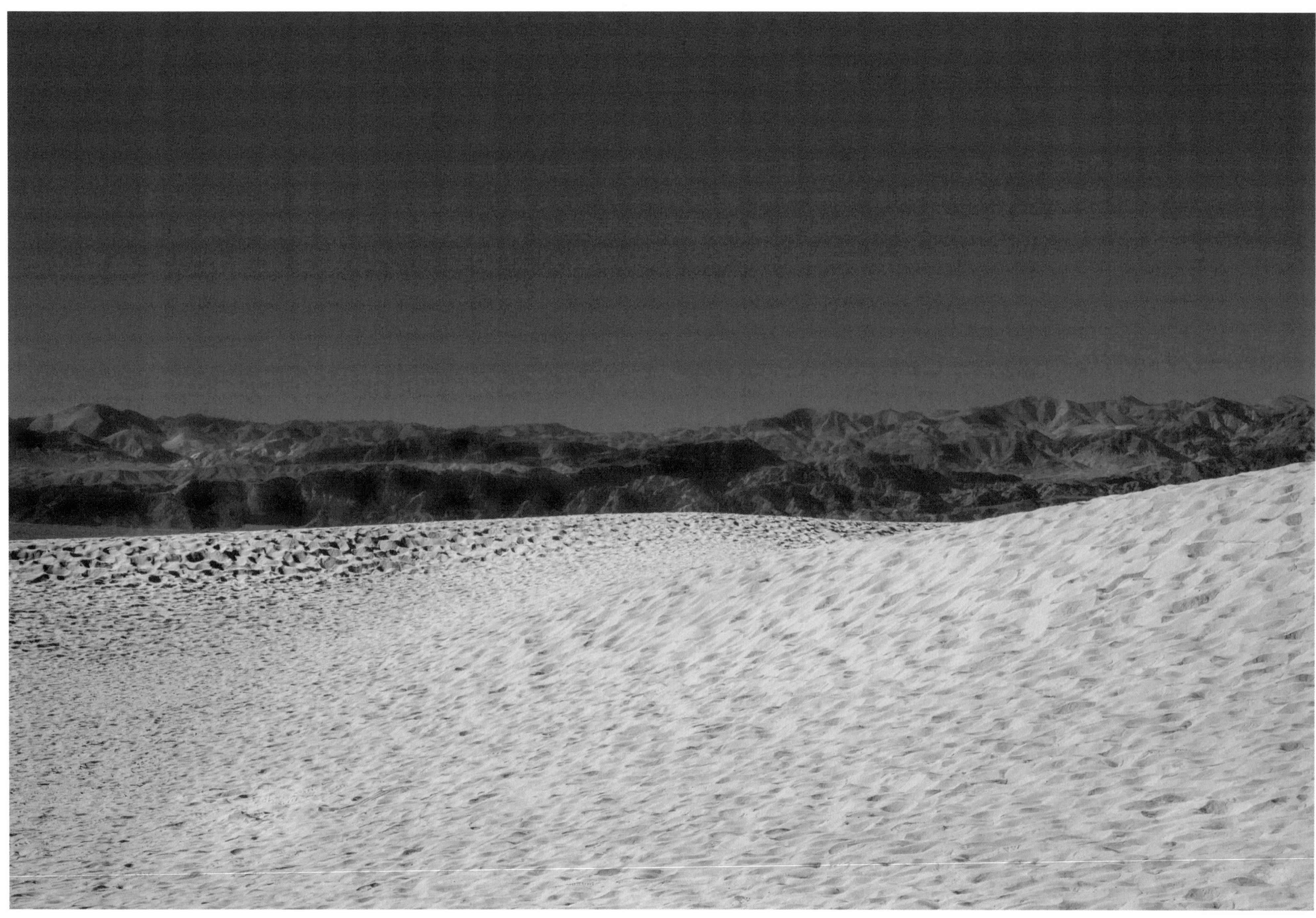

Sand dunes, California

N 36° 12’ 42.4523” W 115° 59’ 12.7392”

PAHRUMP, NEVADA

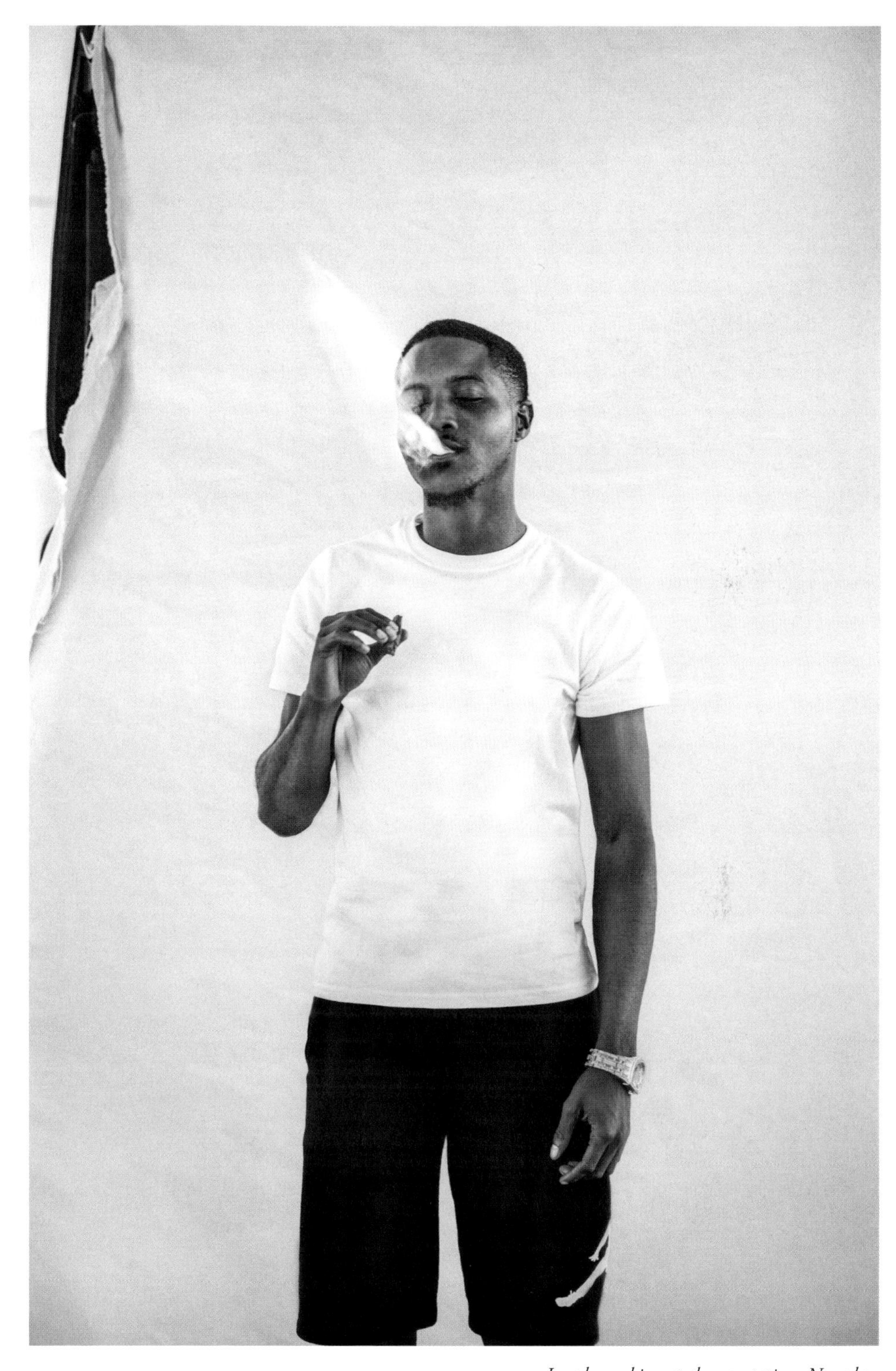

Joseph smoking at the gas station, Nevada

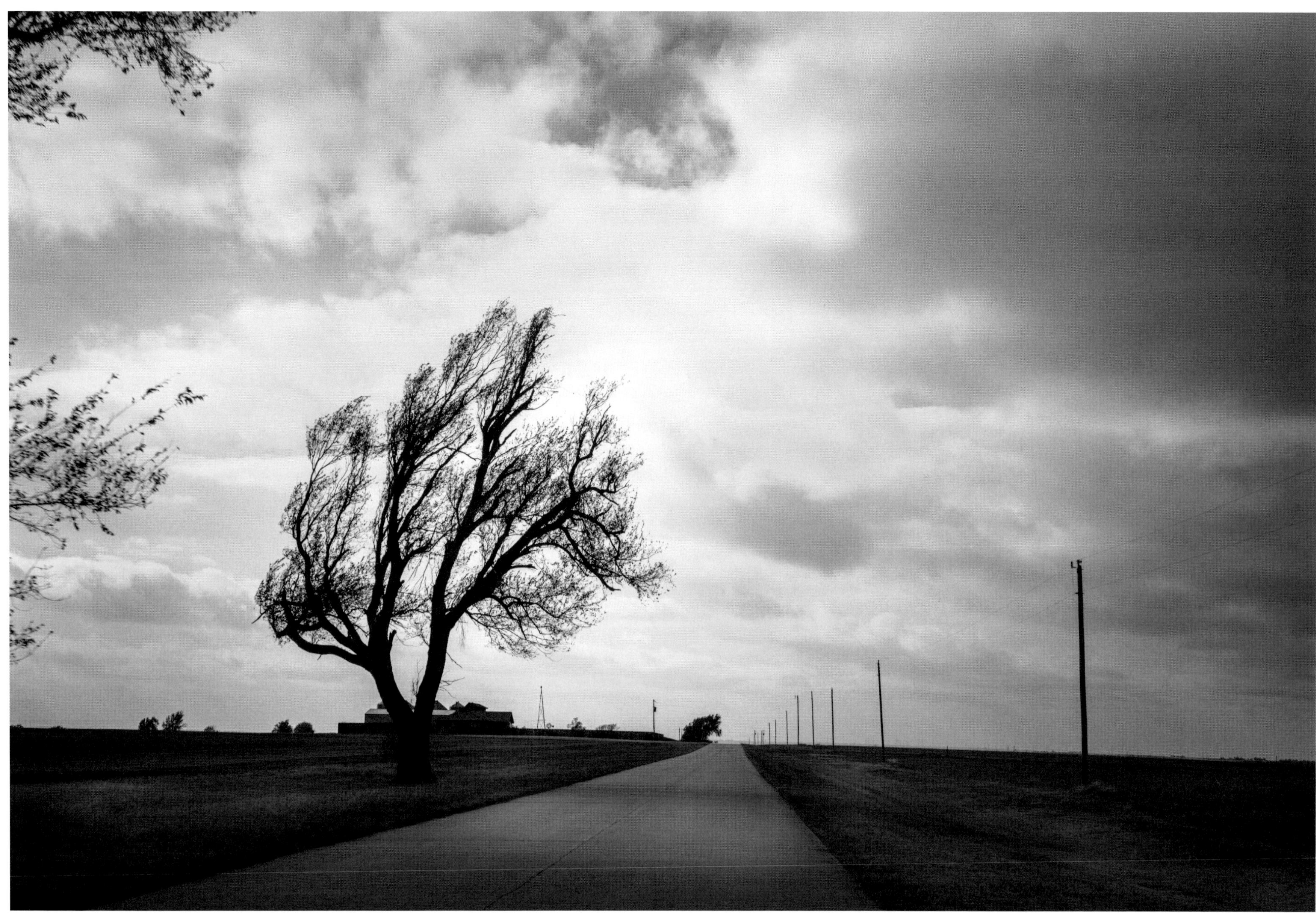

Storm, Oklahoma

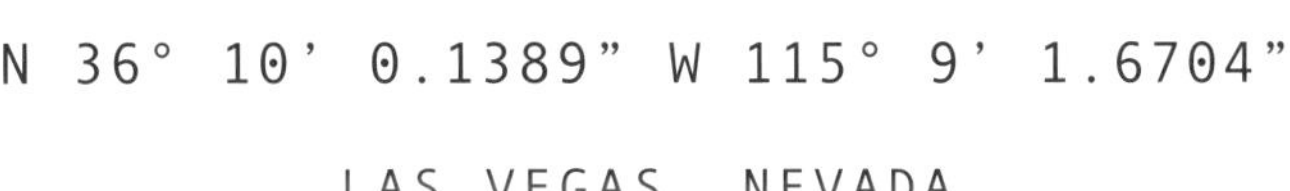

"I'm from Hilo, Hawaii. We're technically not part of the United States. Learning about American history makes me embarrassed. Our queen was held captive in her own palace. It seems like in order to survive the harsh conditions, the Americans had to take. Whereas in Hawaii we were givers. Right now America, is not what I thought it was; I'm confused about what's really going on. It seems greed is the main culprit again."

[Timbelyn]

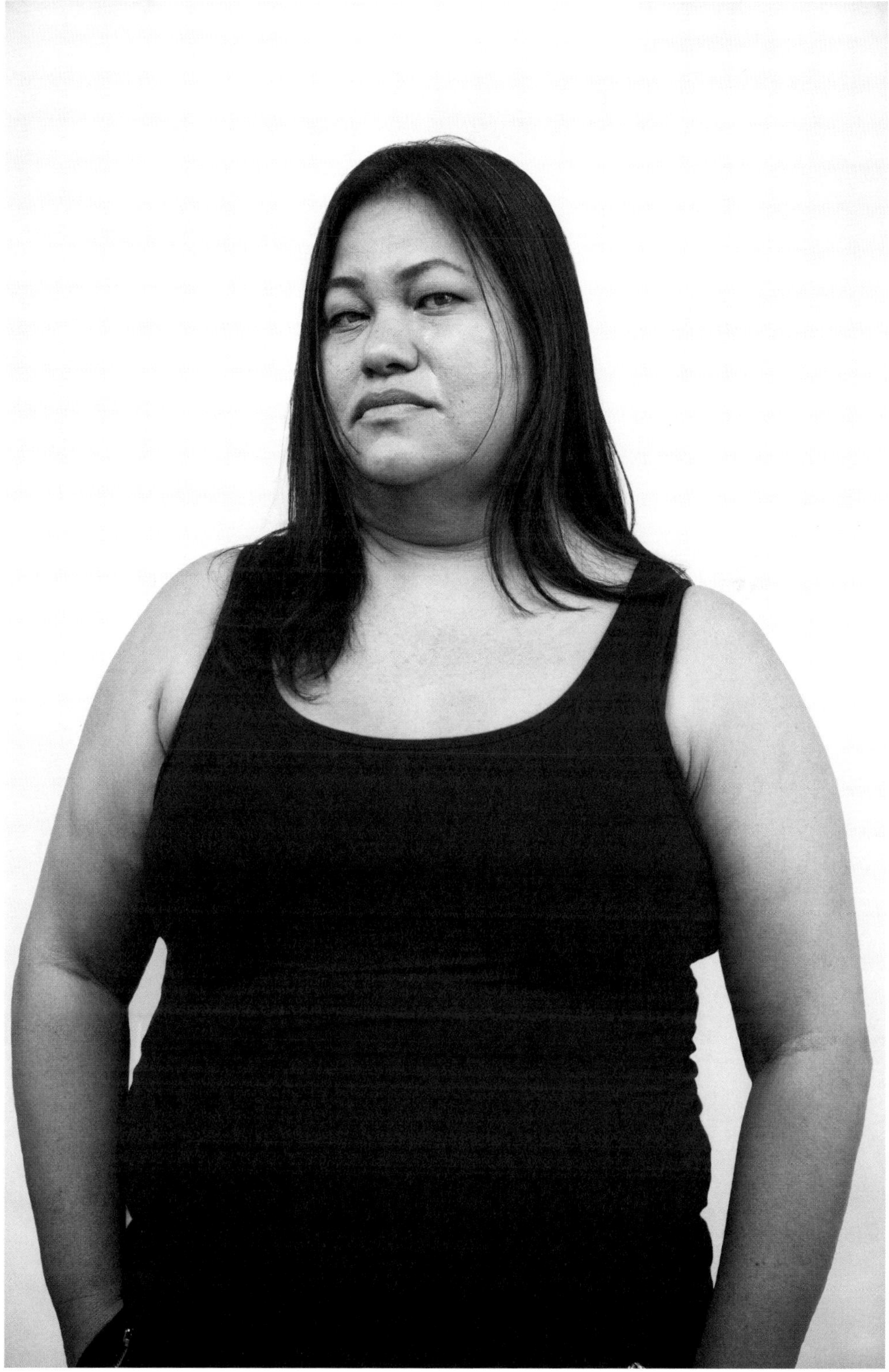

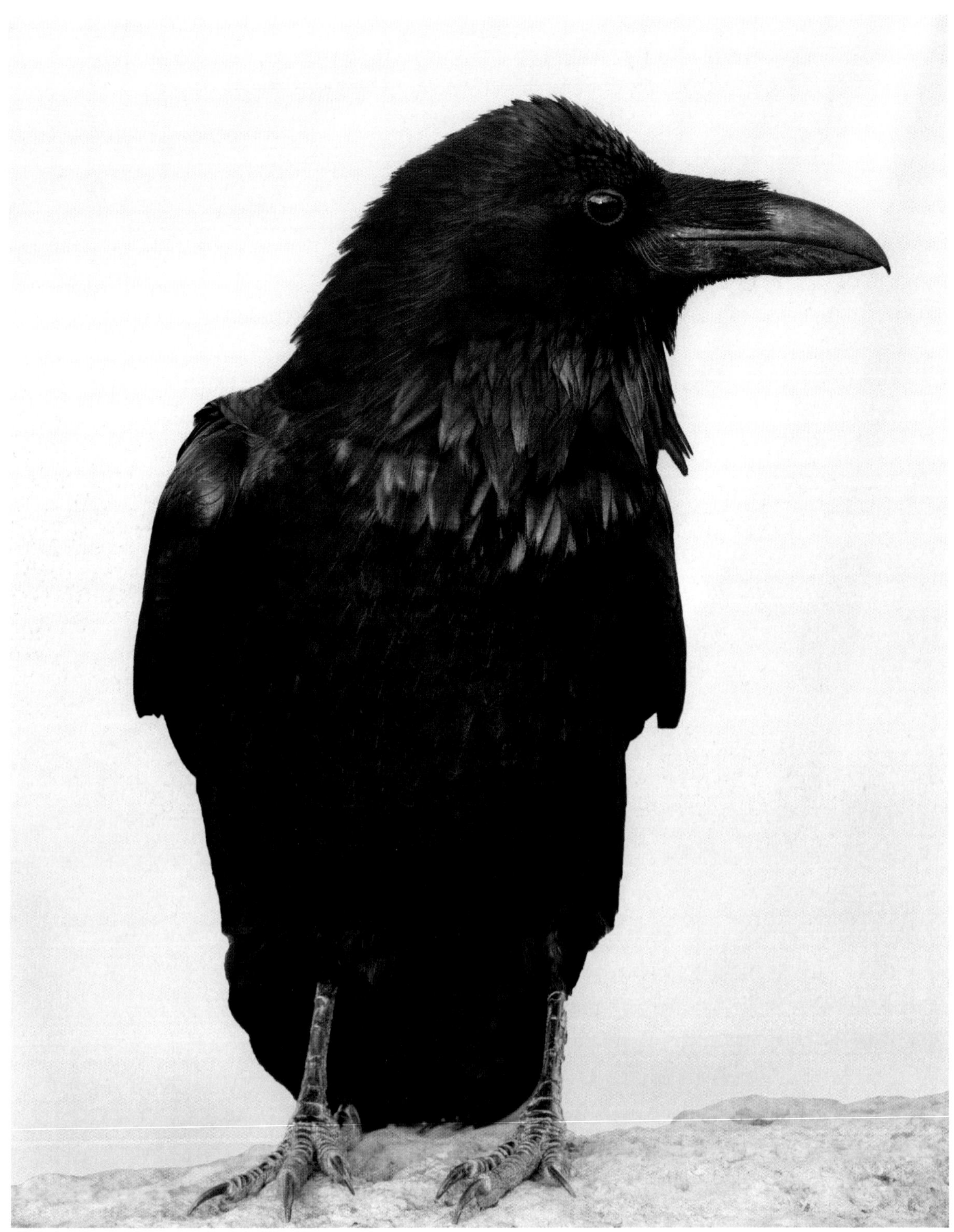

Kraa kraa, Arizona

N 36° 27’ 1.0246” W 116° 51’ 9.2175”

DEATH VALLEY, CALIFORNIA

“I’ve lived in Death Valley my entire life ... I feel so self-conscious. I would smile wide if my teeth were better. My mother ... I loved her so. She had her first child out of wedlock in 1954. She had four boys and five girls, nine total. She was a lounge singer and had to give it up for parenthood ... very rewarding and very discouraging.”

[Gary Roy]

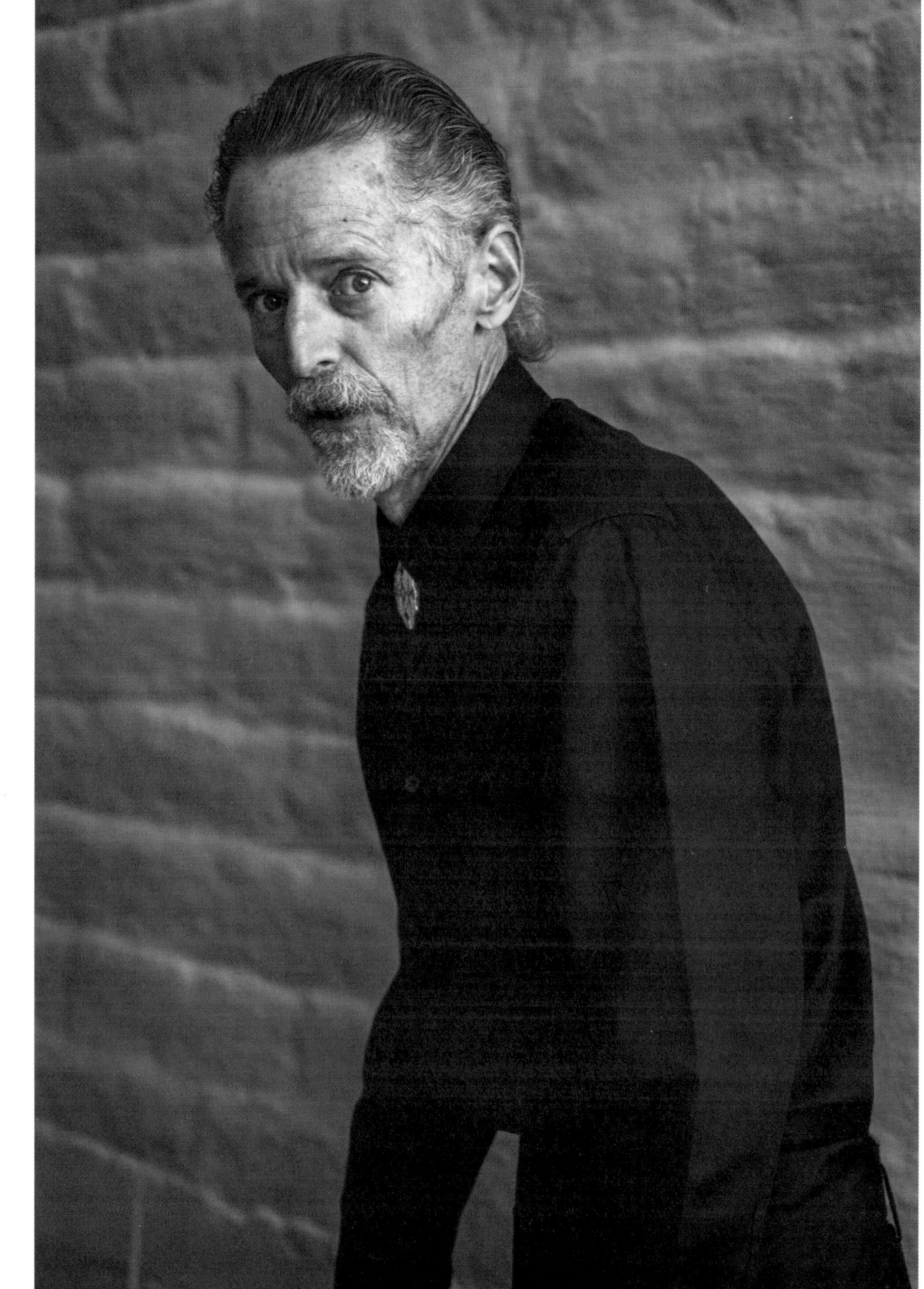

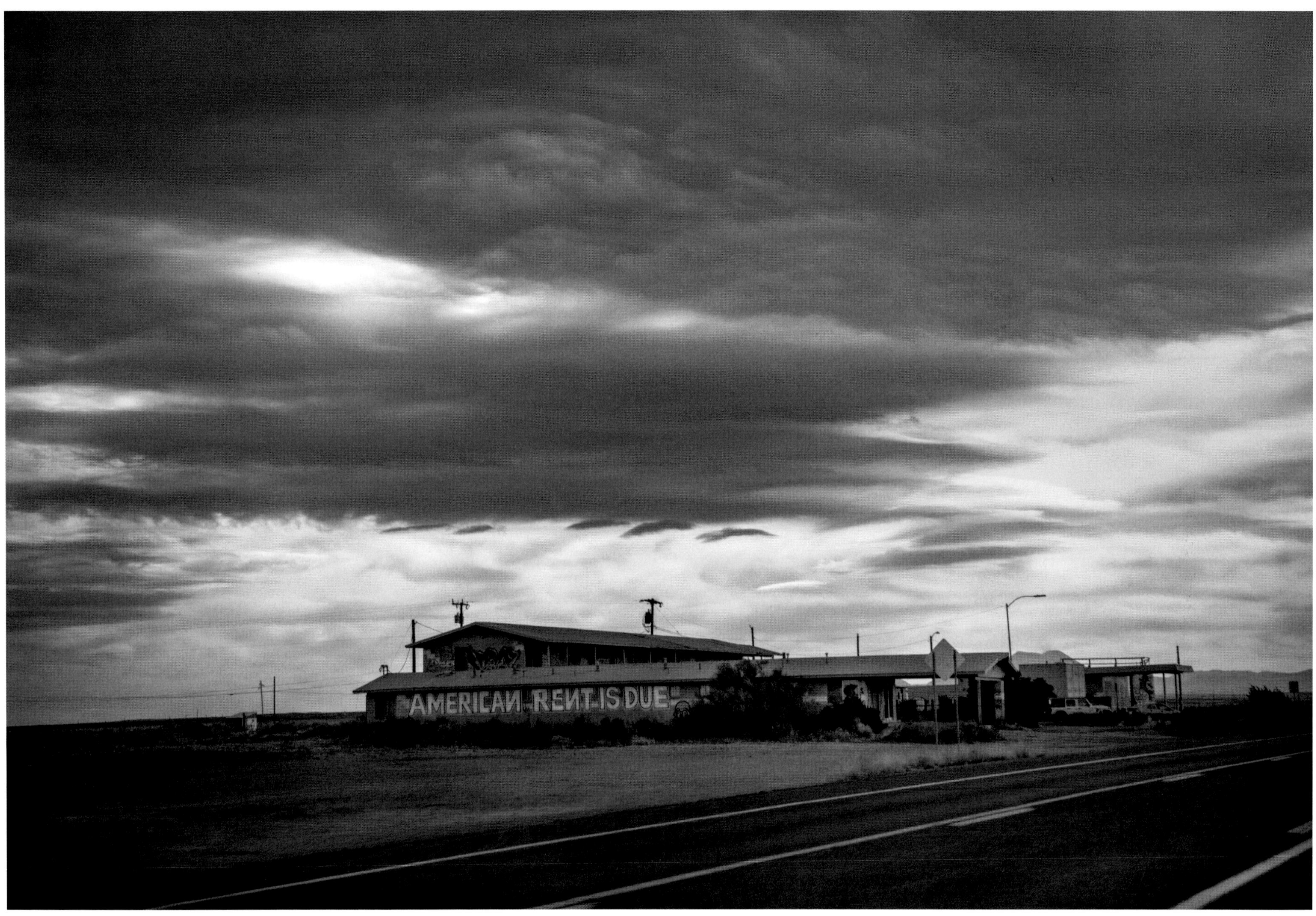

American rent is due, Arizona

N 35° 36' 56.177" W 97° 59' 40.184"

CONCHO, OKLAHOMA

"I'm a foster care caseworker and take care of homes for tribal children, for the Cheyenne and Arapaho tribes. The hurdle is finding tribal homes and keeping our kids connected with our culture. It's generational trauma that goes on and on. It's heartbreaking sometimes, and it's hard to leave work at work. On one hand, I'm thankful to be in this country; on the other hand, there are so many wrongs to be fixed. I'm more worried about my own bubble of my native people, my own tribe and family. It bogs me down to think about the complications of our country."

[Nona]

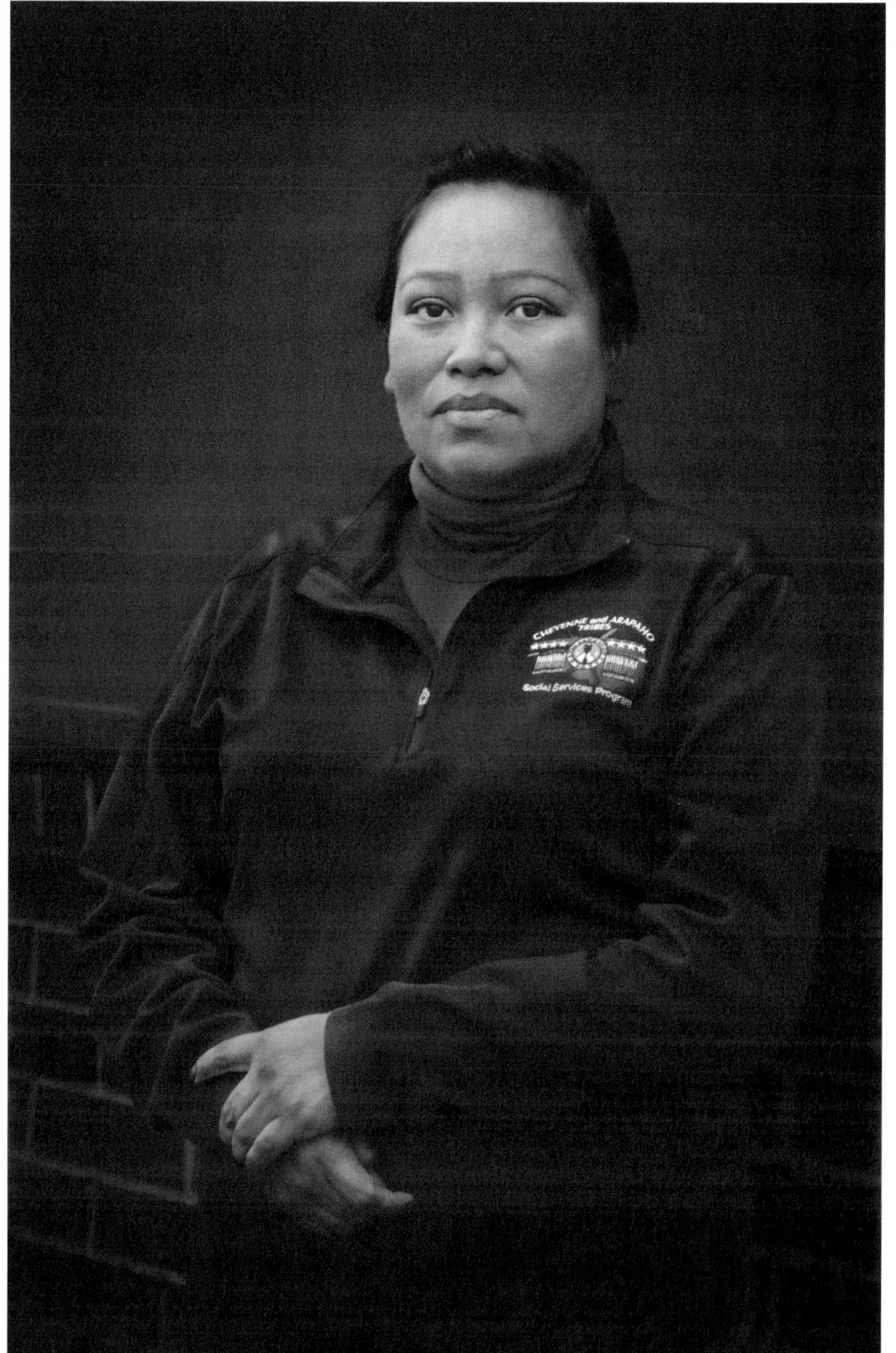

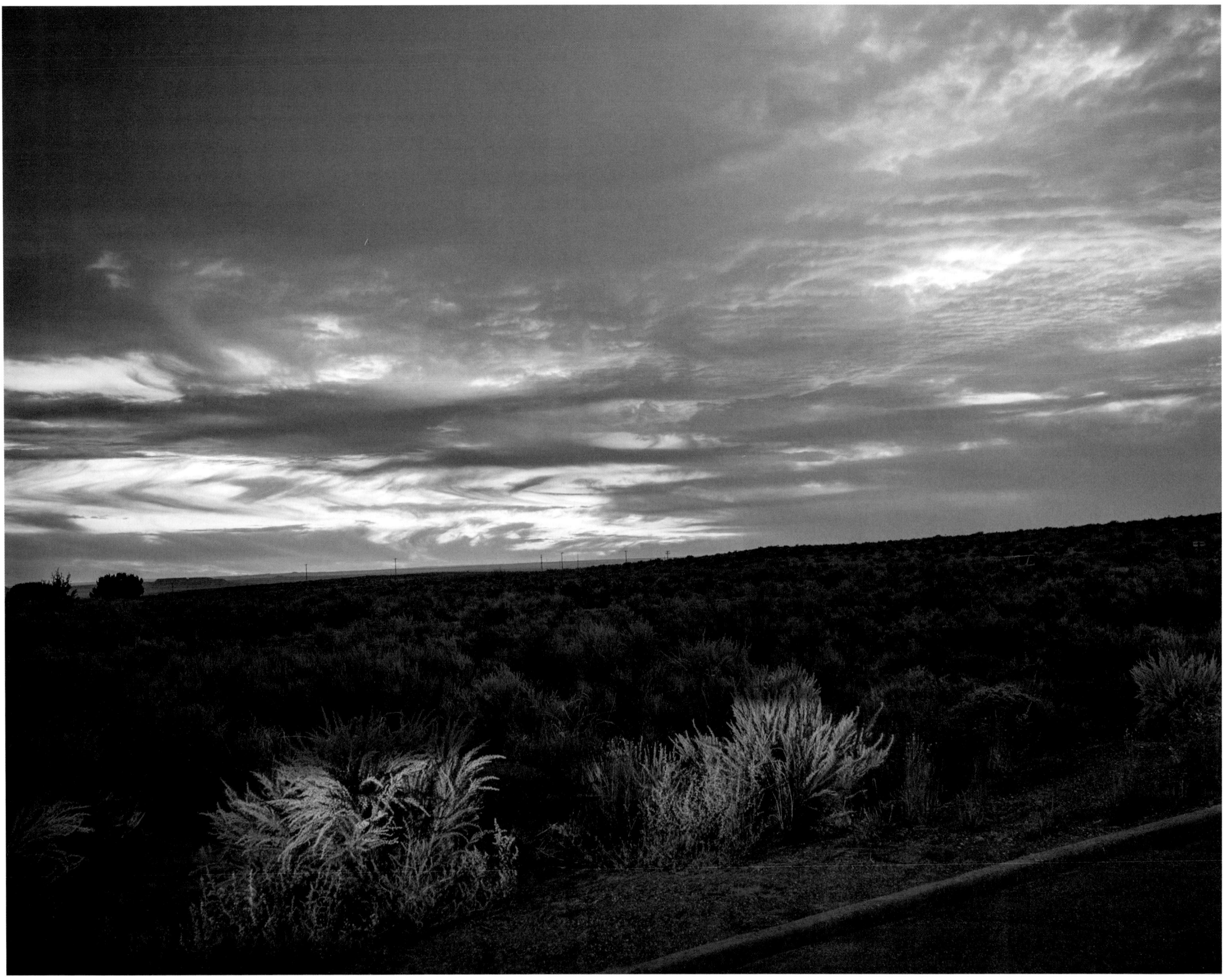

Headlights, Texas

N 31° 41.6431" W 89° 7' 50.2032"

LAUREL, MISSISSIPPI

"I am the world's best turkey caller.
Do you know how to play the ham bone?"

[Charles]

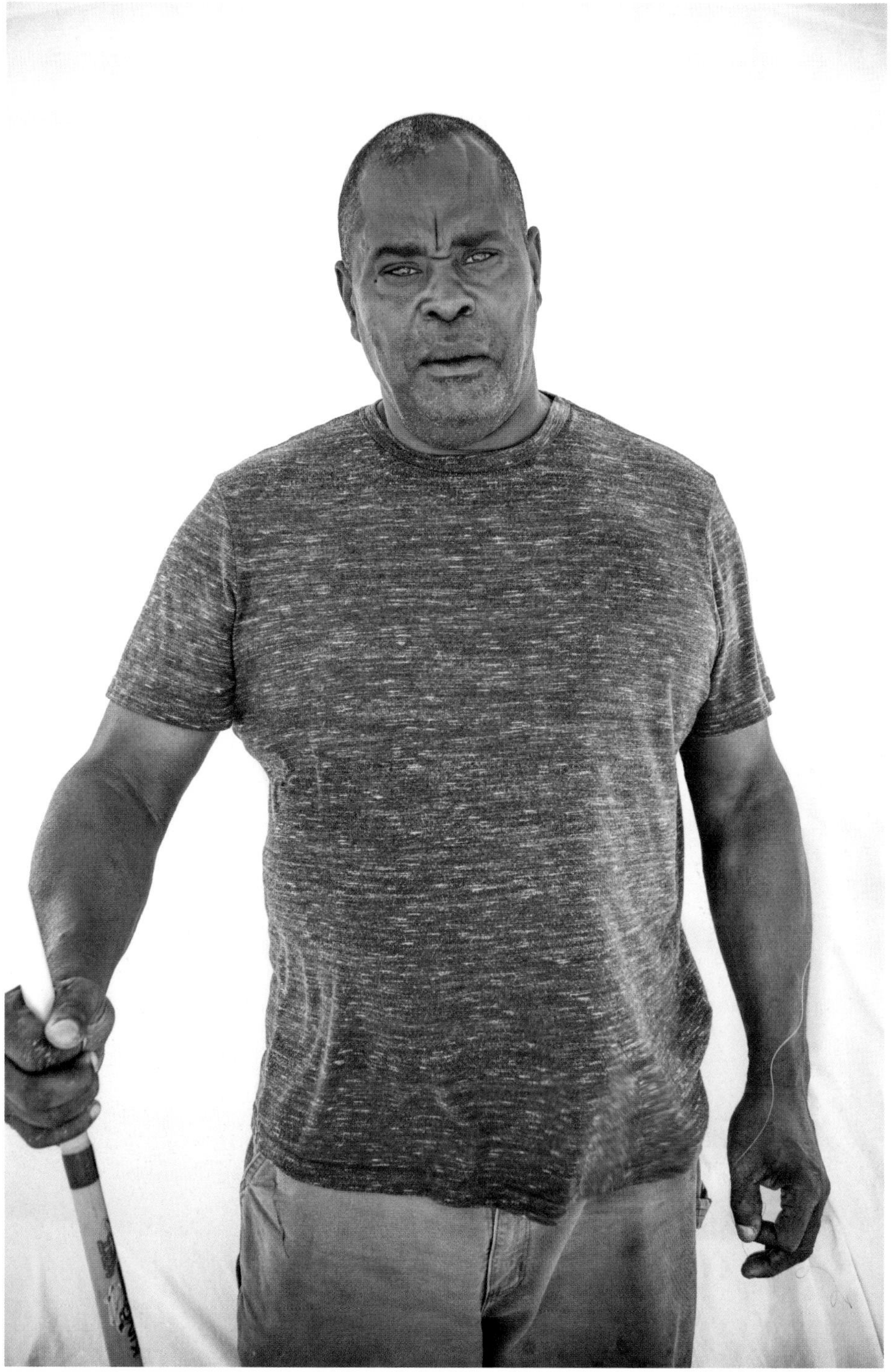

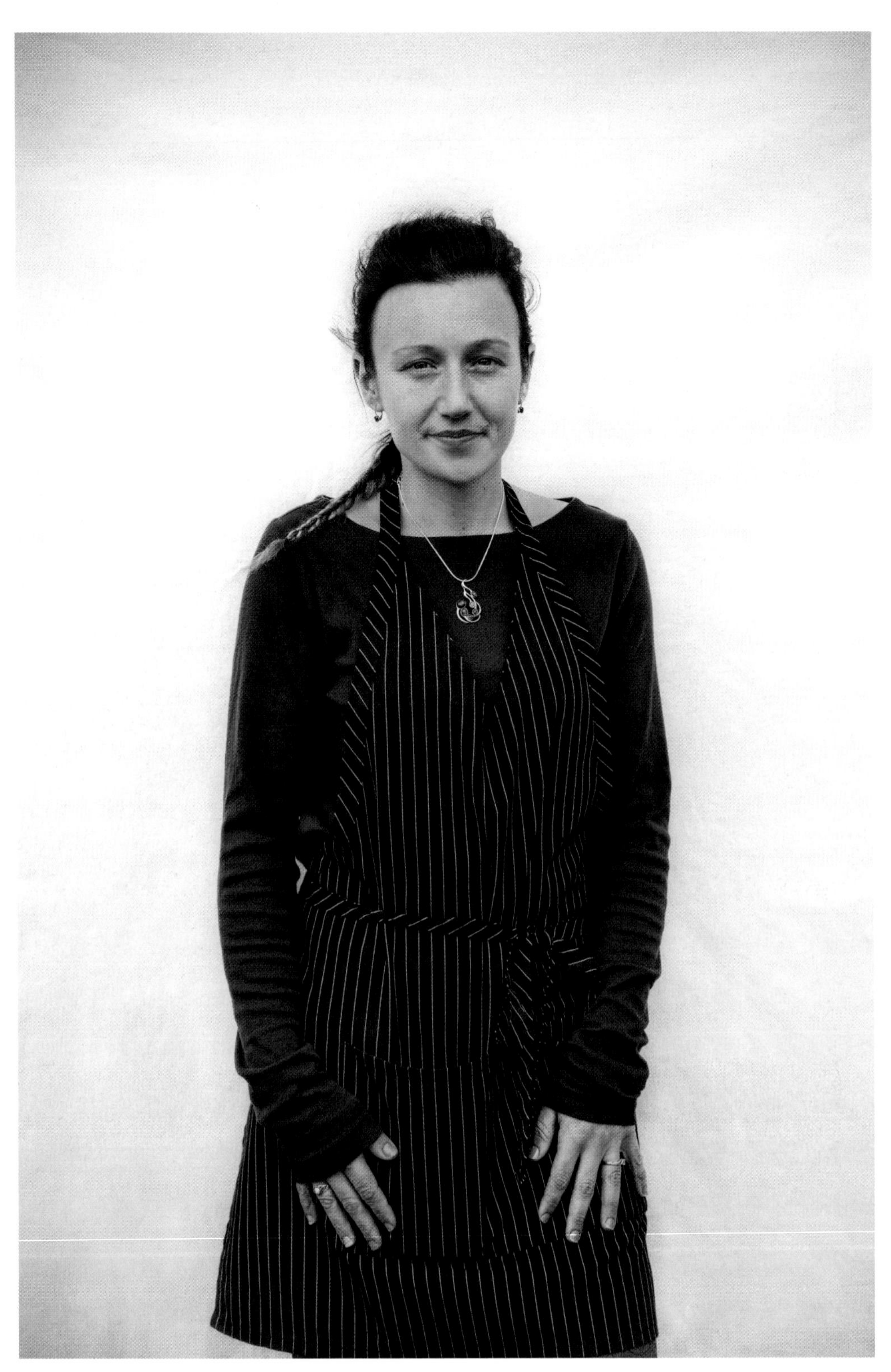

N 37° 56' 18.444" W 75° 21' 41.707"

CHINCOTEAGUE ISLAND, VIRGINIA

"Coming across the causeway is coming into my own life. Being outdoors and not being afraid, I get to enjoy the scenery and no one is bothering me. I love nature and being barefoot. I want to hear birds in the morning and fall asleep to crickets and frogs and nighttime air. I come from a family of artists and take a lot of family traits into account the way I do things. My dream is to be an artist and influence people in a positive way. I want my paintings to be a little more vibrant than my grandfather's and my mother's."

[Berit]

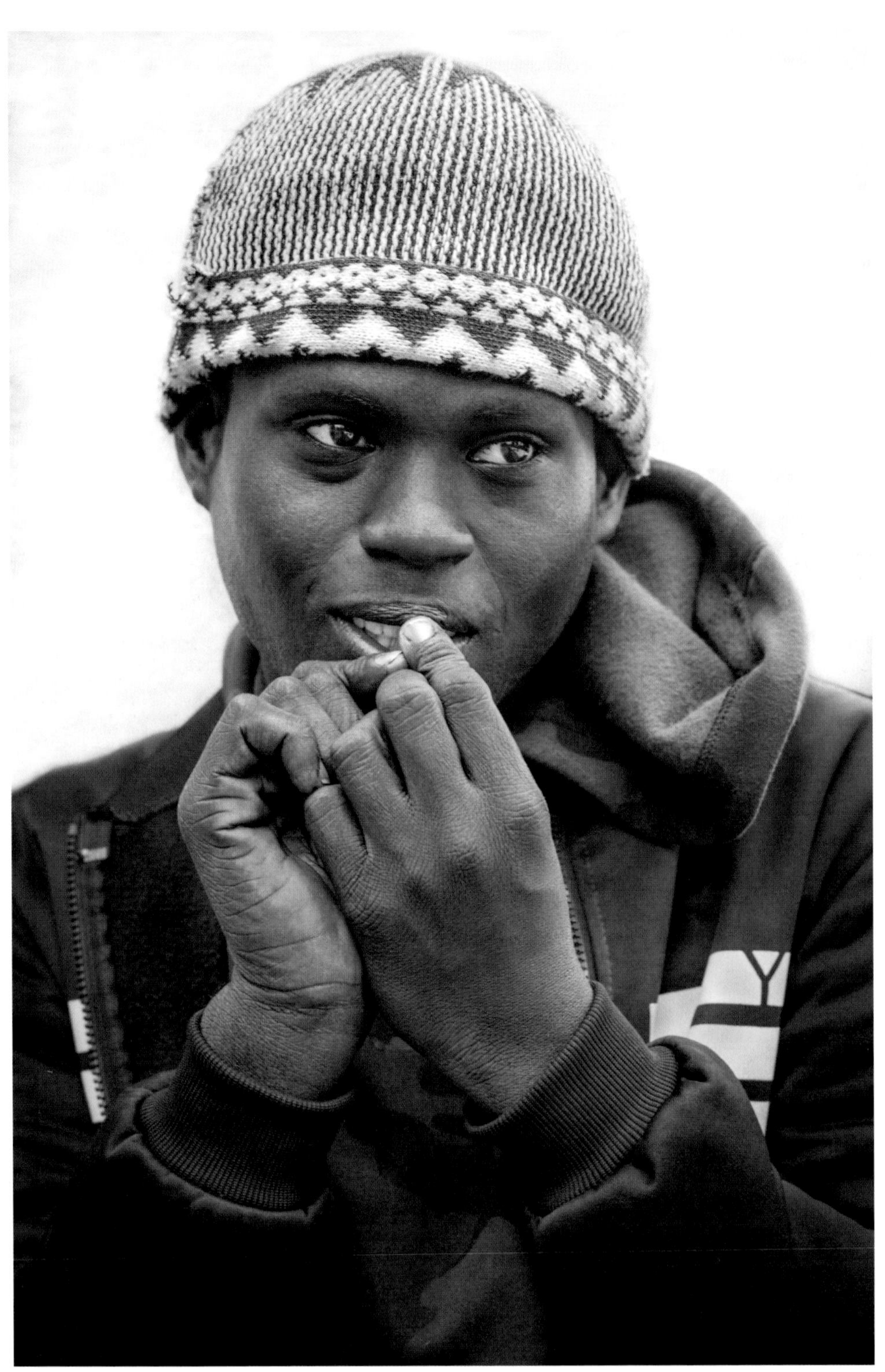

N 40° 44’ 8.3652” W 74° 10’ 20.5212”

NEWARK, NEW JERSEY

“You don’t have to shoot this ... maybe you don’t want to. I was selling candy on the street, carried cash ... I was stabbed and robbed.”

[José]

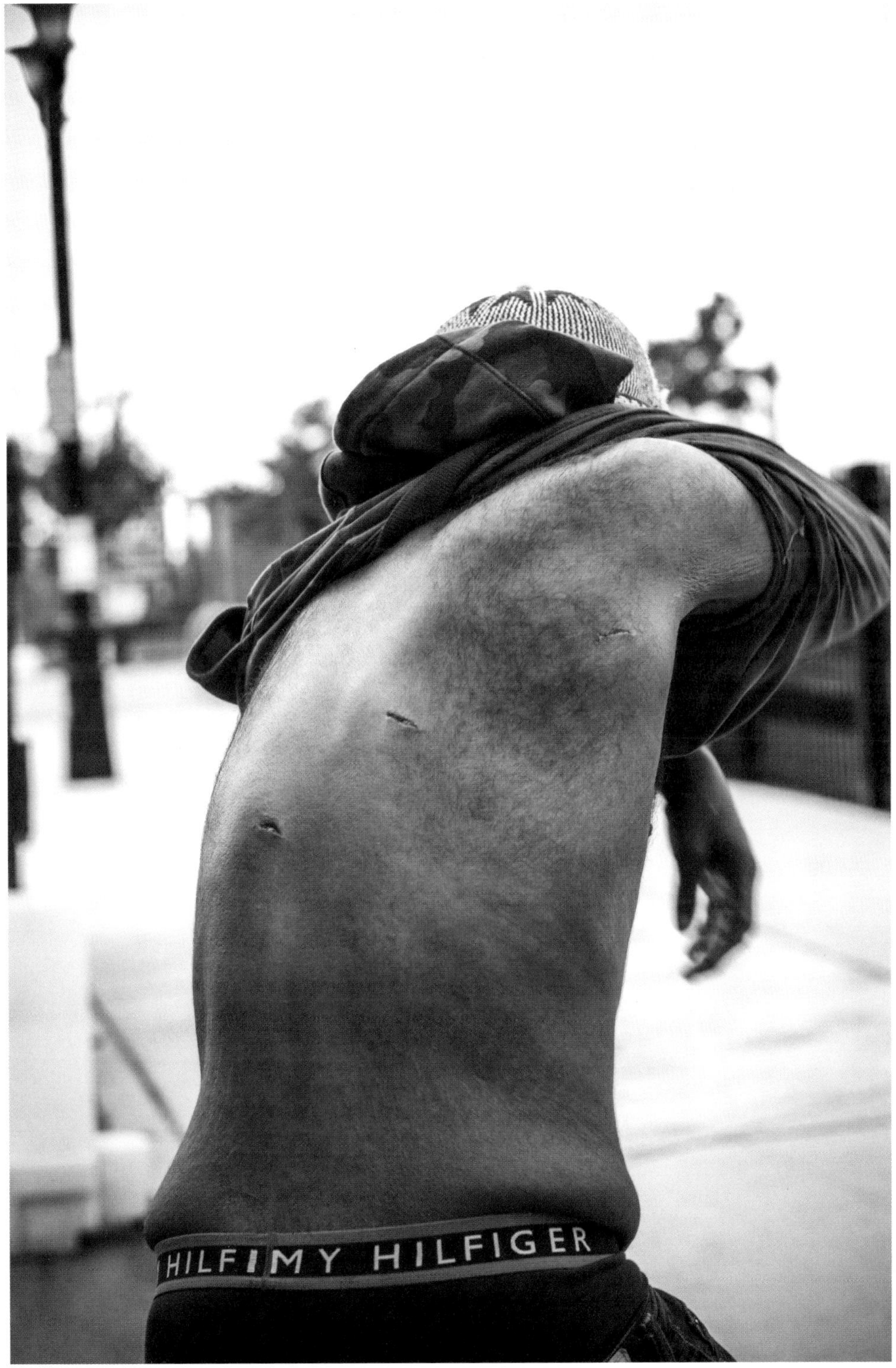

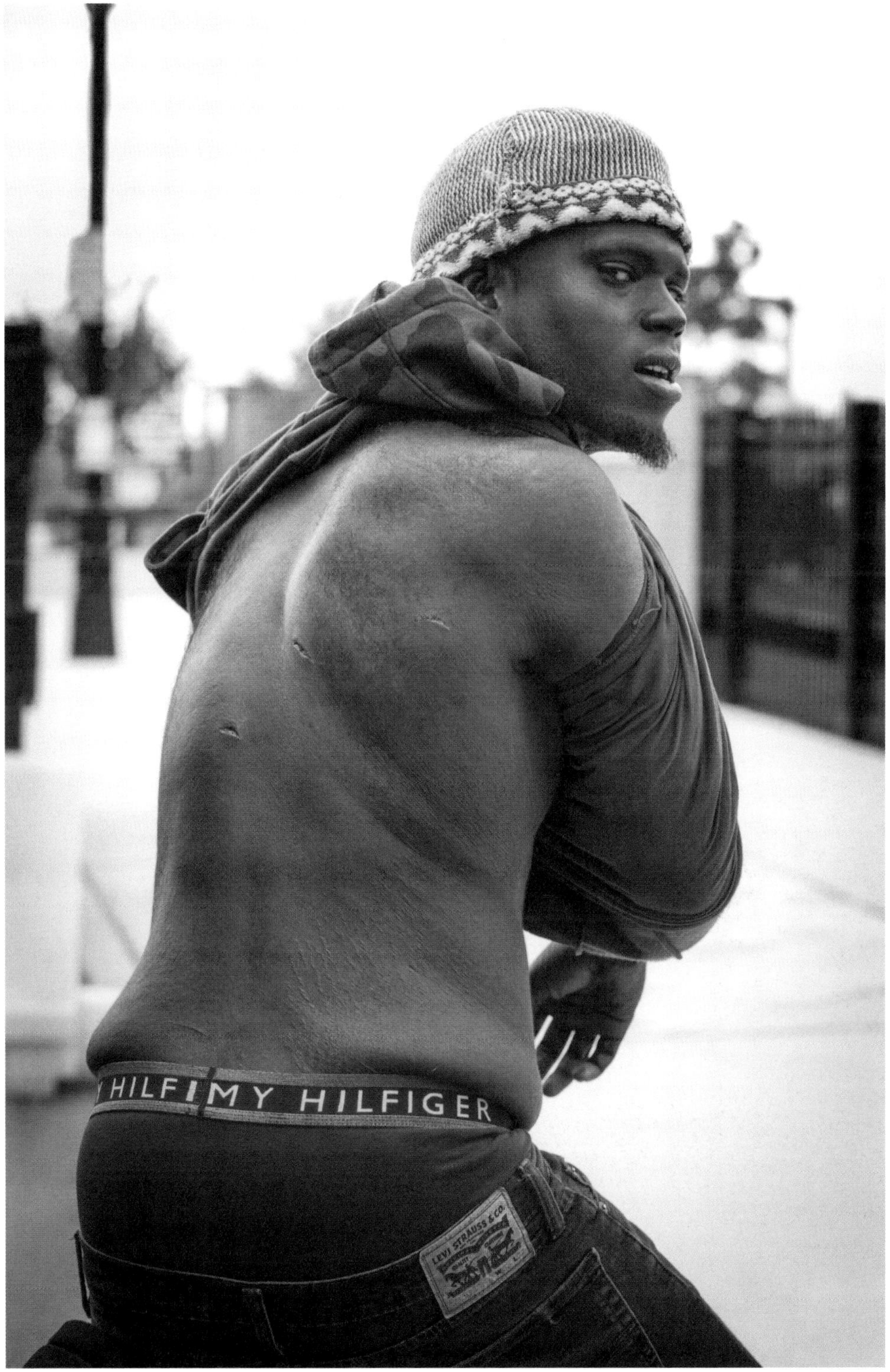

Stab marks, New Jersey

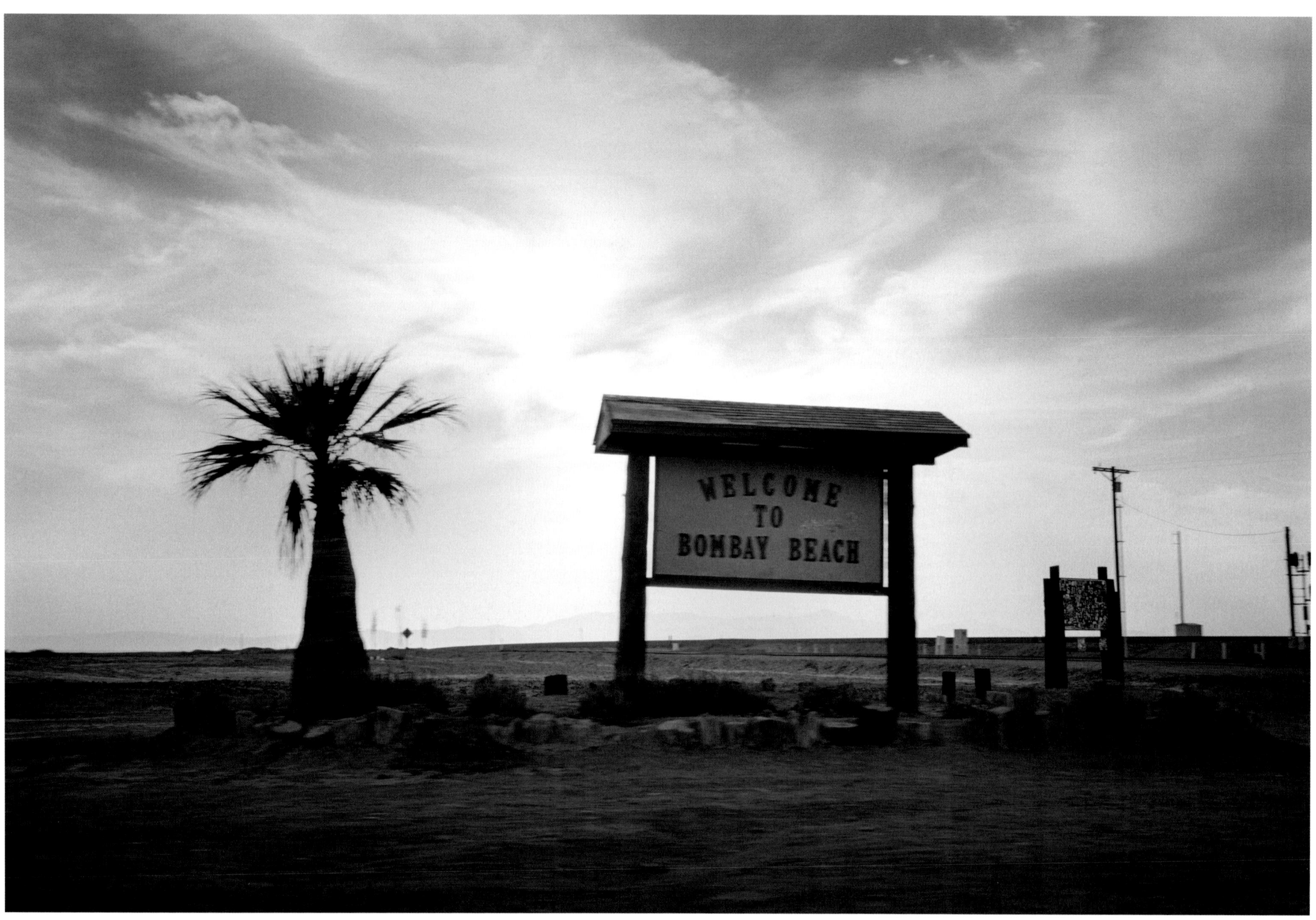

Bombay Beach, California

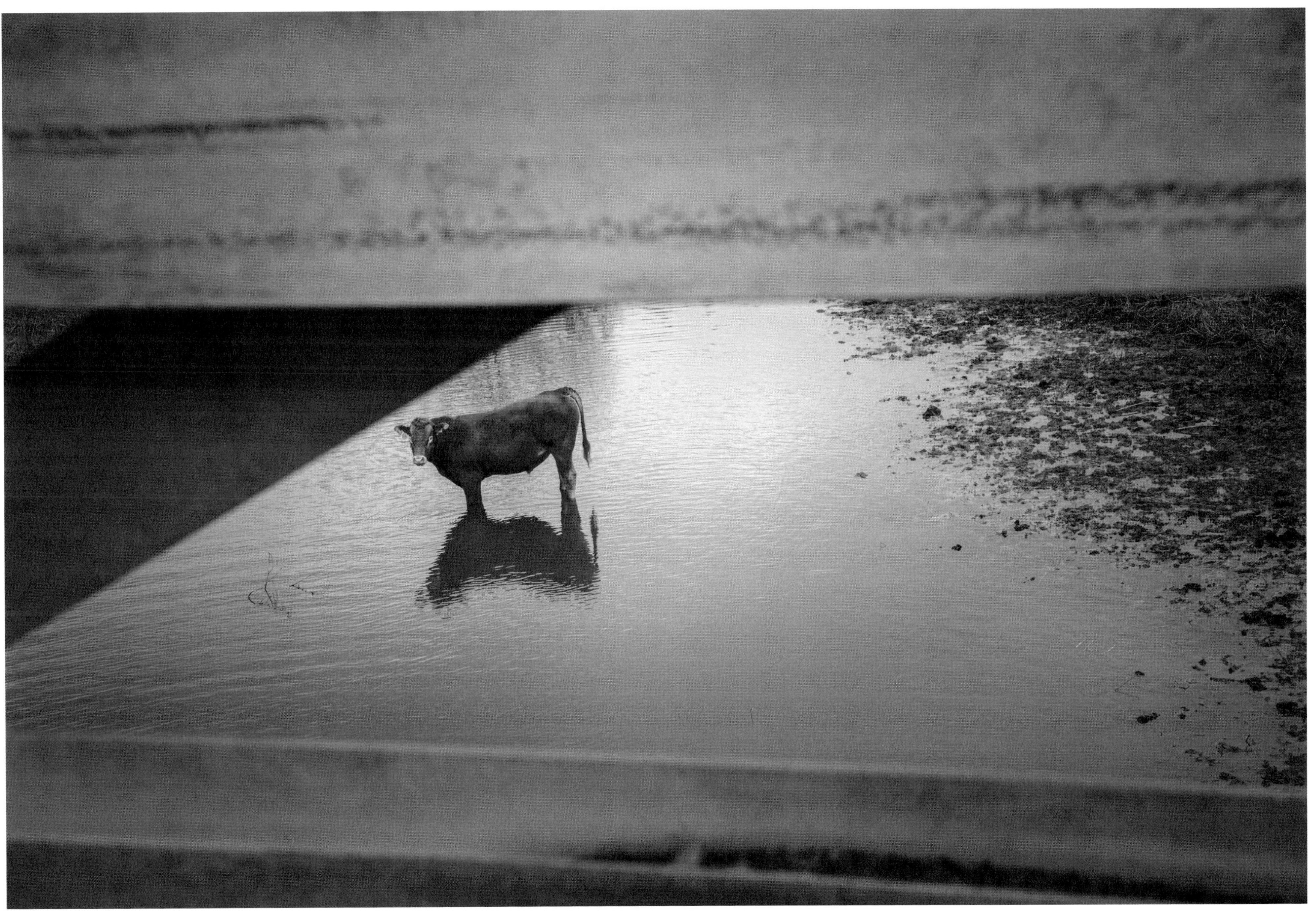

Number 490, Oklahoma

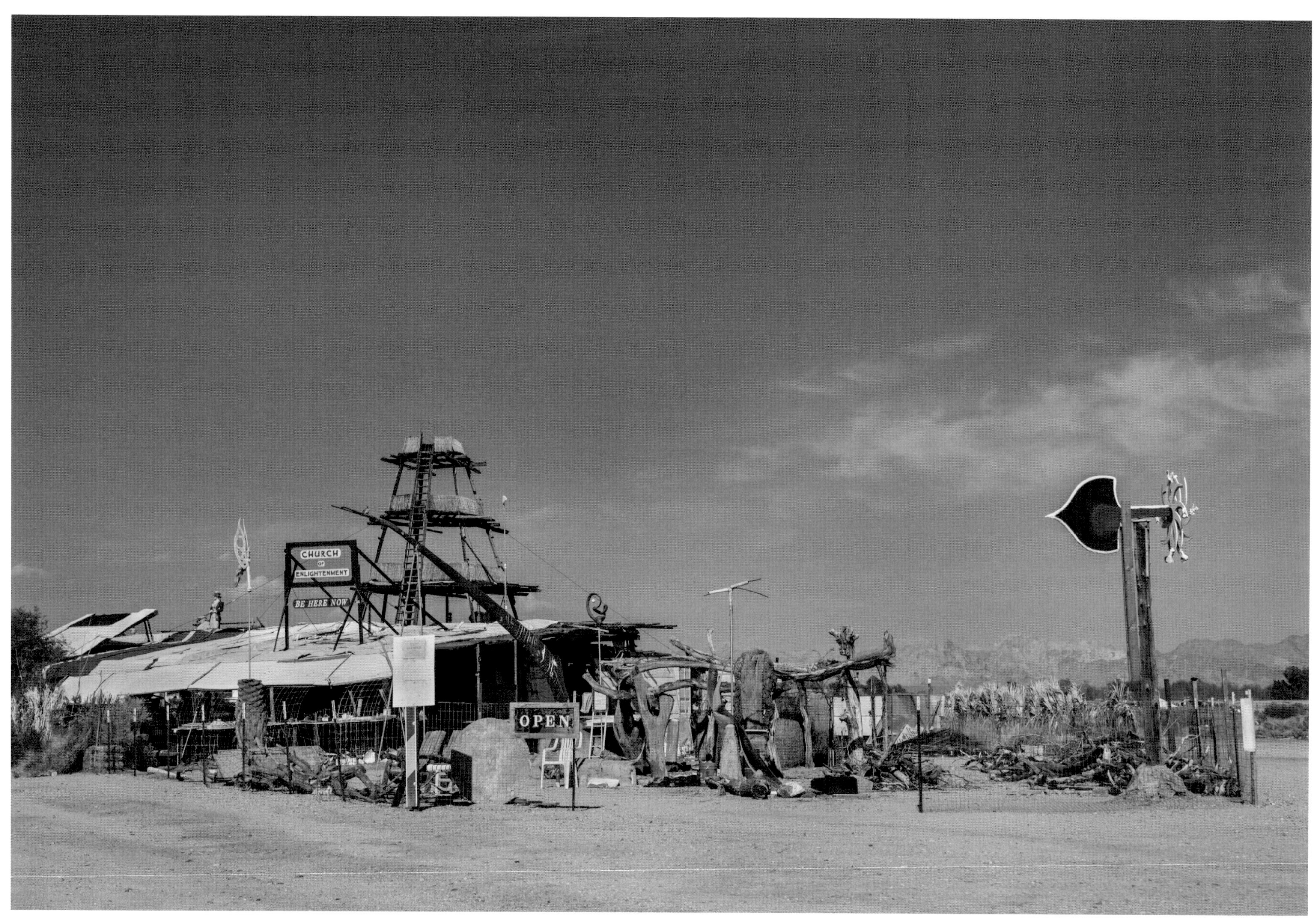

Church of Enlightenment, California

N 33° 15‘ 8.94” W 115° 28‘ 12.83”

SALVATION MOUNTAIN, CALIFORNIA

“I heard about this place from ‘Into the Wild.’ I was homeless in Washington and decided to come here and build a life from scratch. I have the freedom to live my life the way I want to, and the government leaves me alone because I live out here. Most of the Salton Sea is abandoned now, and the areas that have dried out have a layer of toxic dust. We have earthquakes throwing the dust up in the air, then the wind blows it around everywhere. They’re talking about pumping brine down into the lithium reservoirs. It is going to degrade those caverns underneath us and cause the earthquakes to get worse. If you can survive here, then you’re pretty much good. I could live anywhere after living here.”

[Eohkka]

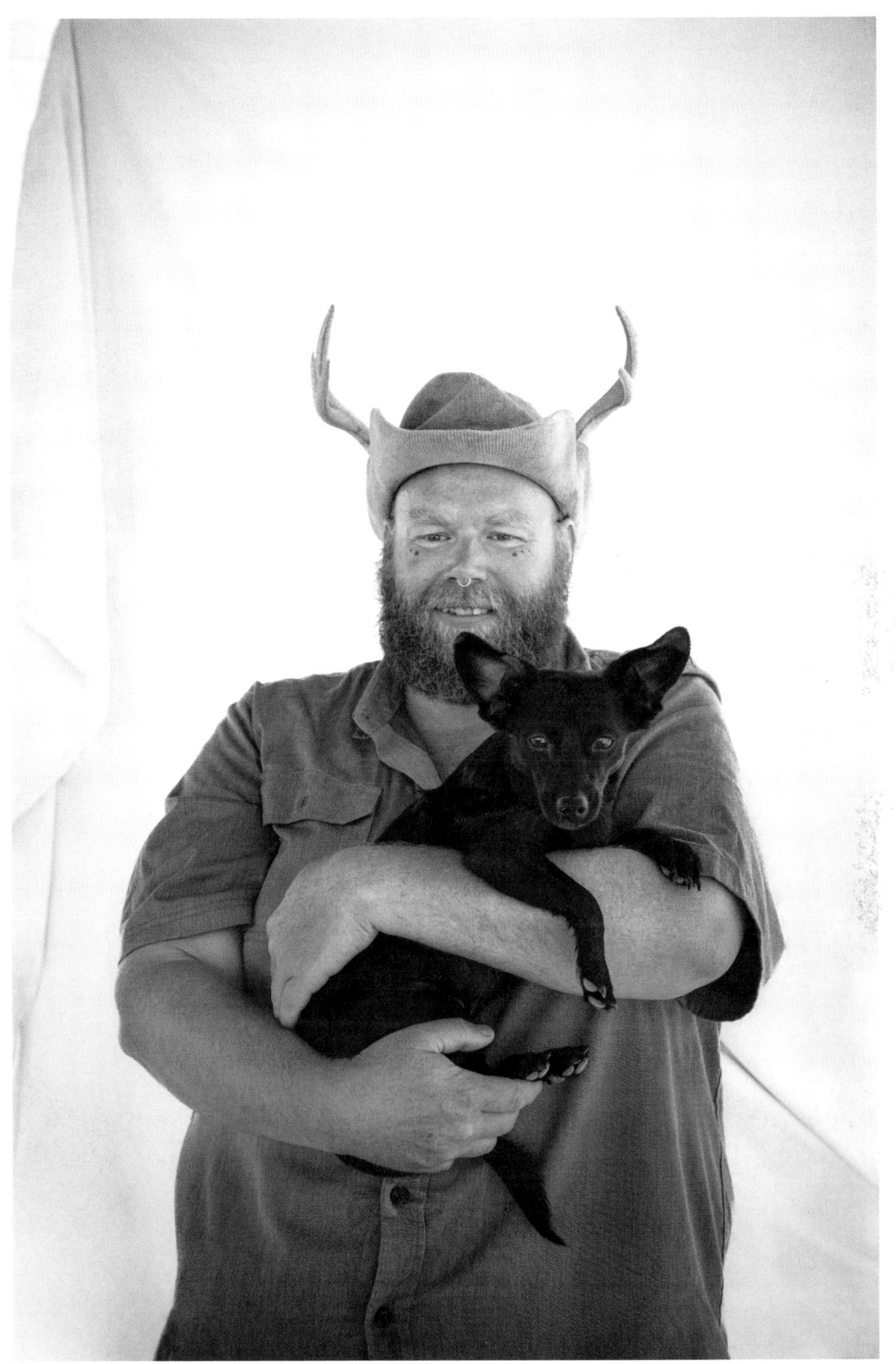

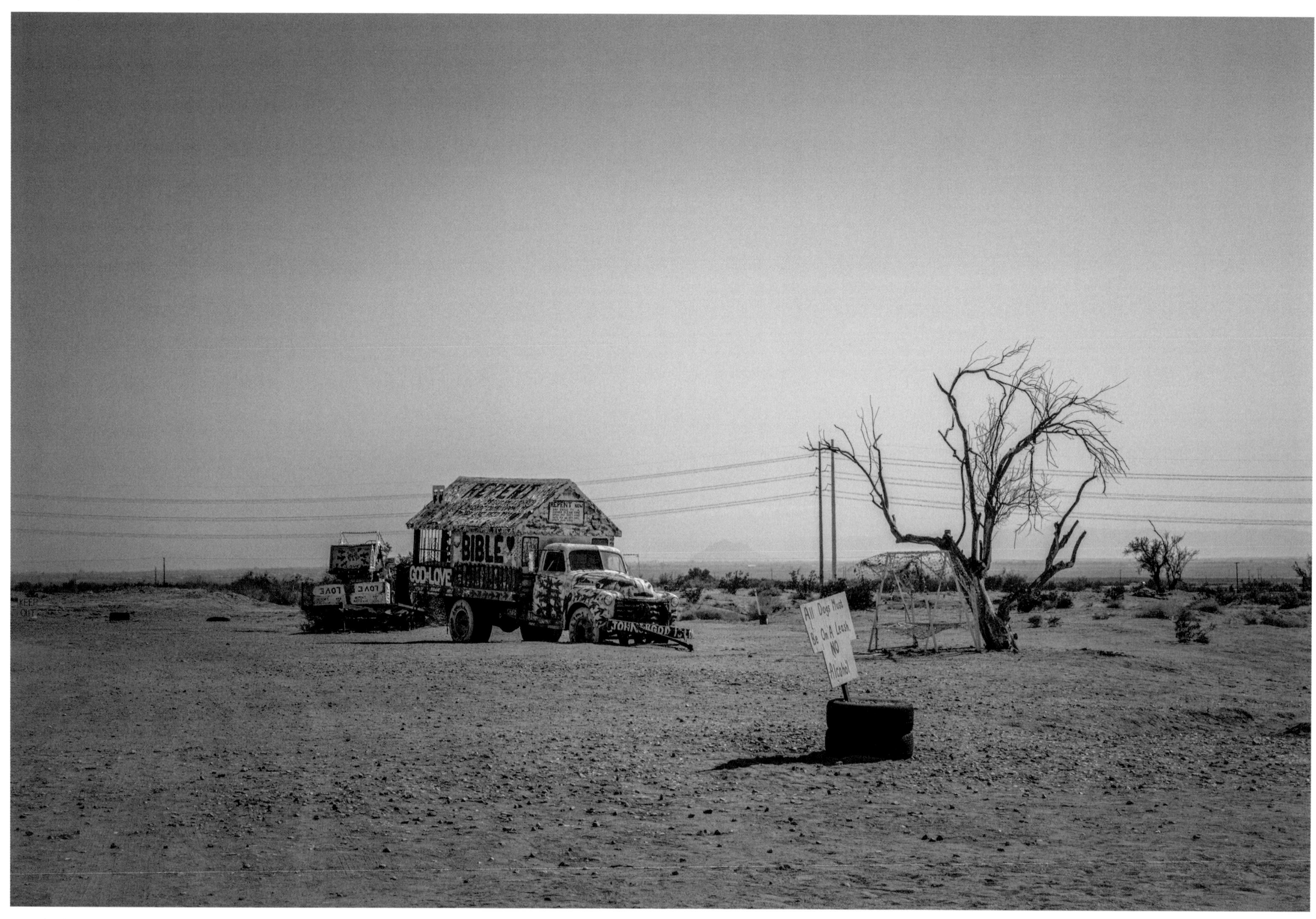

God is love, keep out, California

N 36° 13' 46.866" W 116° 46' 4.5084"

BADWATER BASIN, CALIFORNIA

"Maybe you should be chasing the sun. As you keep up with the sun, it will never set. Therefore the day will always last, the year never really ending."

[Nathan]

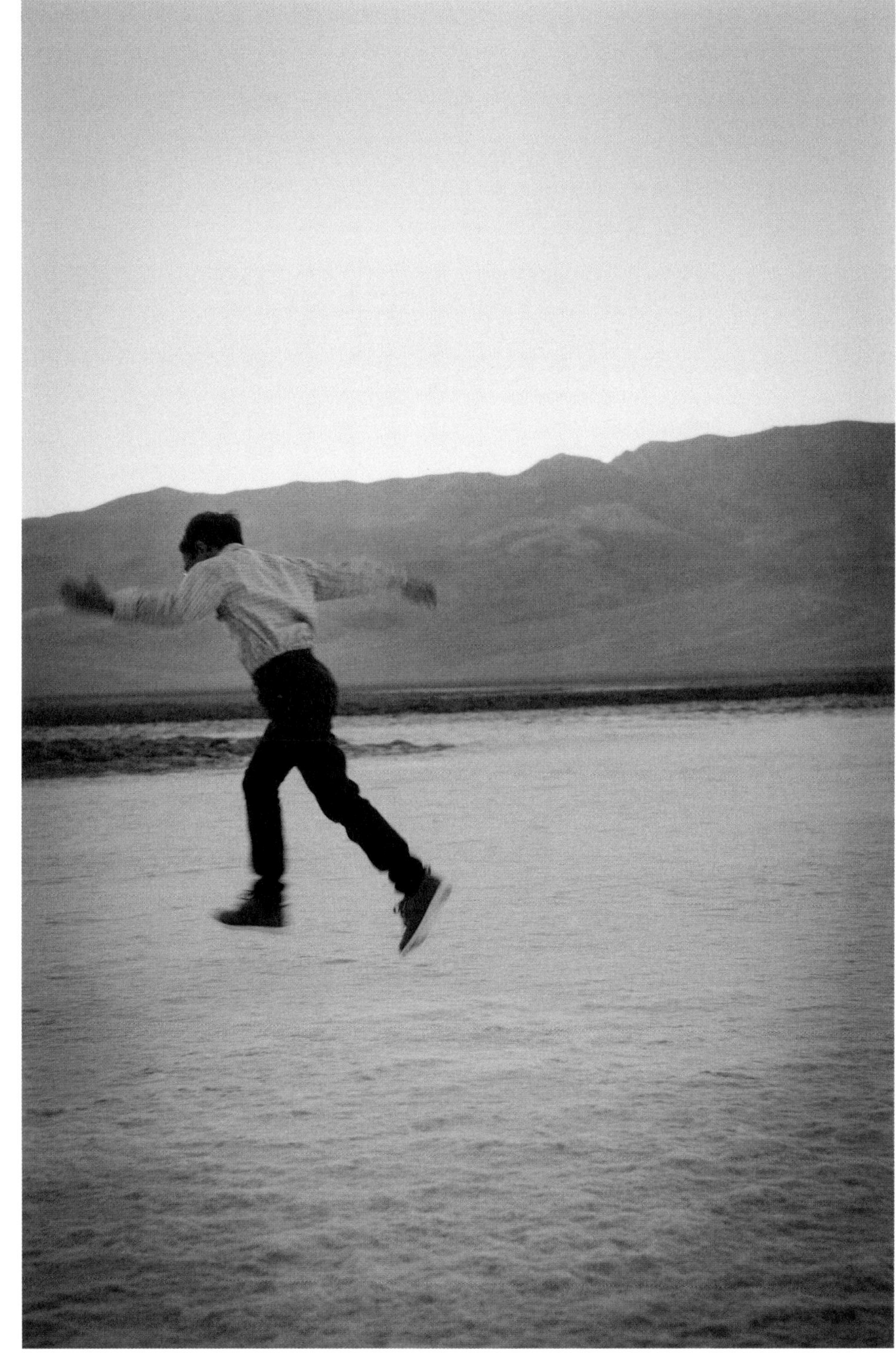

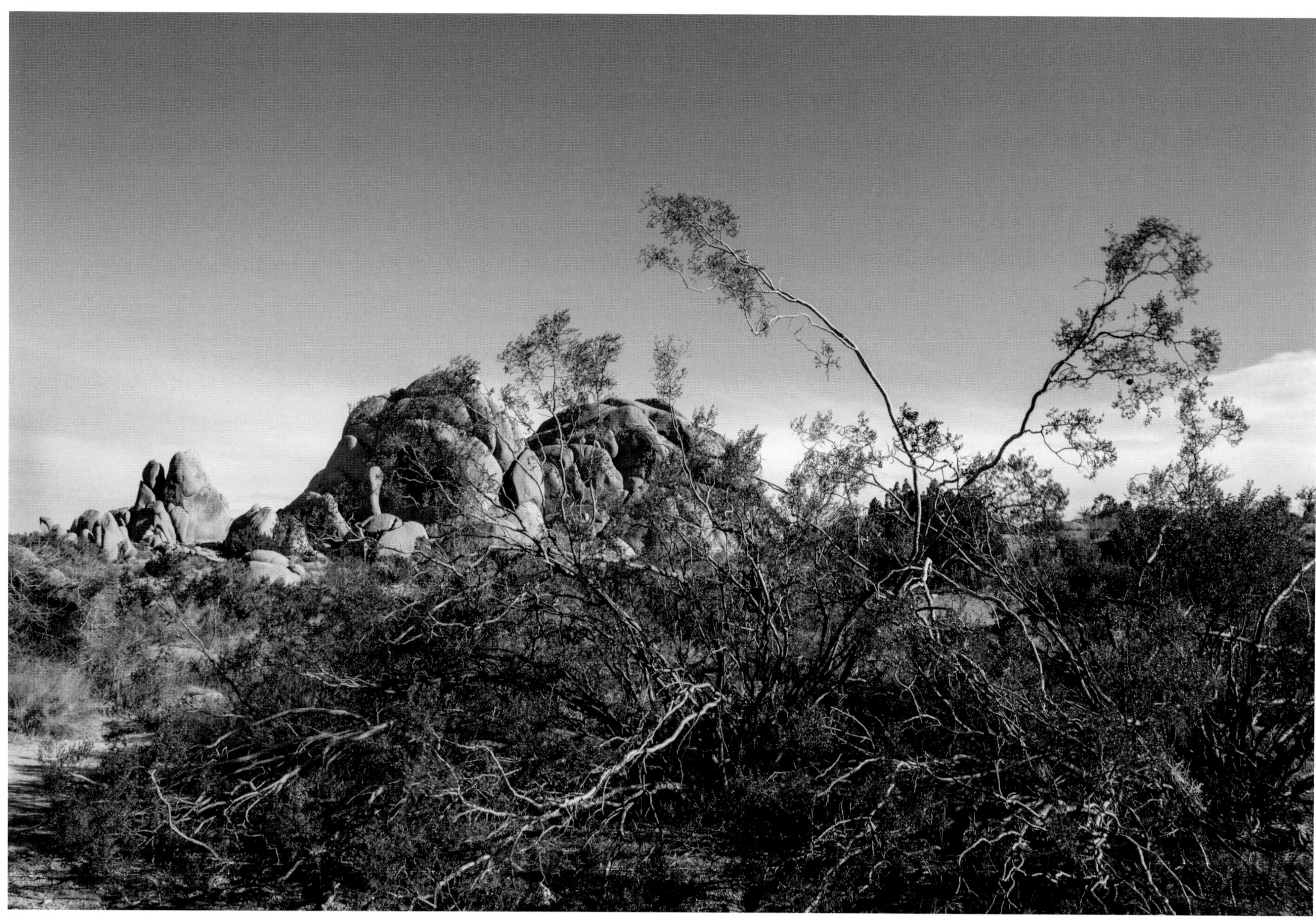

Boulders, California

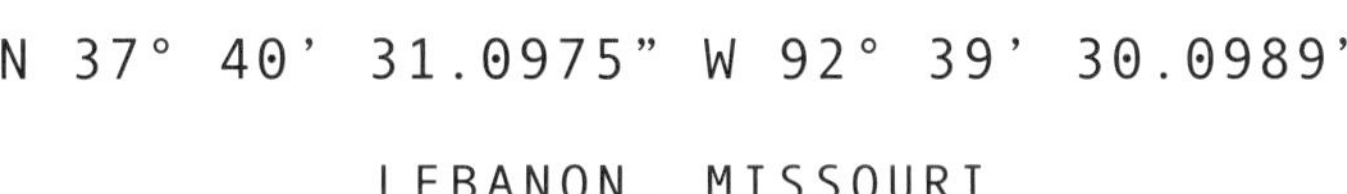

N 37° 40’ 31.0975” W 92° 39’ 30.0989”

LEBANON, MISSOURI

“I was born in Memphis, Tennessee, raised in the Chicago suburbs and live in Lebanon. It took me a lifetime of searching to find myself. I dream of one more West Coast trip, but I am very grateful for the life I led when I was young, foolish and a free spirit on the road in the ’70s and ’80s. It was a different world then. My dream is for some type of real peace in the world, but I doubt that will happen in my kids’ or my grandkids’ lifetime.”

[Larry]

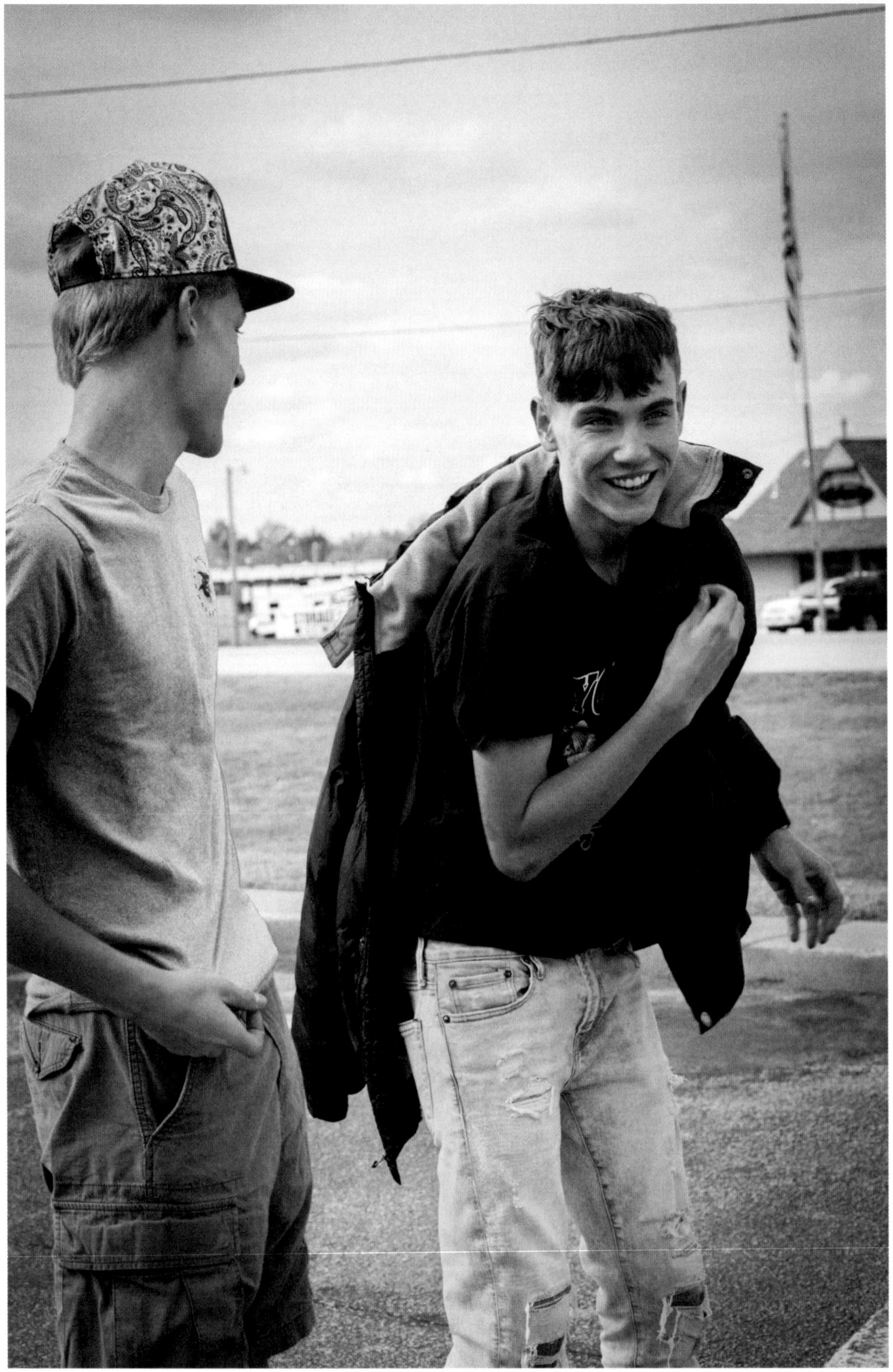

Josh and Braden, Oklahoma

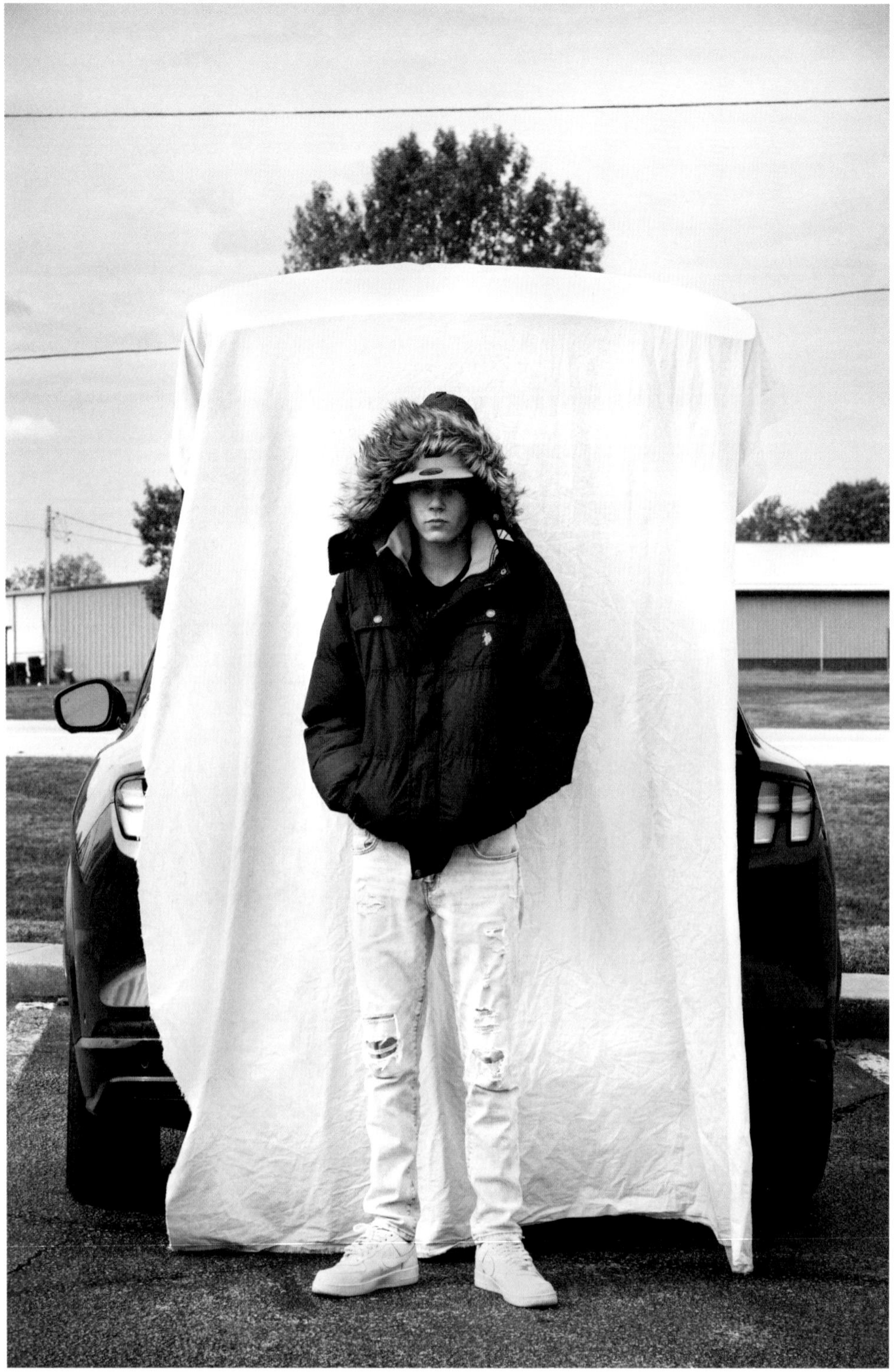

N 36° 56’ 0.2472” W 94° 52’ 22.8324”

COMMERCE, OKLAHOMA

“I would love to be a model.”

[Braden]

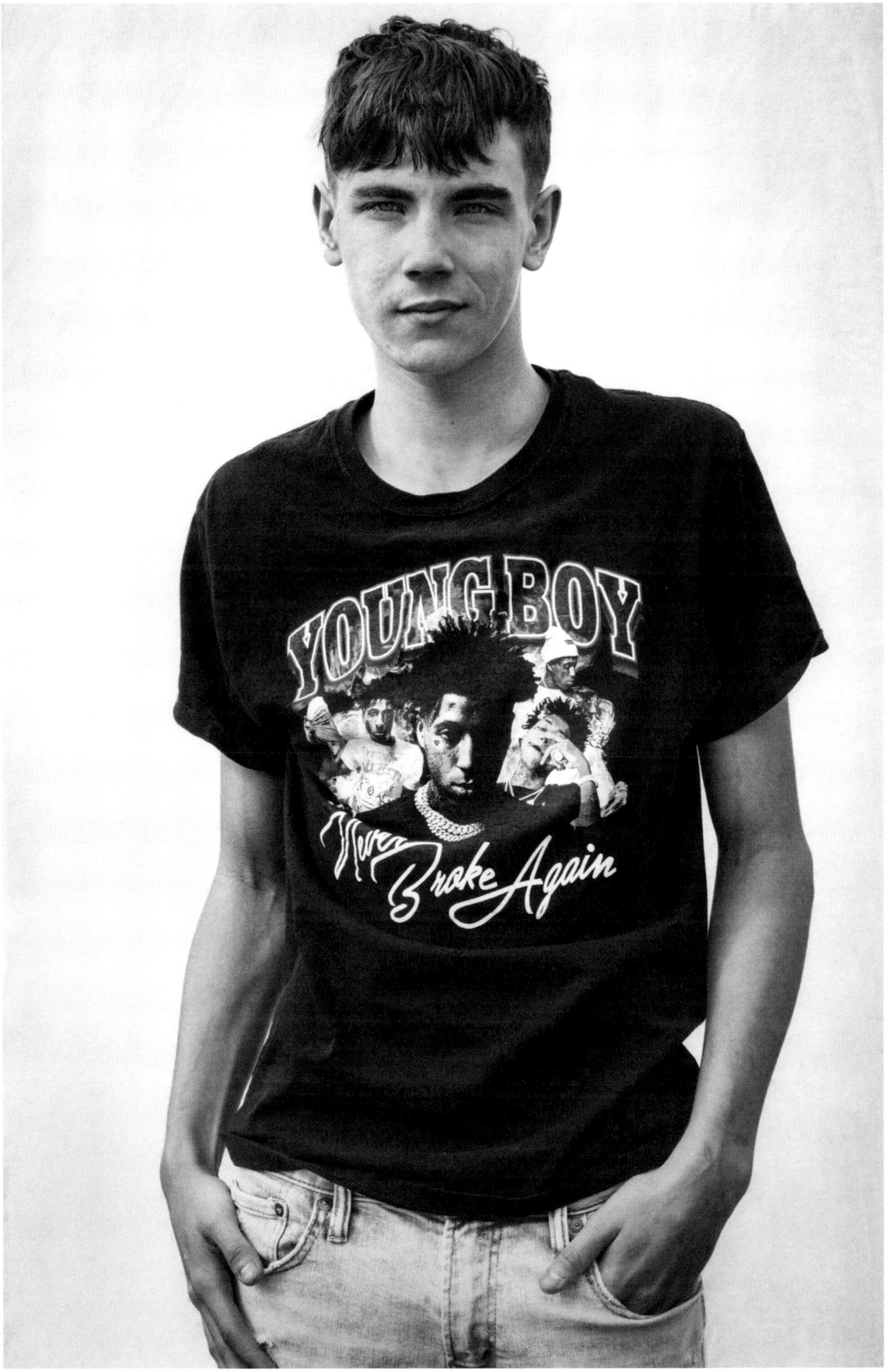

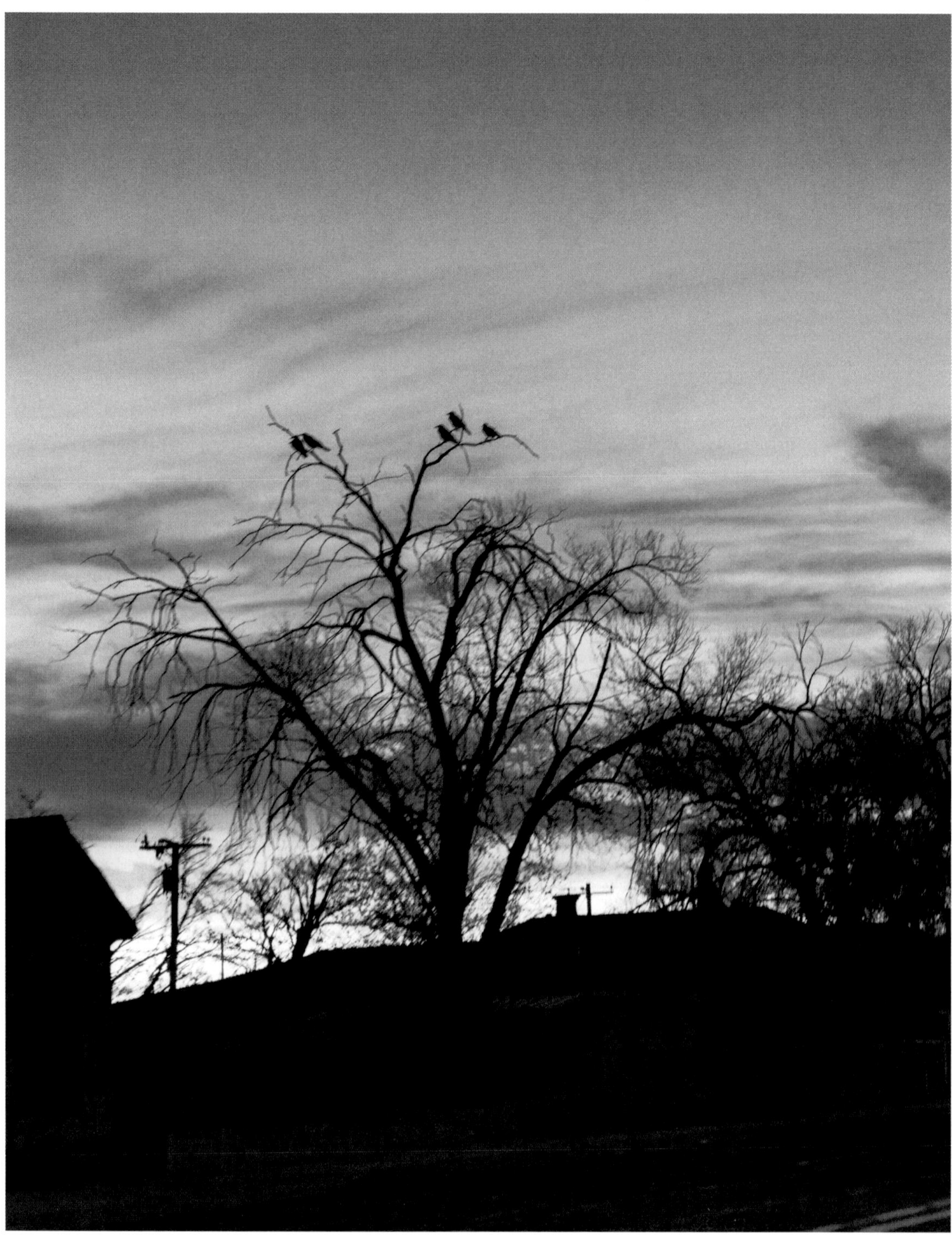

Dusk, California

"Here in Craig County, it's hard to find housing. I had a basement full of water and got into an argument with my landlord. Then I got evicted, so me and my wife and my son have been living in a motel for two years now. What can you do? I used to work in mental health and saw a lady trying to hang herself. I haven't been right in the head since. Then this kid hung himself, bad drugs or something. He was only 19. I got kids that age, so it hit me really hard. After that I kind of lost it. Trying to keep a job, but I believe that I can fix this."

[Don, Oklahoma]

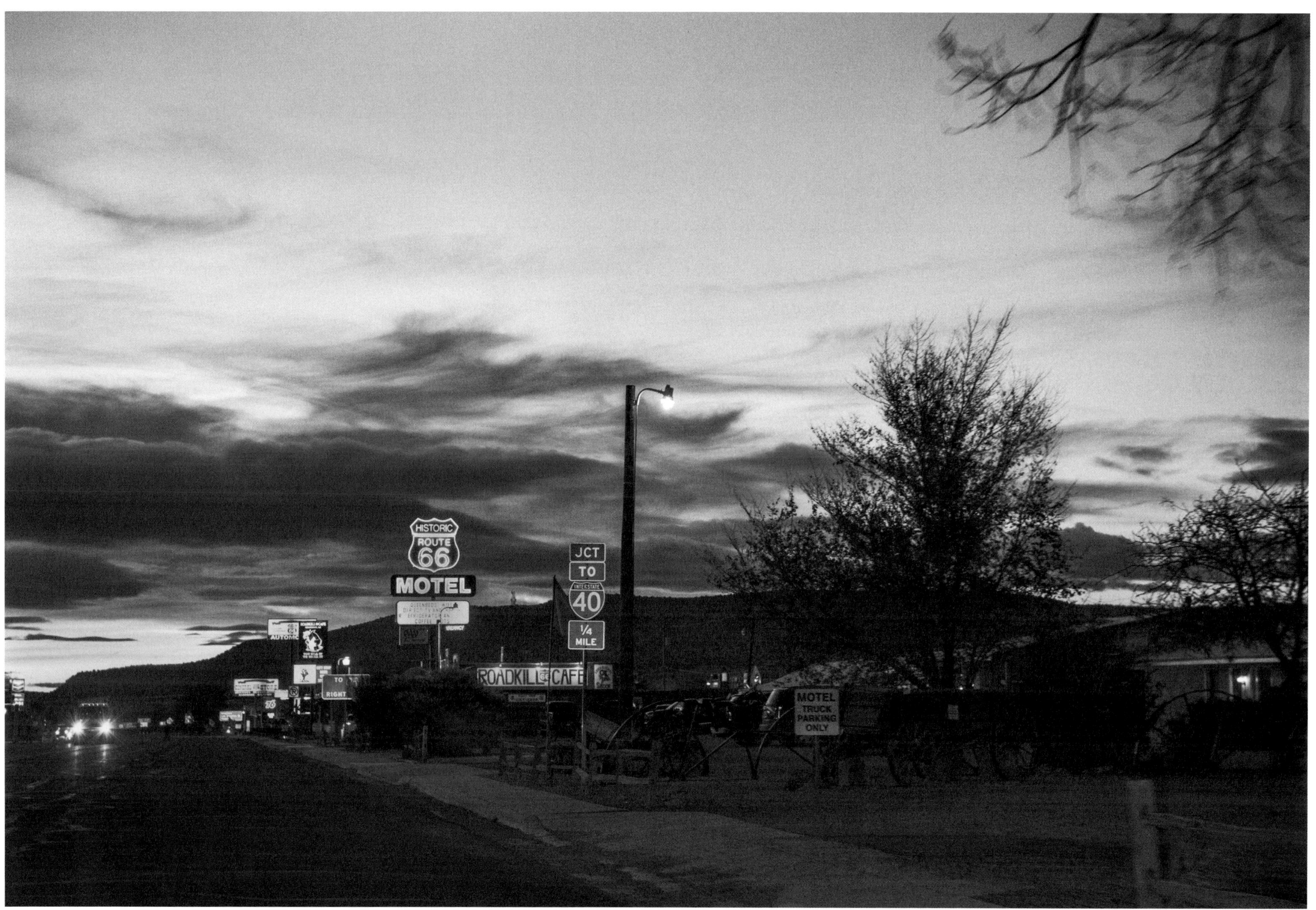

Mojave Drive, California

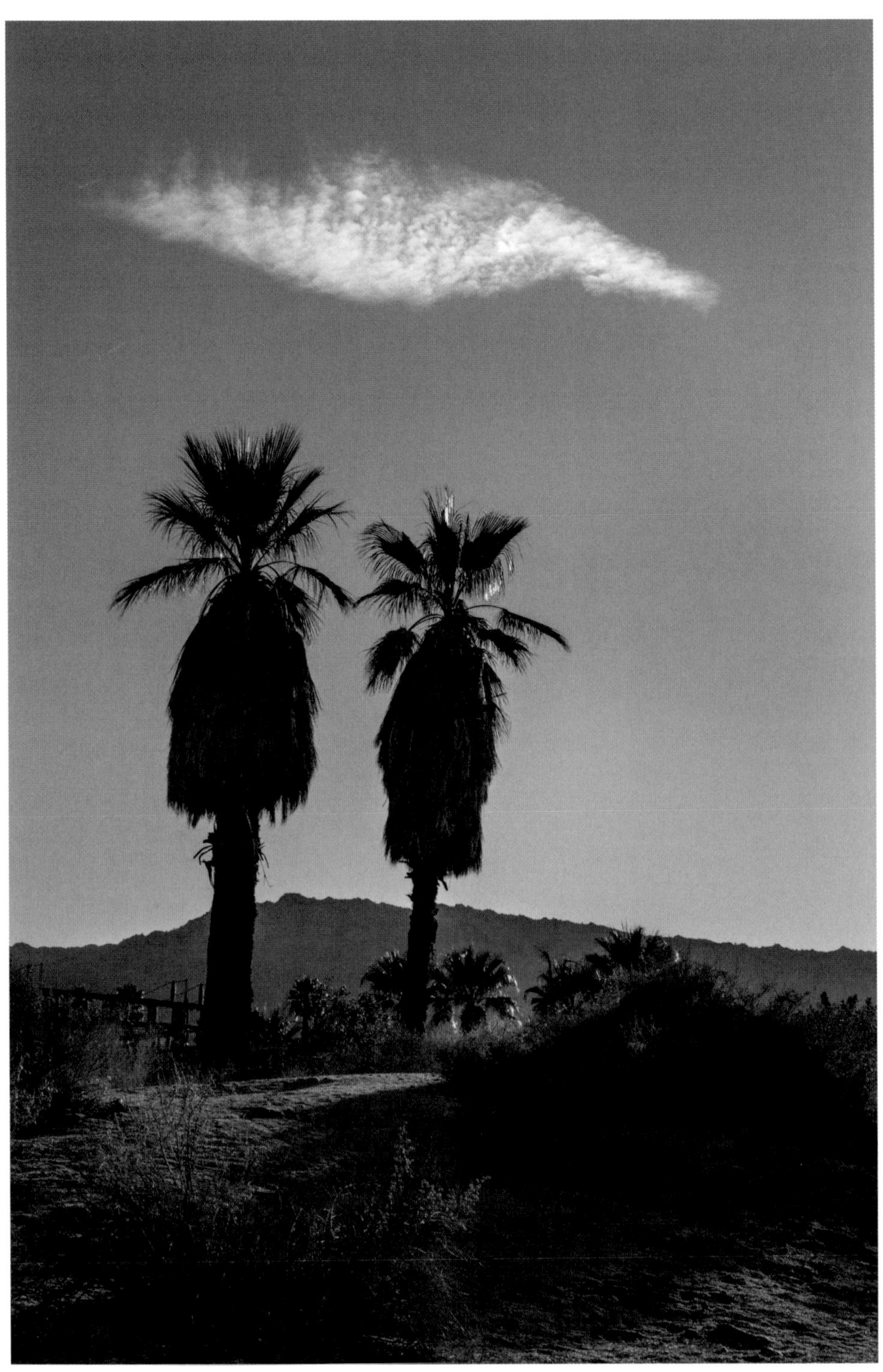

Lip cloud, California

N 33° 43' 20.082" W 116° 22' 28.0416"

PALM DESERT, CALIFORNIA

"I followed in my father's footsteps; we are stone workers. There are so many misunderstandings in the world because we don't realize we are nature and also matter. We are split from ourselves. Whatever we're creating, it's not only for us — it should have an echo that goes on forever and breaks the barrier between the matter and the soul. There could be many futures, and we create them with every decision. America is a journey. America is a lesson and hard work. America is an idea of a people. But for real — America is Atlantis."

[Carlos Jr.]

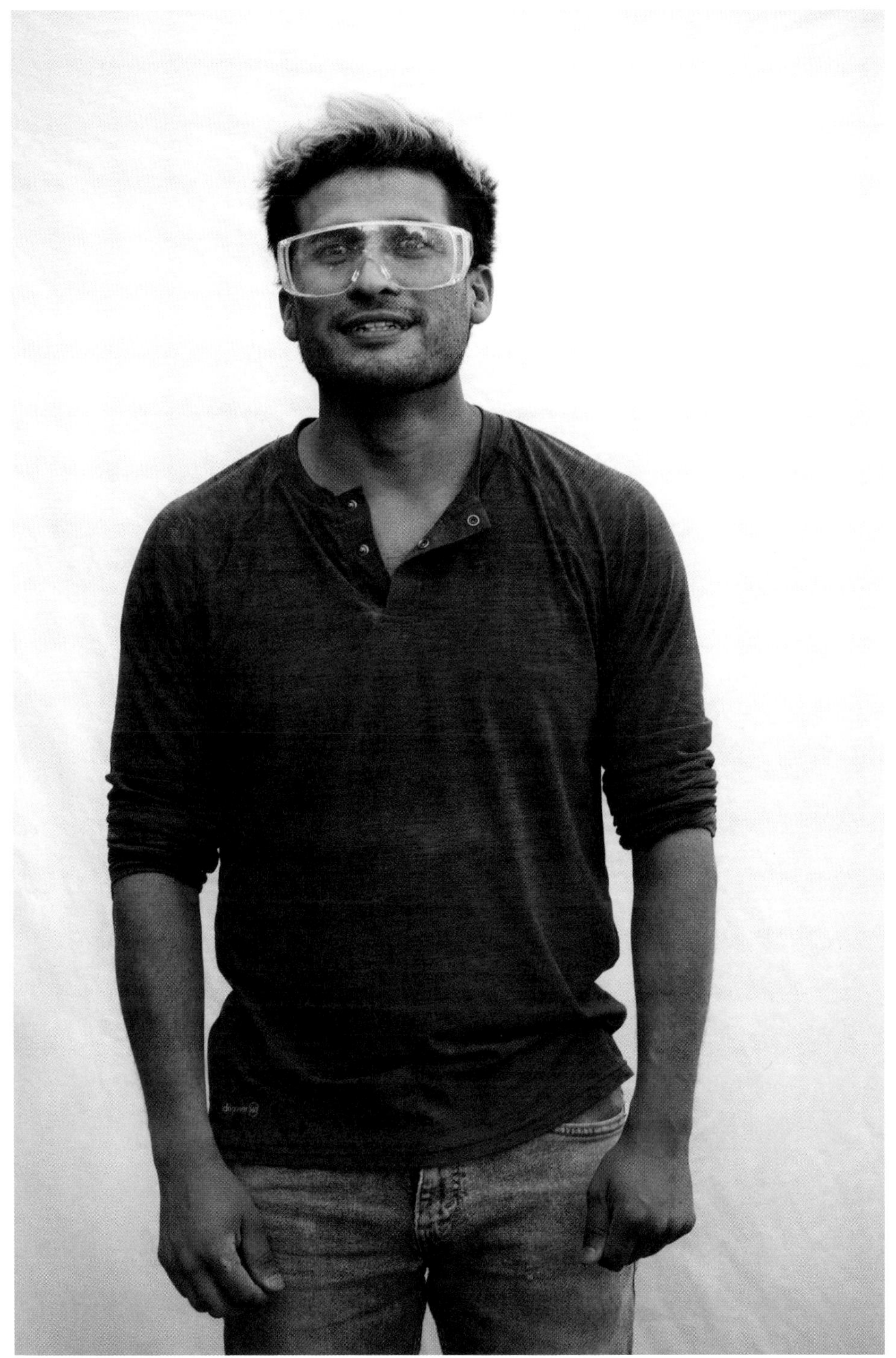

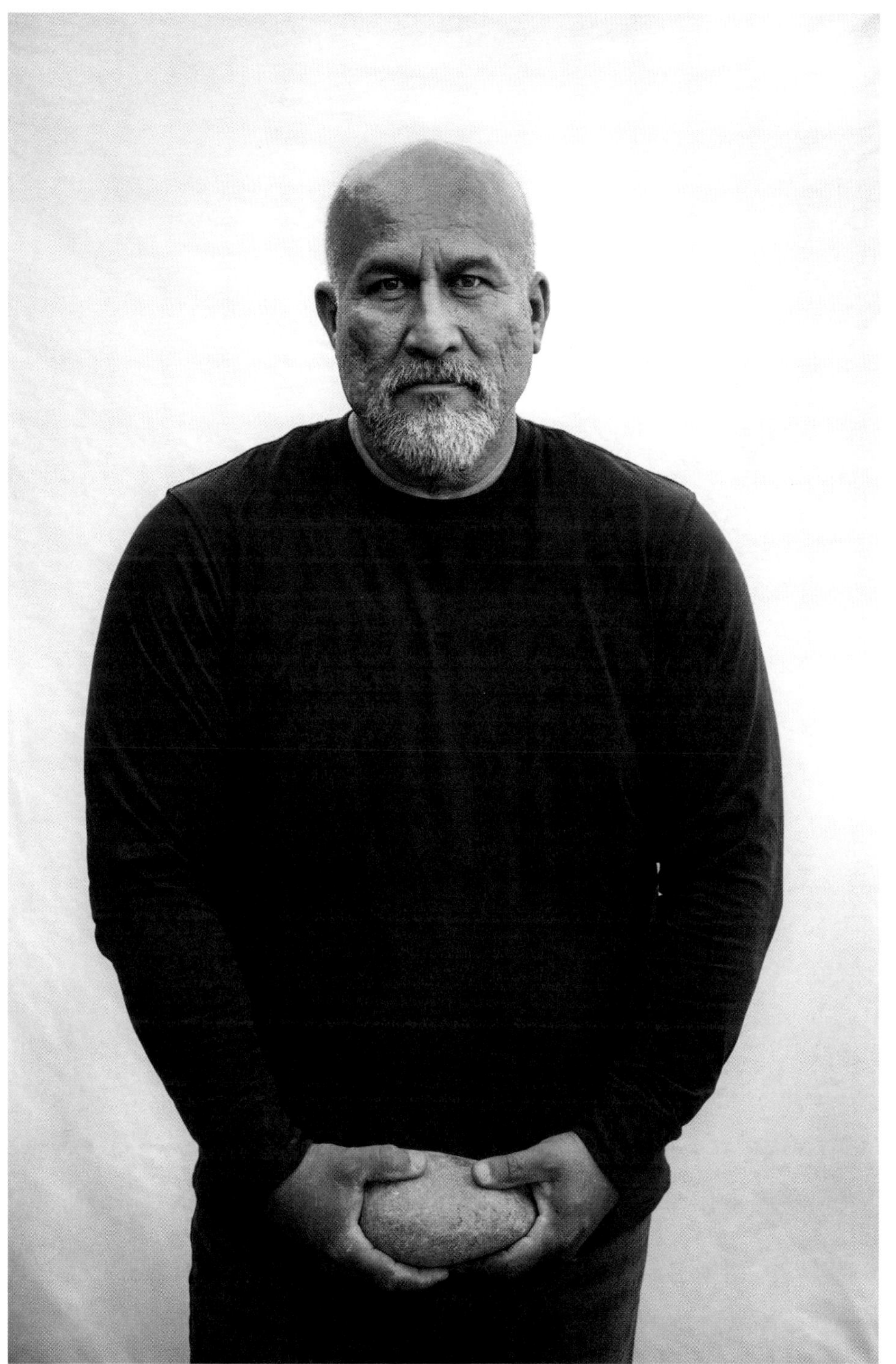

Carlos Jr., and Sr., California

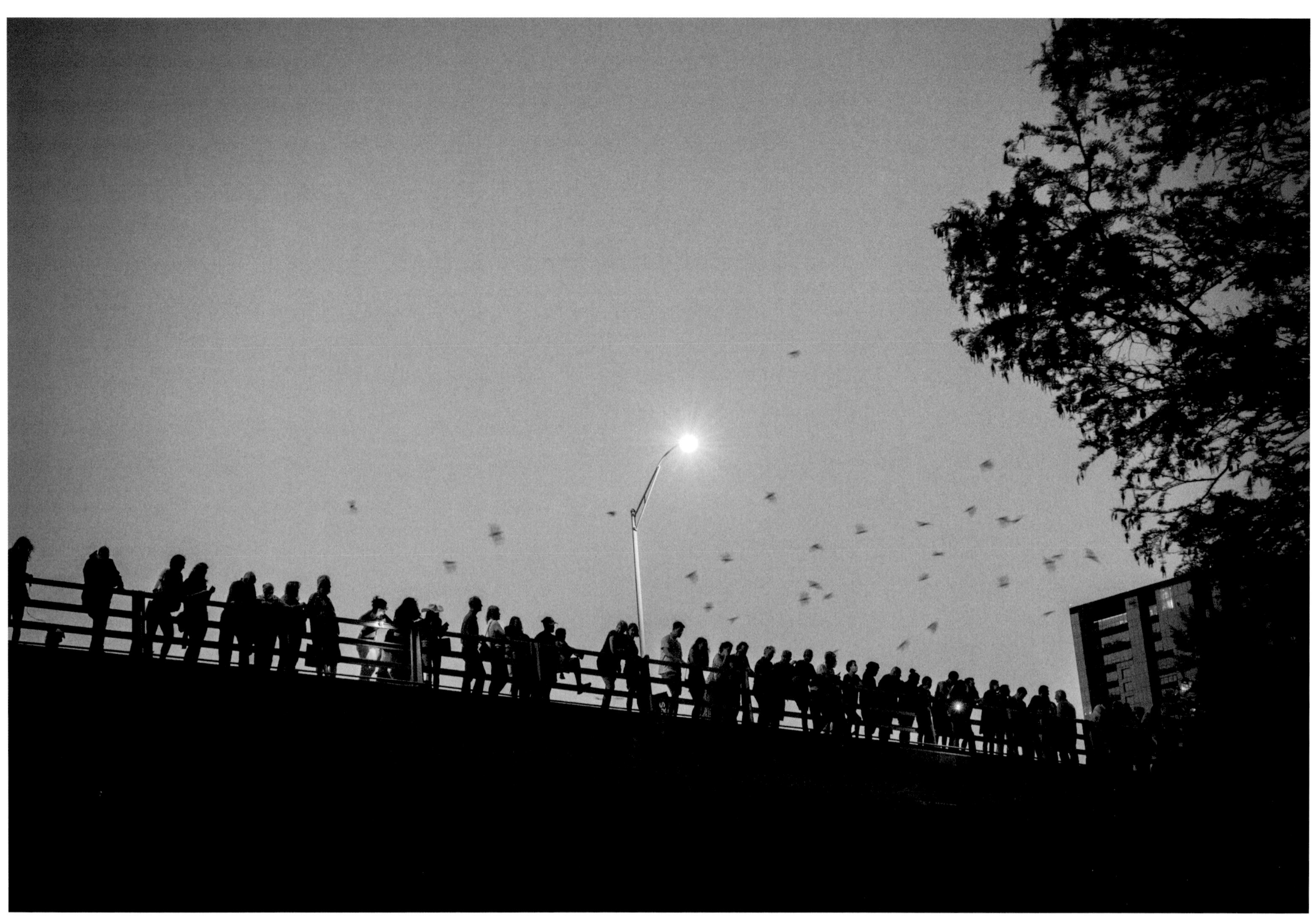

Bats and people, Texas

N 41° 52’ 41.2104” W 87° 37’47.2728”

CHICAGO, ILLINOIS

“Motherland is the earth, forces, ecosystem ... everything. I wish we could save energy and gas and not have to put pollution out into the world. I have asthma and helping the environment helps me, and it helps my daughter. I hope for things to be different in the future, that the forests get saved. There’s a lot of things I hope for.”

[Danisha]

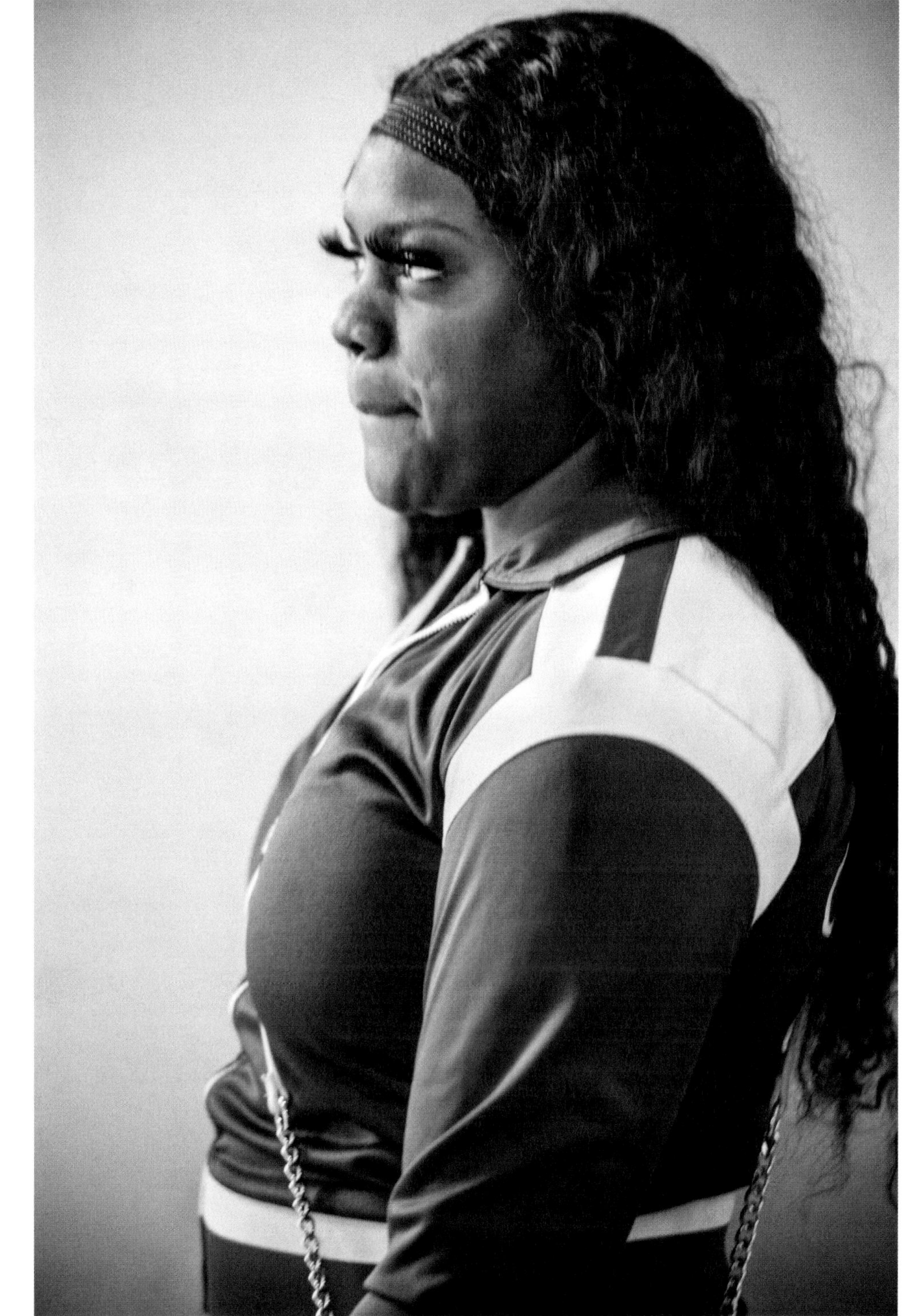

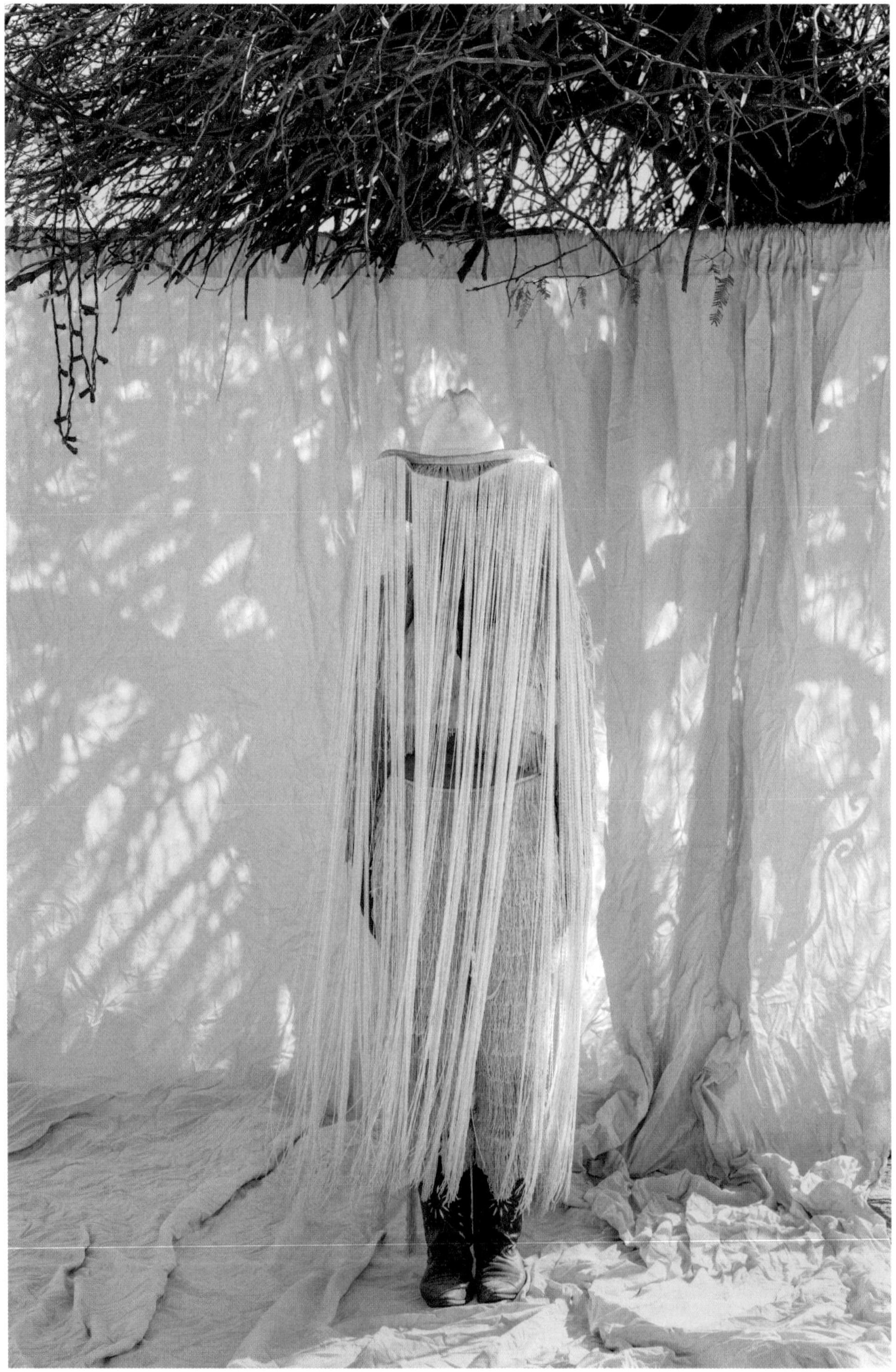

Fringe, California

"Terra Madre ... connection to the land is really important out here in the West. My mother came here from Brazil to get a better life. This country represents hope for the future and a better life for people who come from places of poverty and oppression. America wants authenticity. It was founded on people being who they are. I like that people don't really have to apologize for who they are here or explain themselves."

[Sarah, New Mexico]

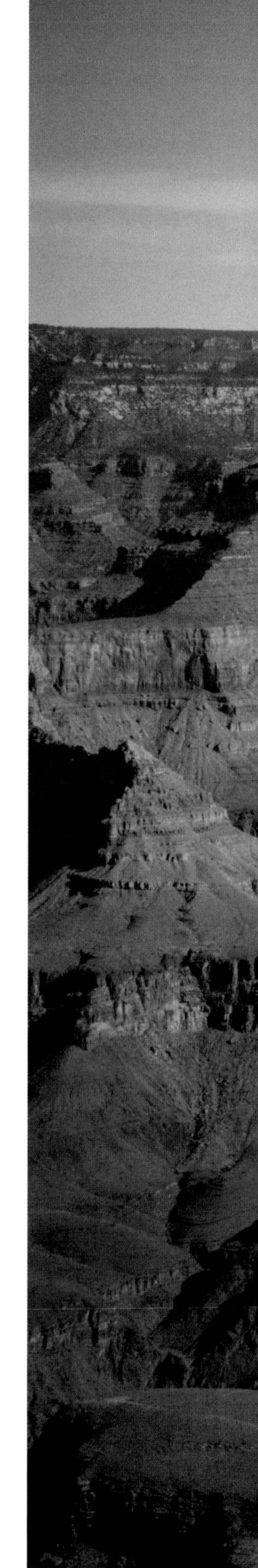

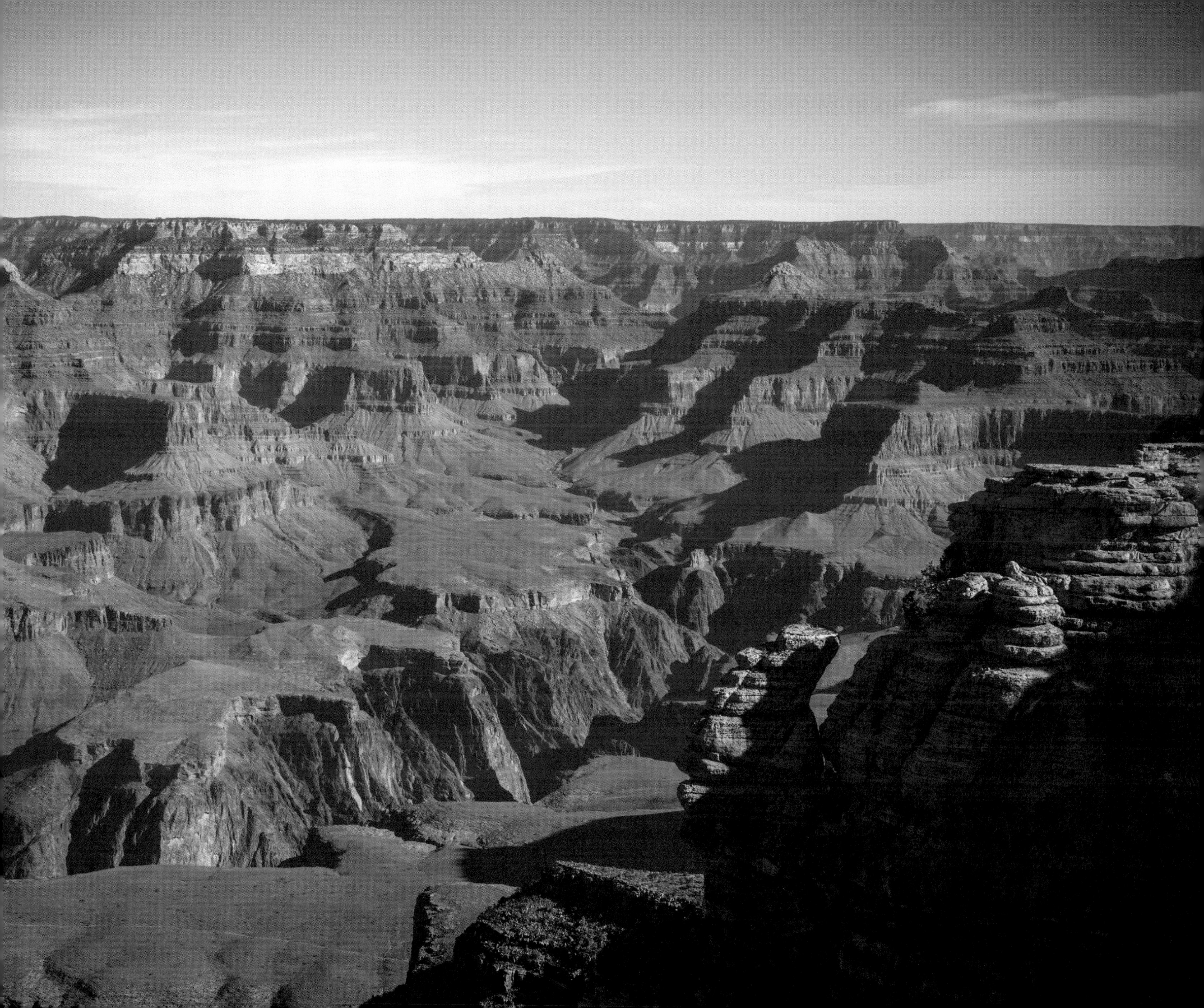

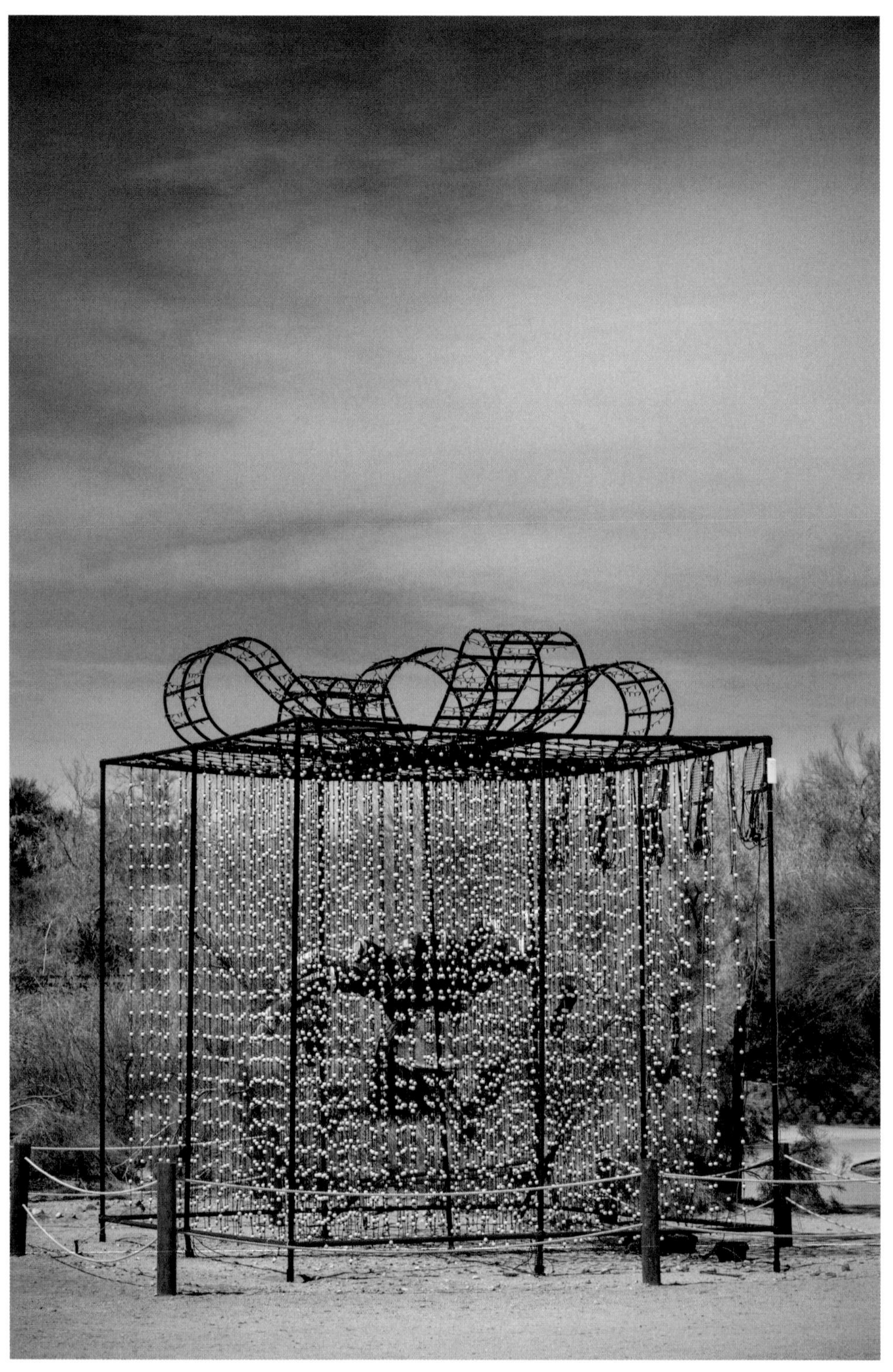

Desert cage, California

N 33° 42' 47.452' W 116° 11' 56.086"

INDIO, CALIFORNIA

"Ever since I lost my husband, I've dedicated my time to rescueing wild birds."

[Linda]

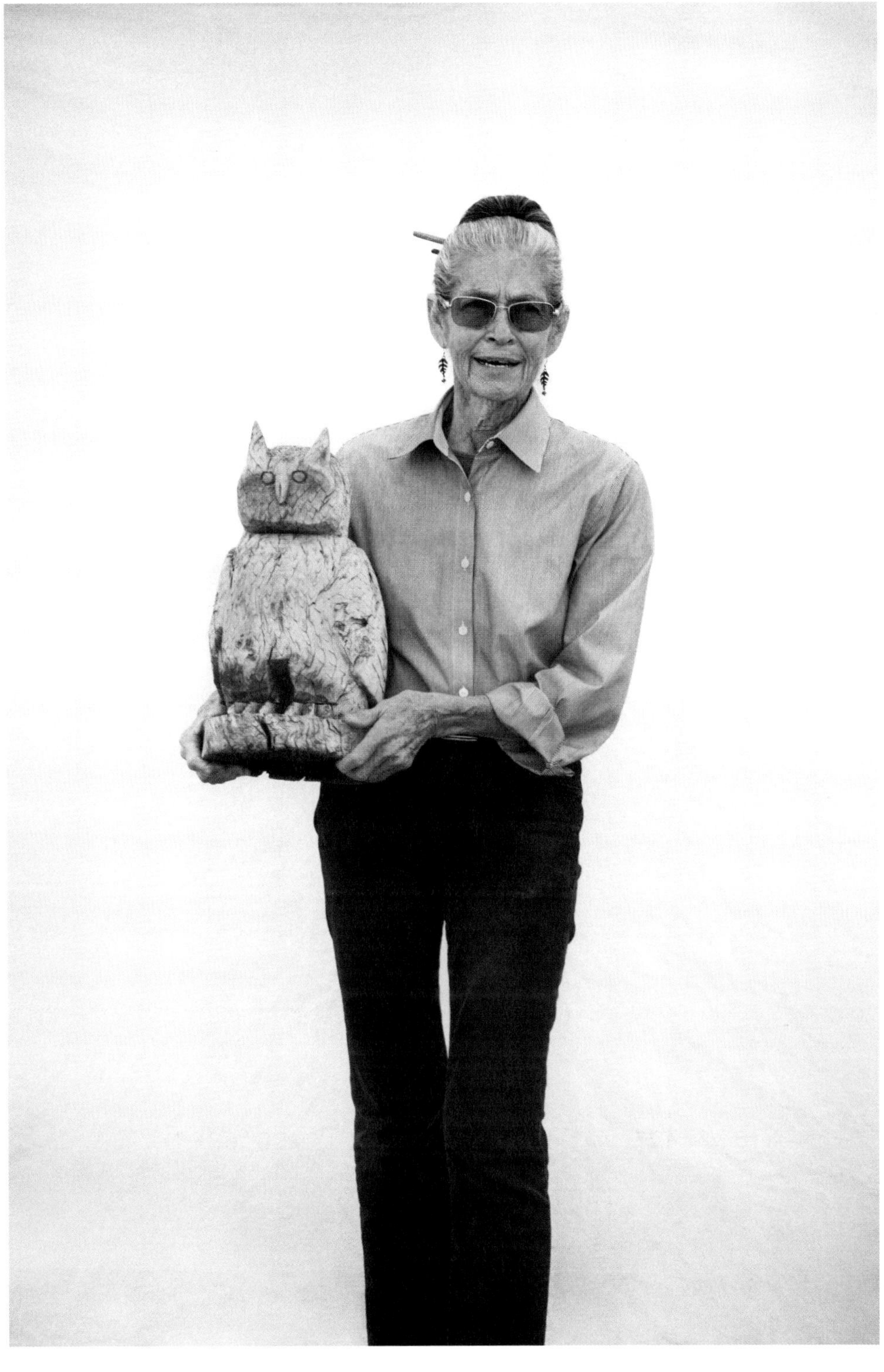

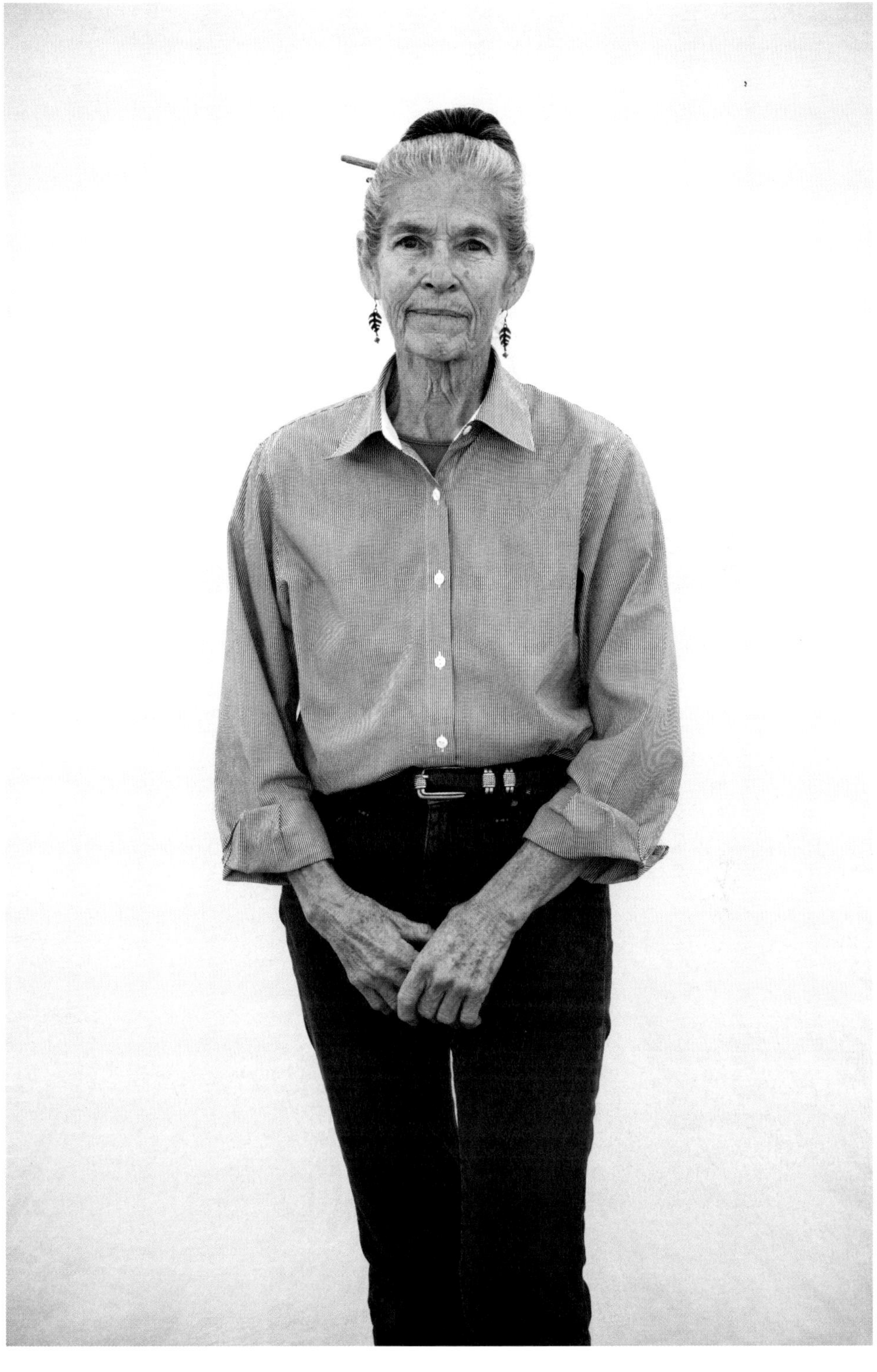

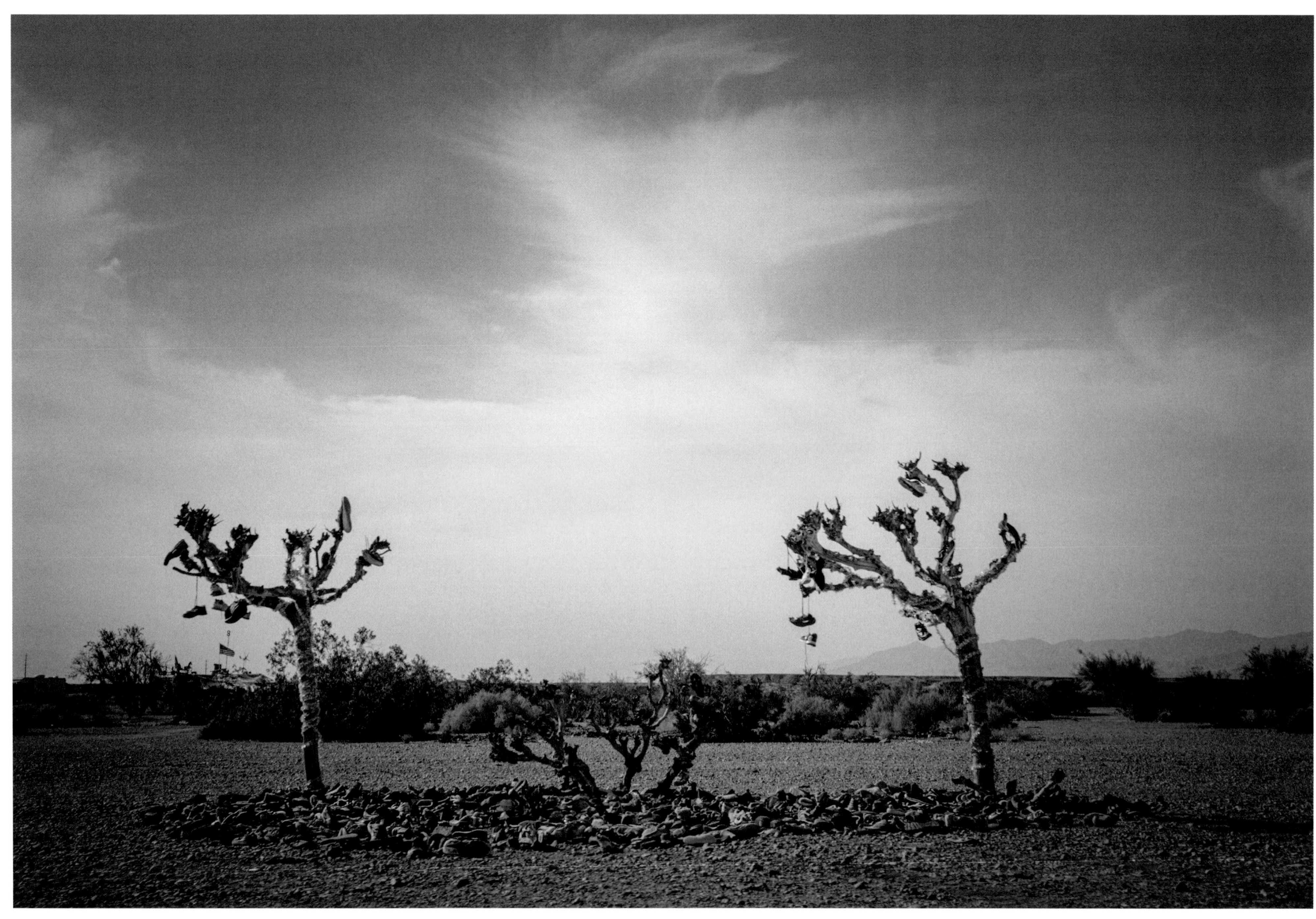

Shoe trees, California

N 33° 15' 12.7188" W 115° 42' 36.6444"

SALTON SEA, CALIFORNIA

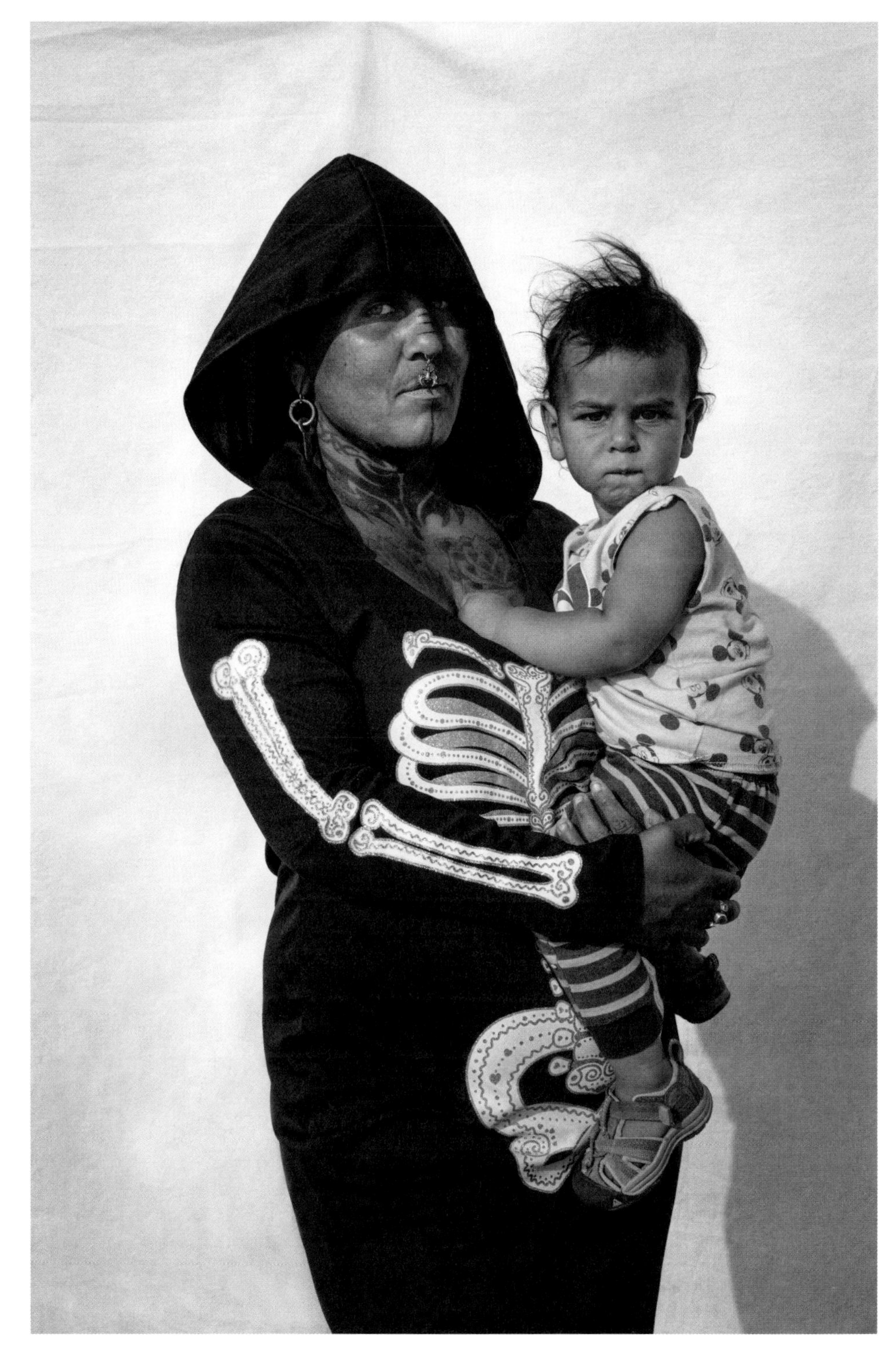

Vida and Prince, California

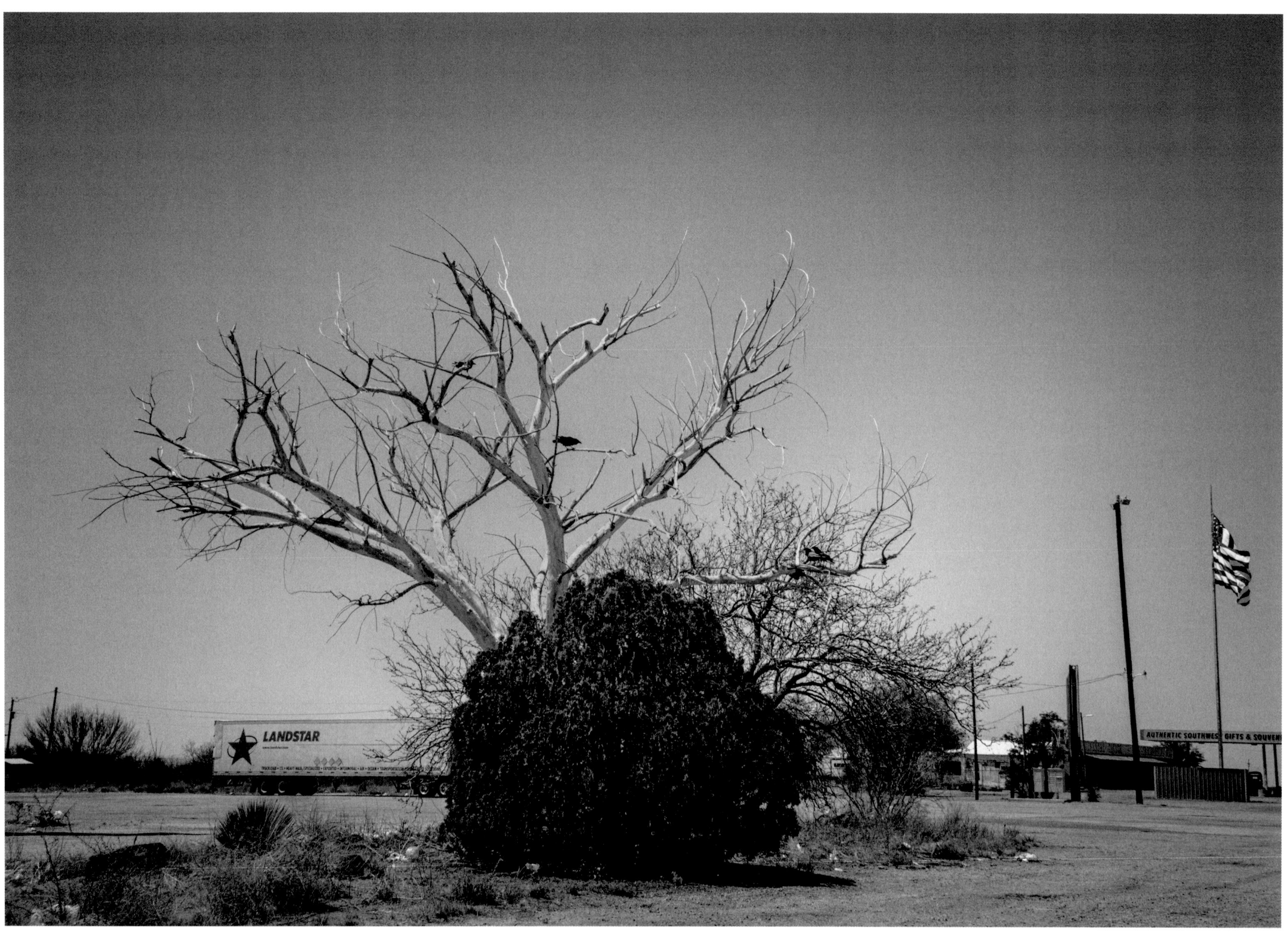

Land Star, Texas

N 33° 15’ 12.7188” W 115° 42’ 36.6444”

SALTON SEA, CALIFORNIA

“I drove to Reno every day, played slot machines and got paid. My job was to test the programs and play the games. I fell into it, a high school kid with just two computer classes under my belt … and I went into engineering. We bought a bus because of my daughter’s handicap, but she ended up moving to Pennsylvania. Now what are we gonna do? So we took the bus, put the semi on a trailer and went up to Washington. By the time we got back home, we were convinced that this was a good bus to convert to live in. The rest is history, because here we are. If you blow up Google maps big enough, you’ll see I’m here.”

[Jaimee]

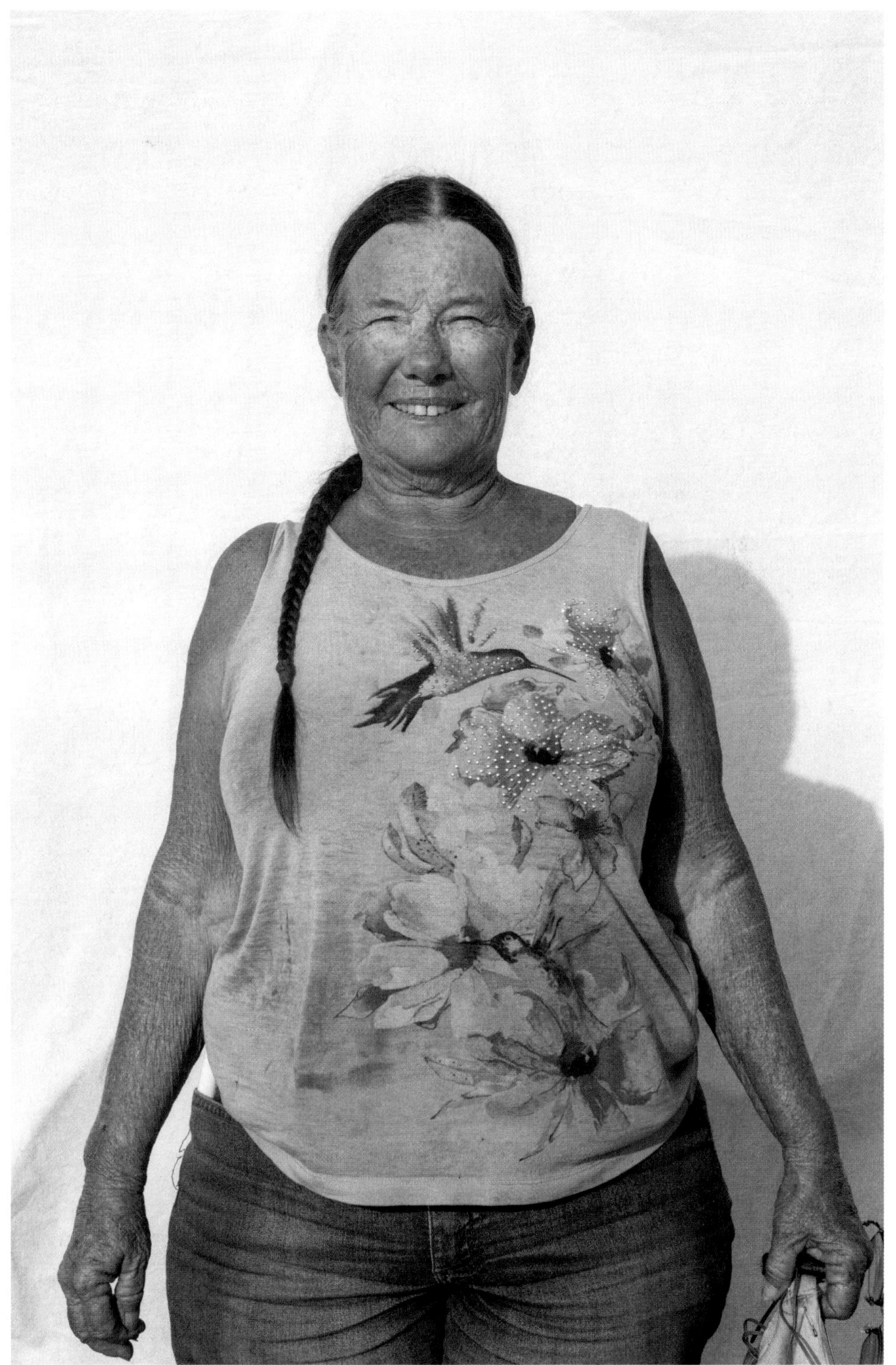

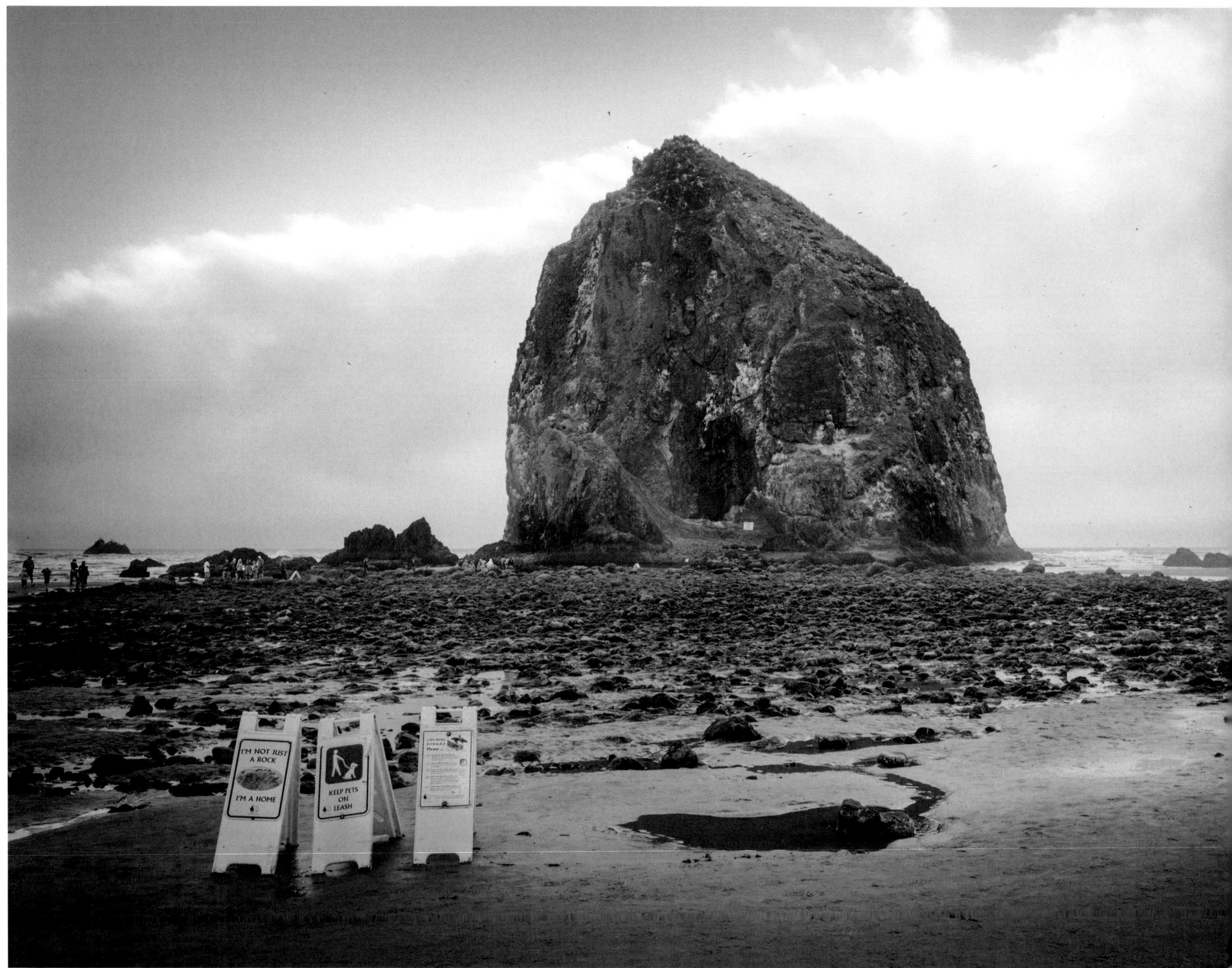

I'm a home, Oregon

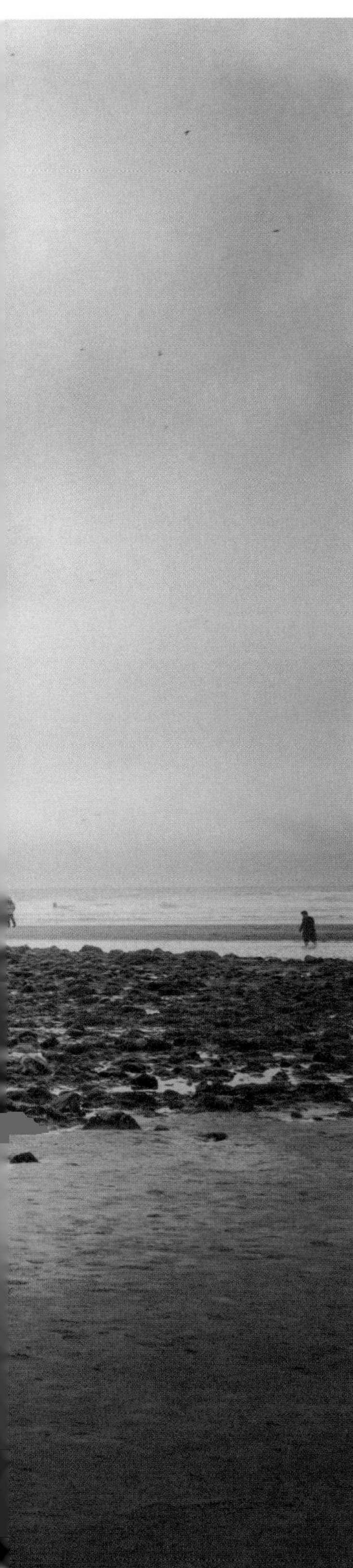

"I long for the end of capitalism and colonialism across the world. America is stolen land. I'm tired of liberals with their outrage but no action to try to help save their democracy."

[Keith, Oregon]

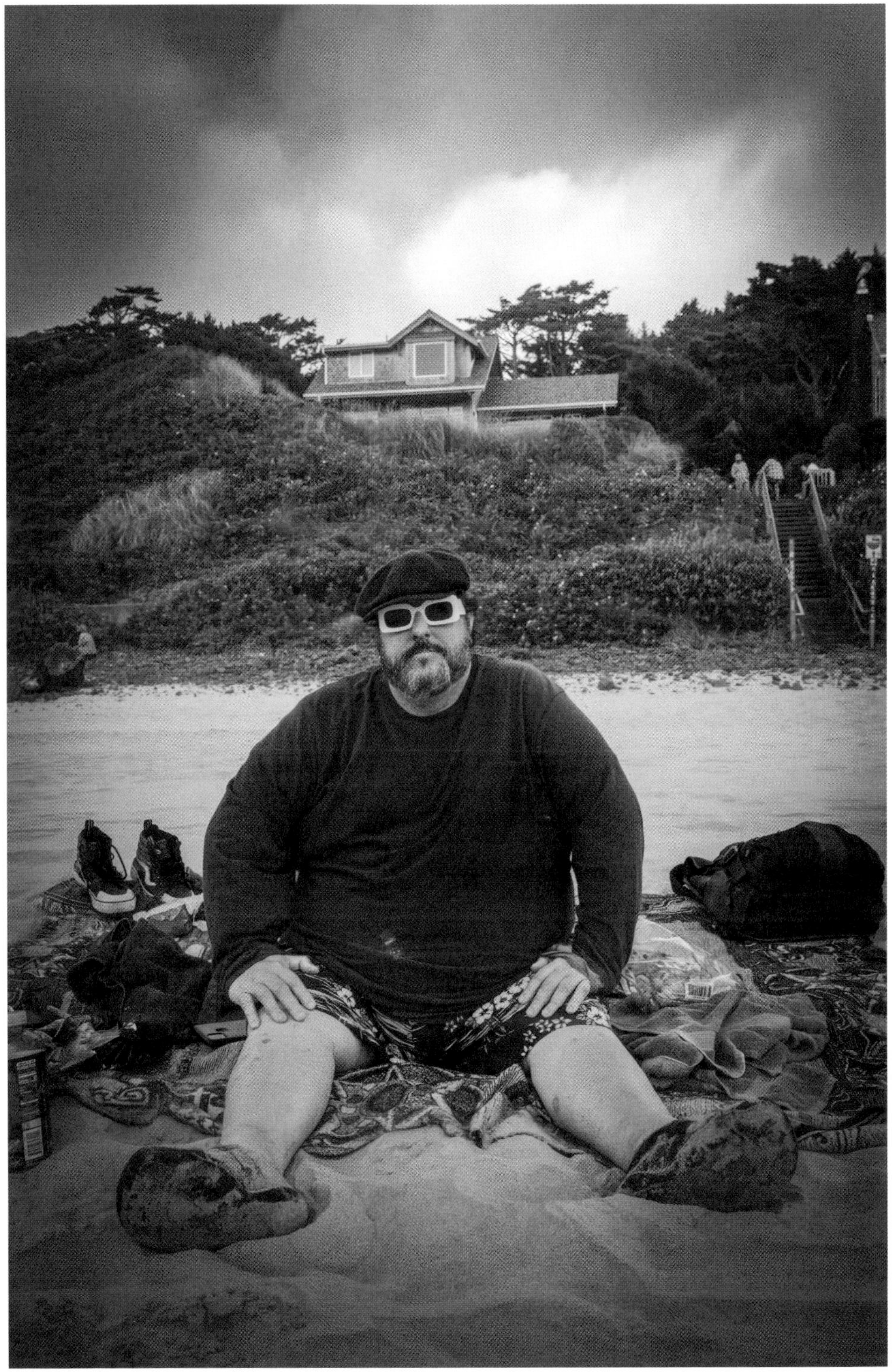

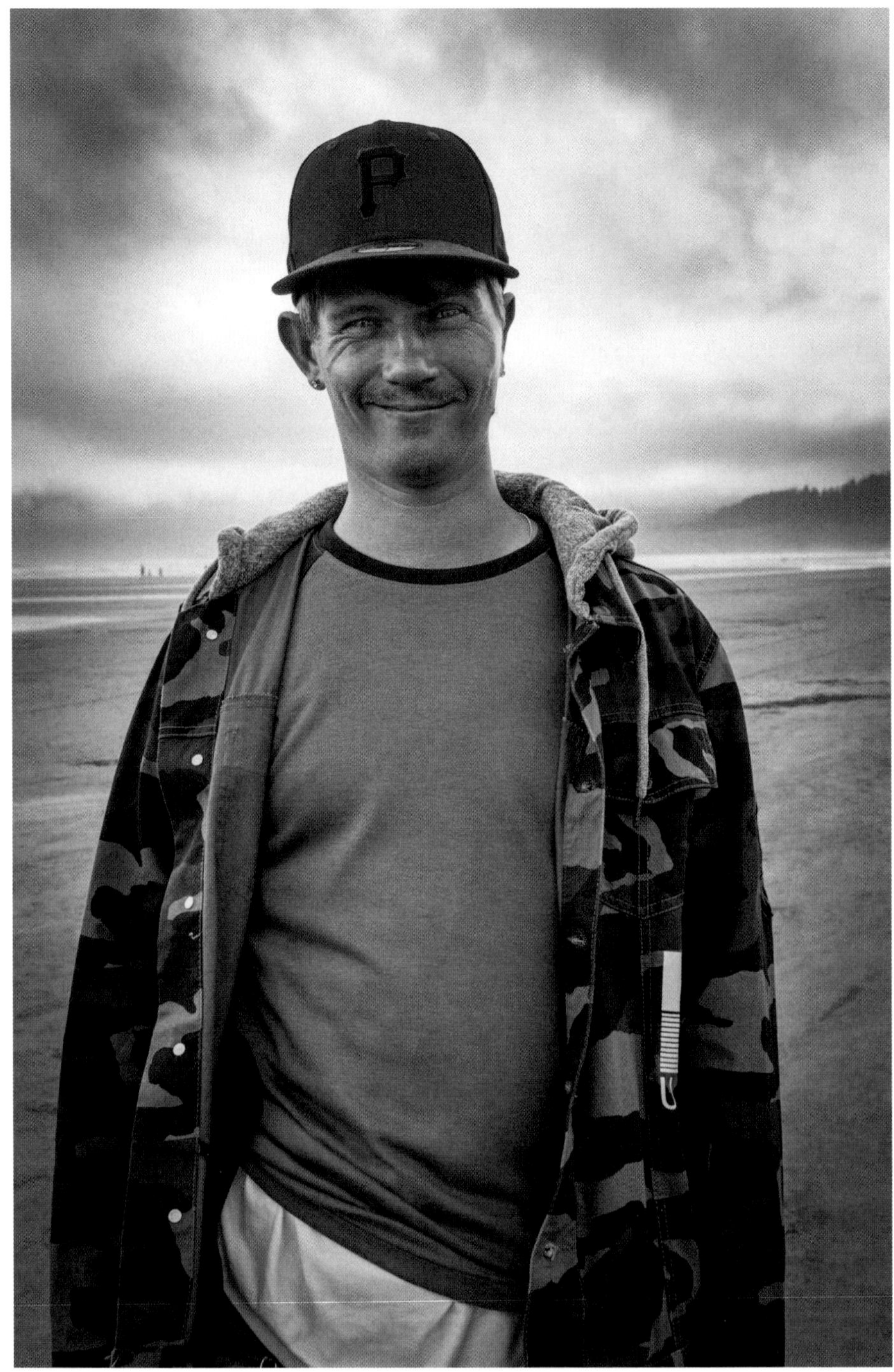

Michael, Oregon

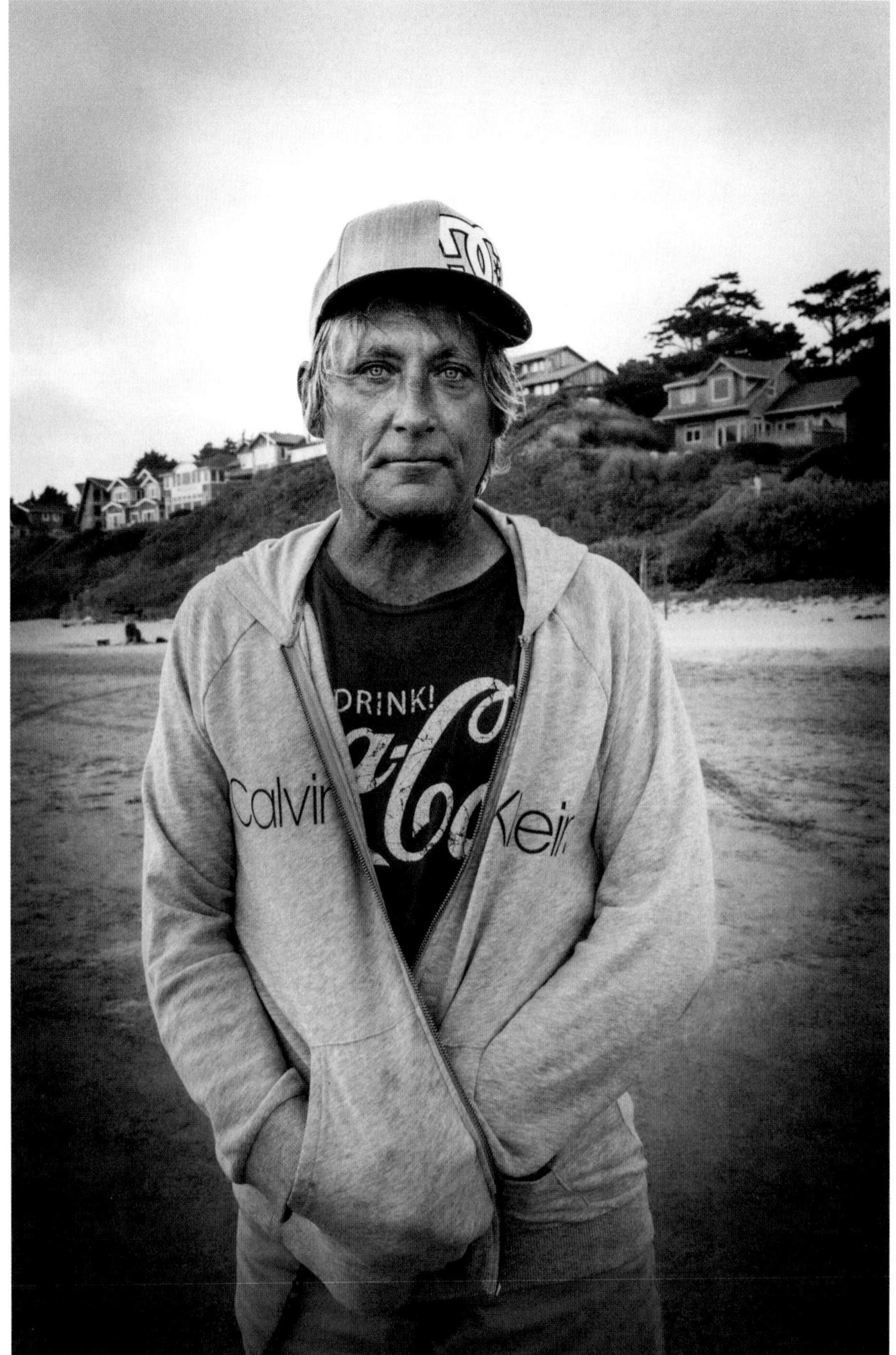

Drink Calvin Klein, Oregon

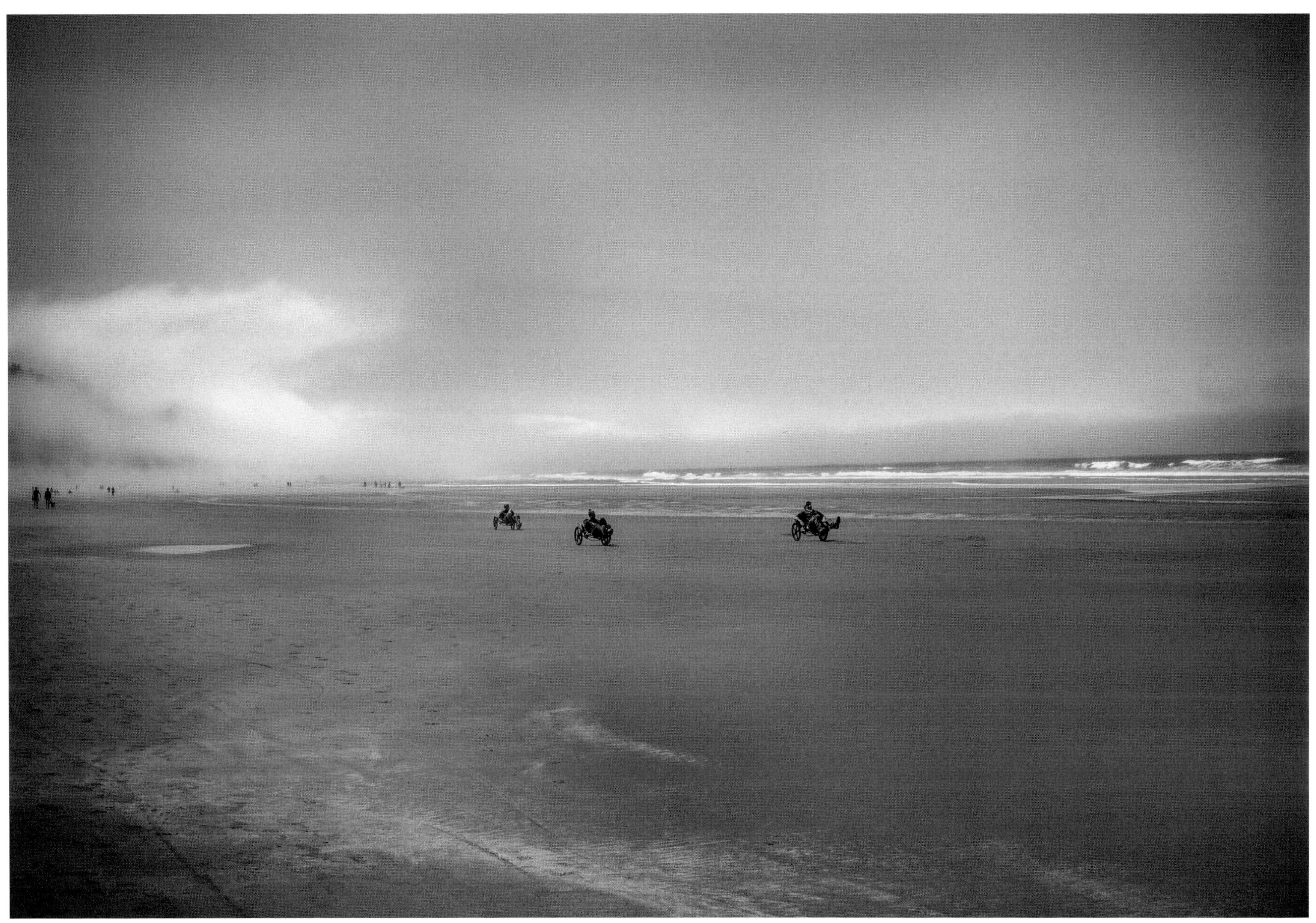

Recumbent tricycles, Oregon

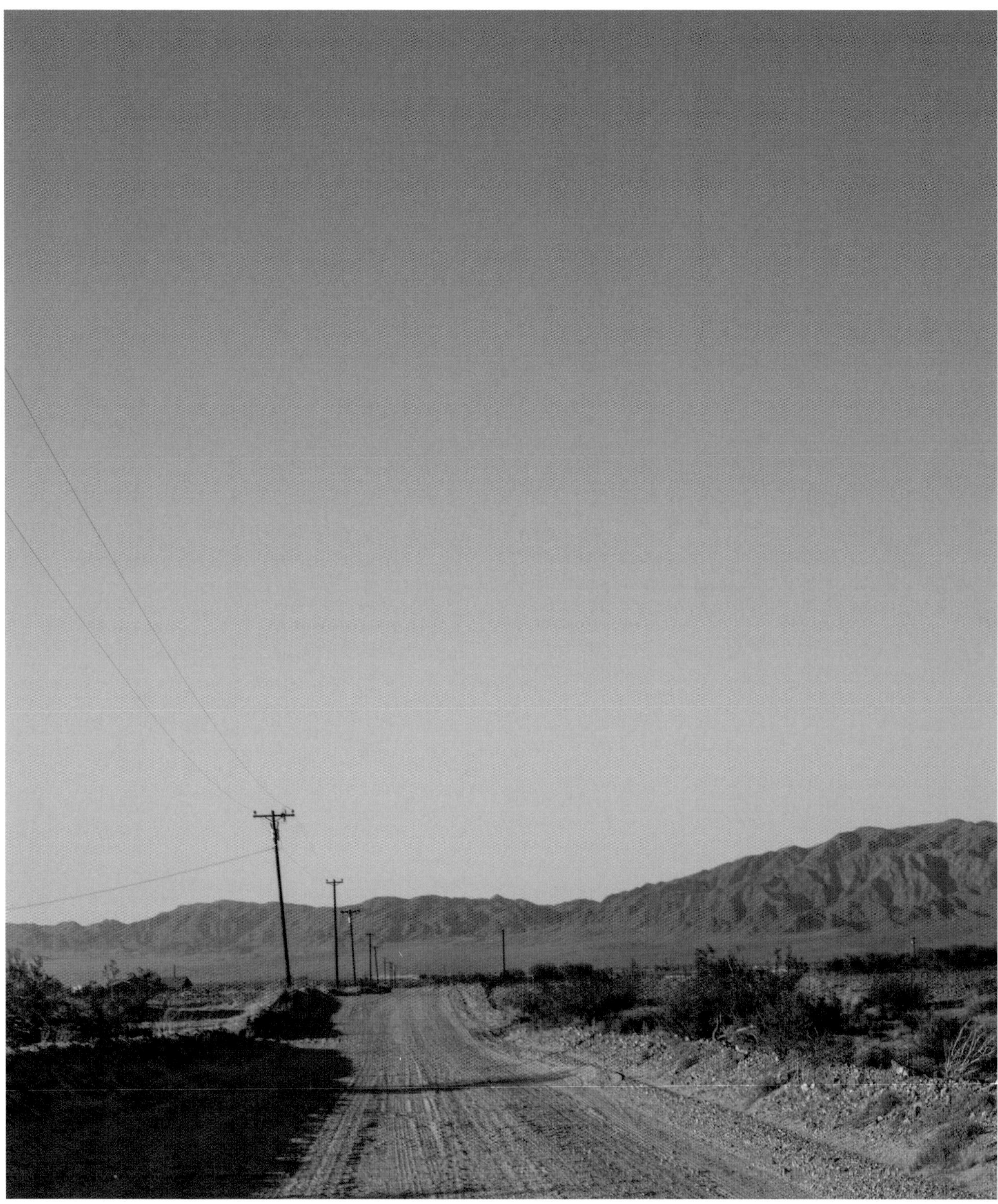

High desert road, California

NEW ORLEANS, LOUISIANA

N 29°57'16.72" W 90°04'30.25"

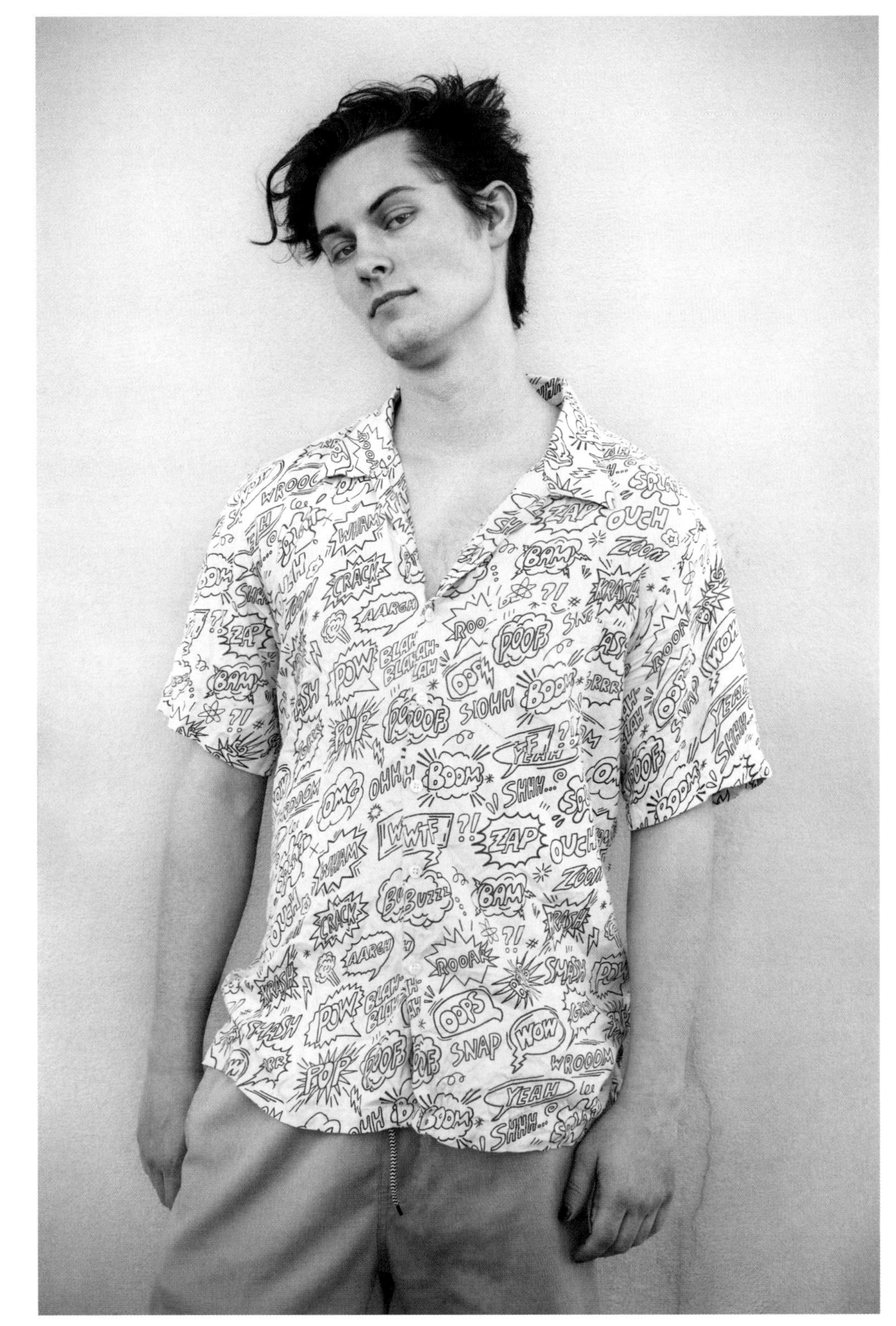

Nathan, Louisiana

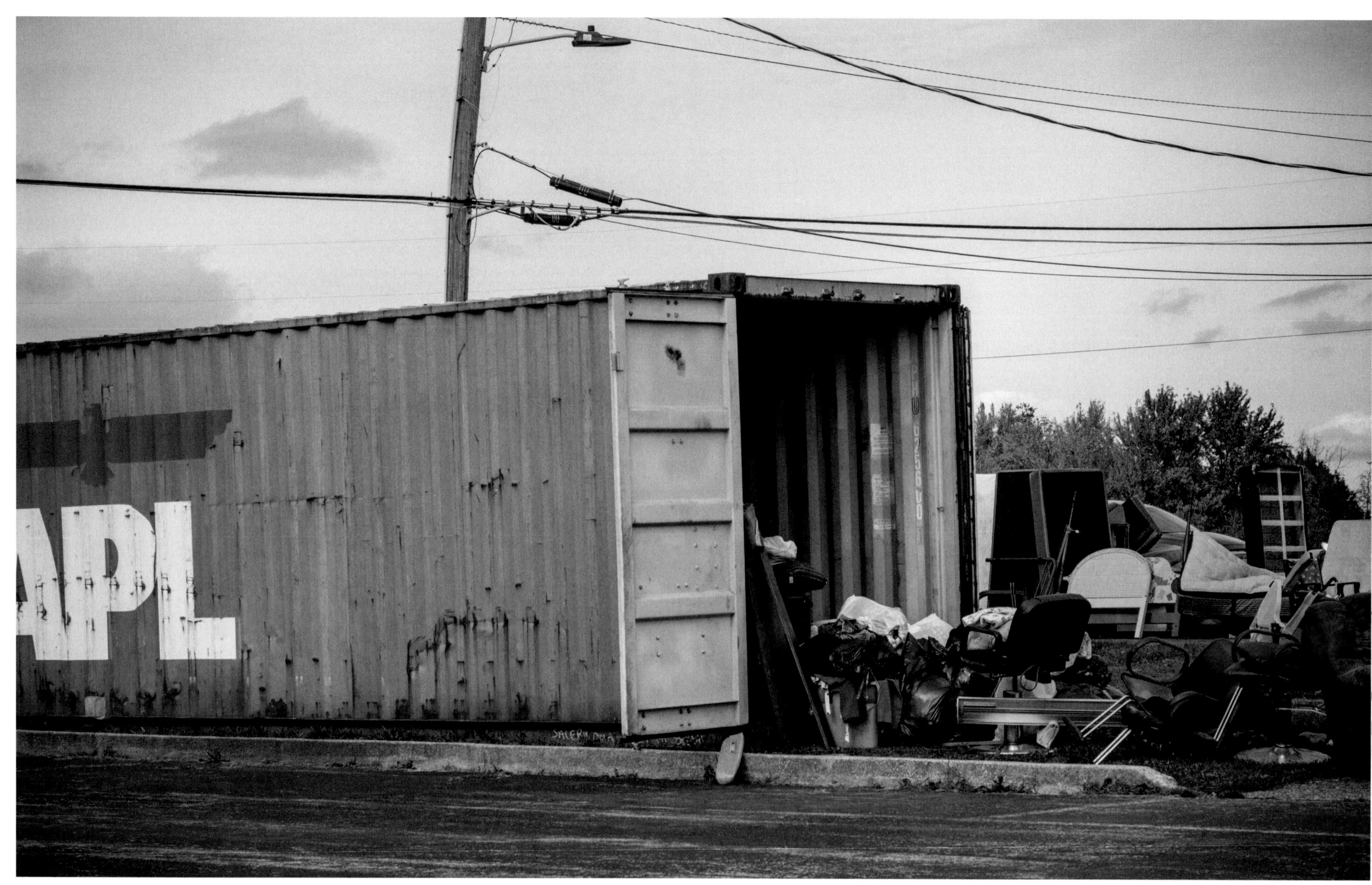

Container ministry, Missouri

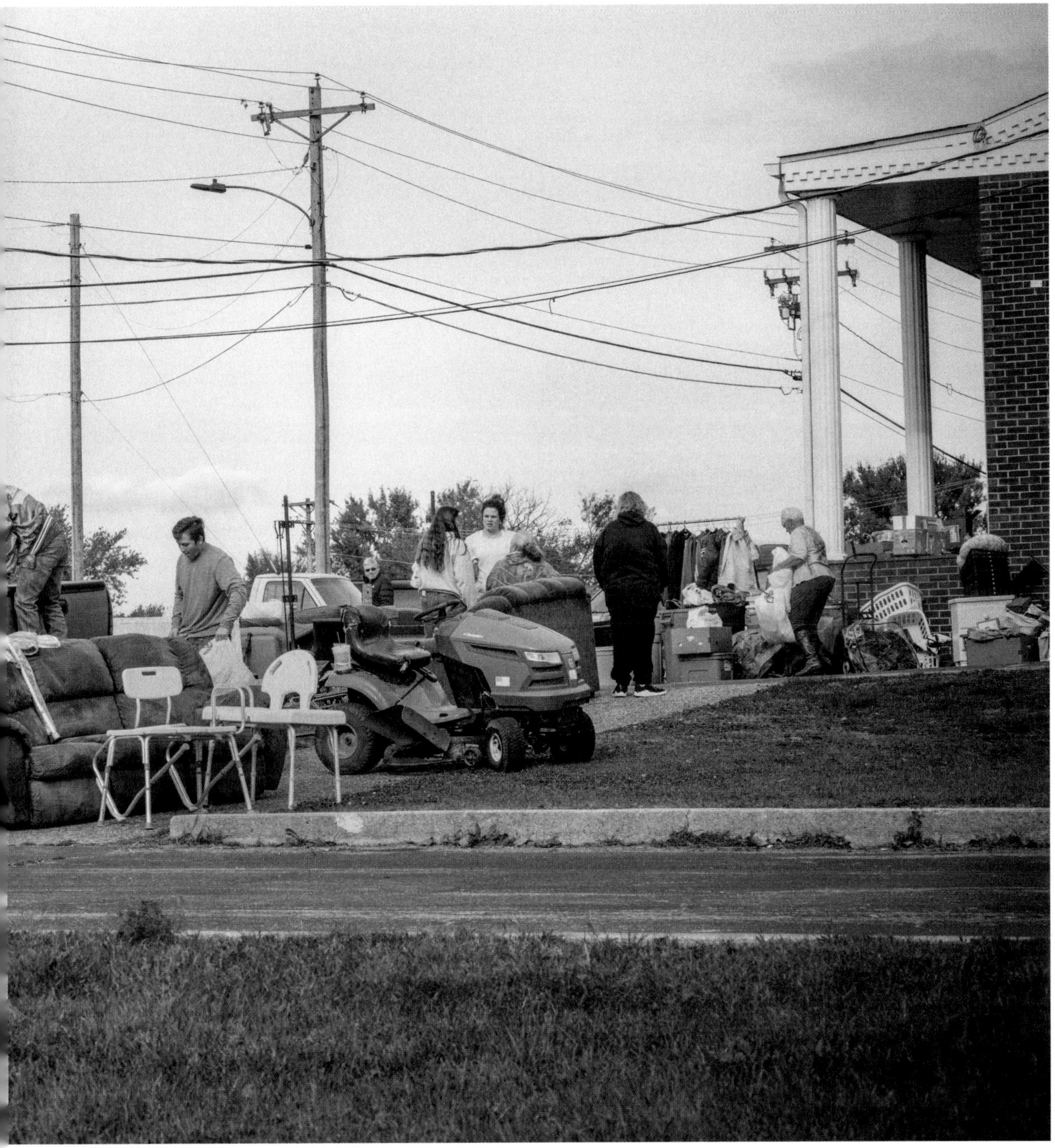

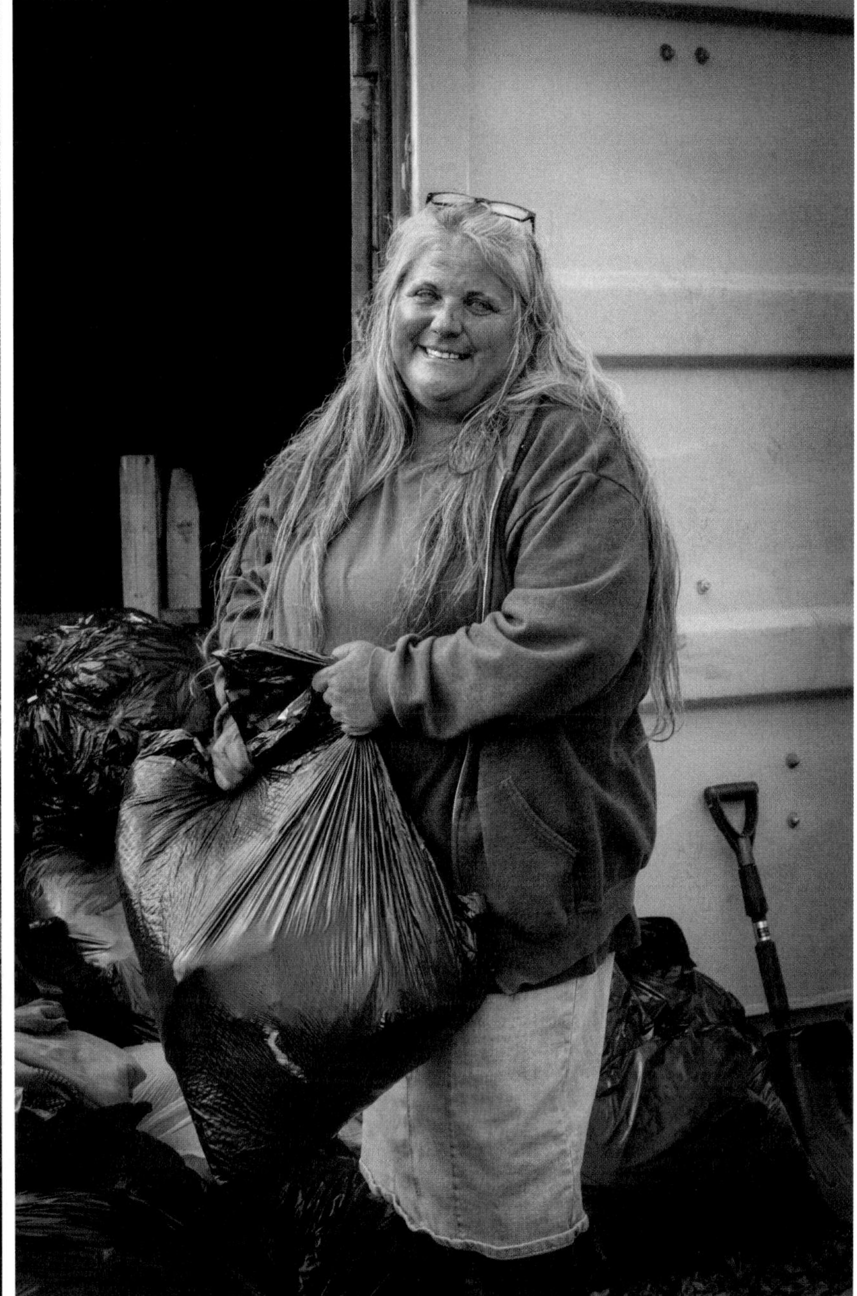

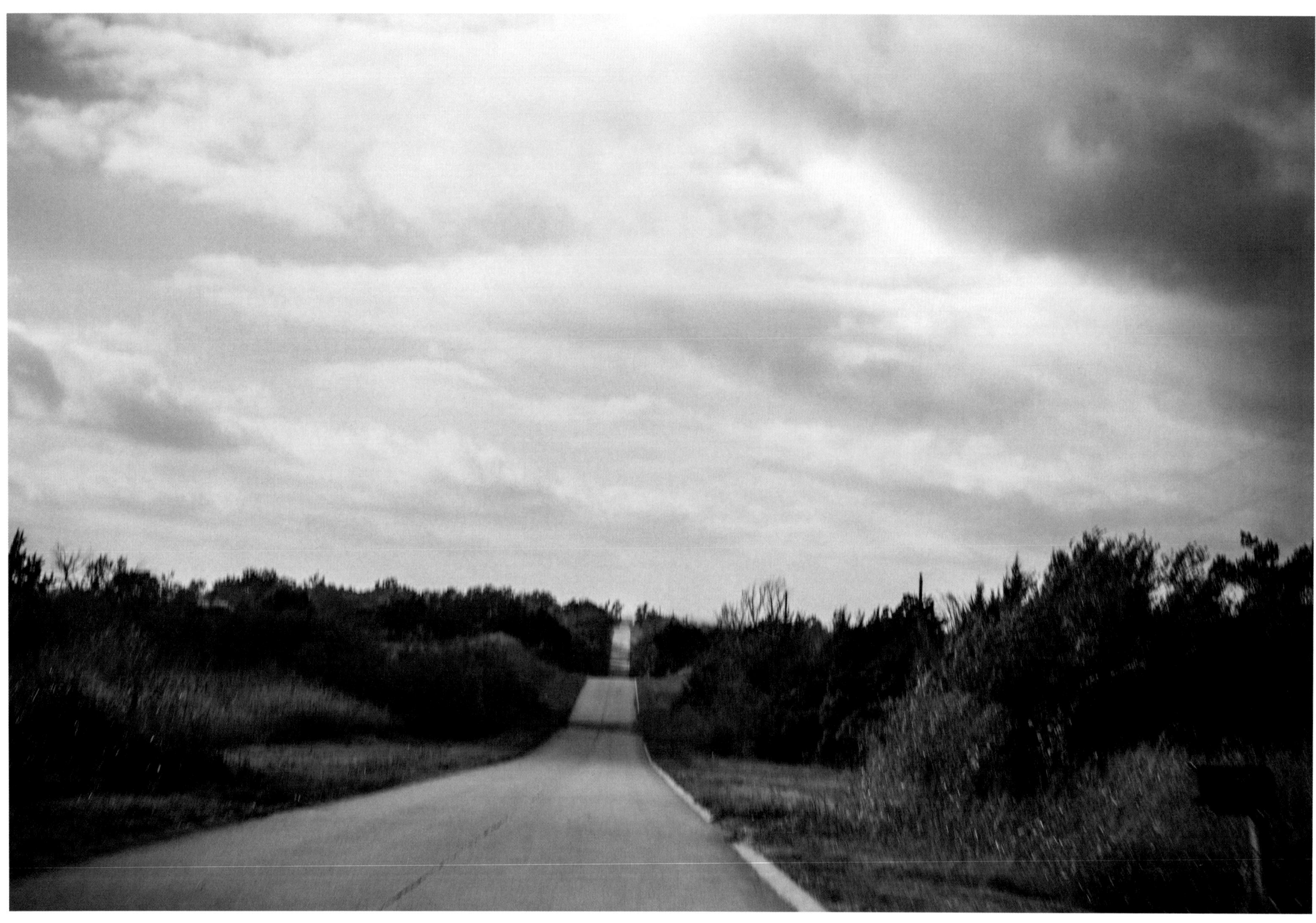

Country road, Missouri

N 37° 40' 31.0975" W 92° 39' 30.0989"

LEBANON, MISSOURI

"I started the ministry with my family. I get to see God's miracles happen here every day with people. It's about helping people have access to all of God's blessings, so that they have the same opportunities as everybody else."

[Amber]

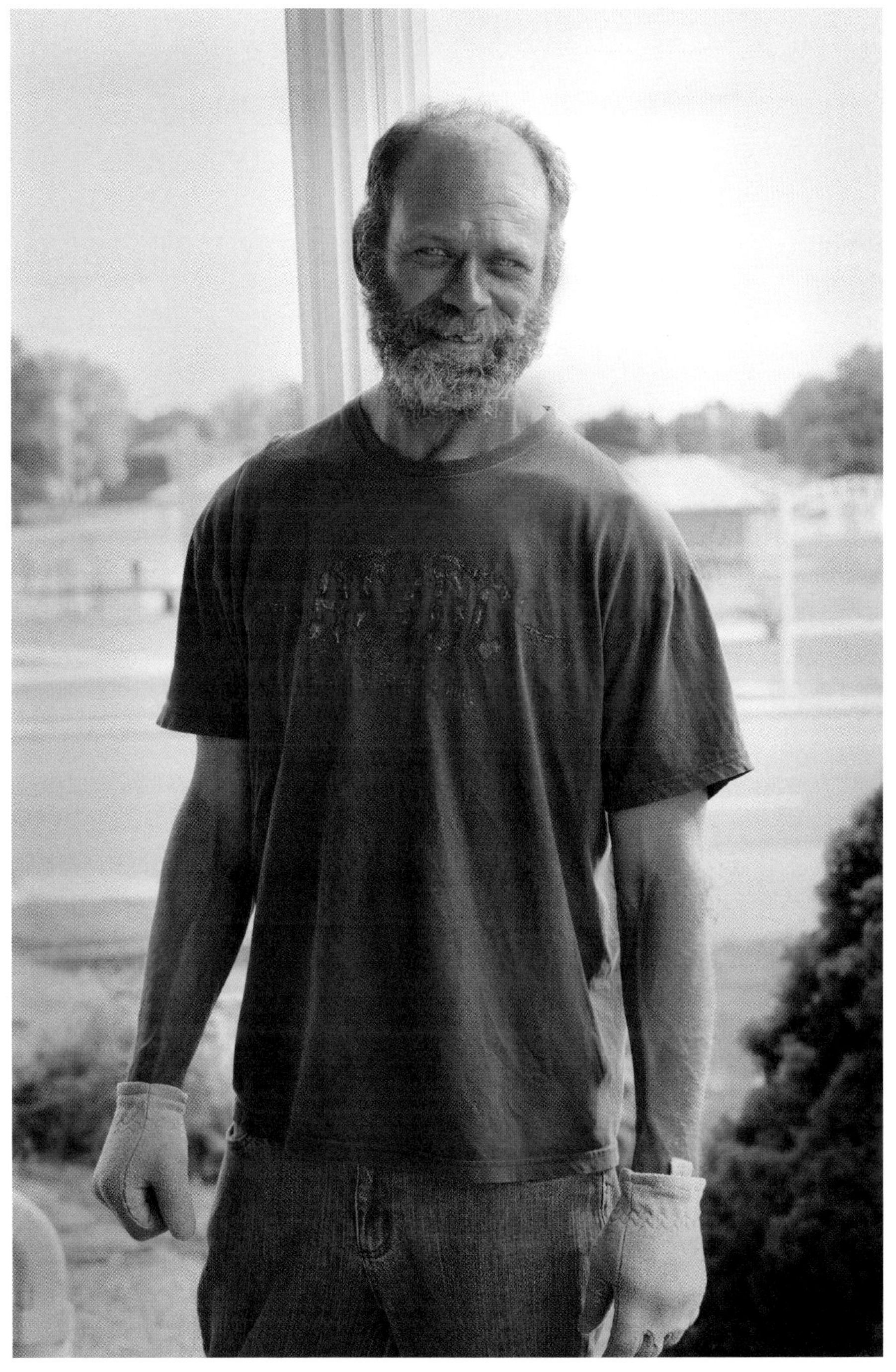

Volunteer, Missouri

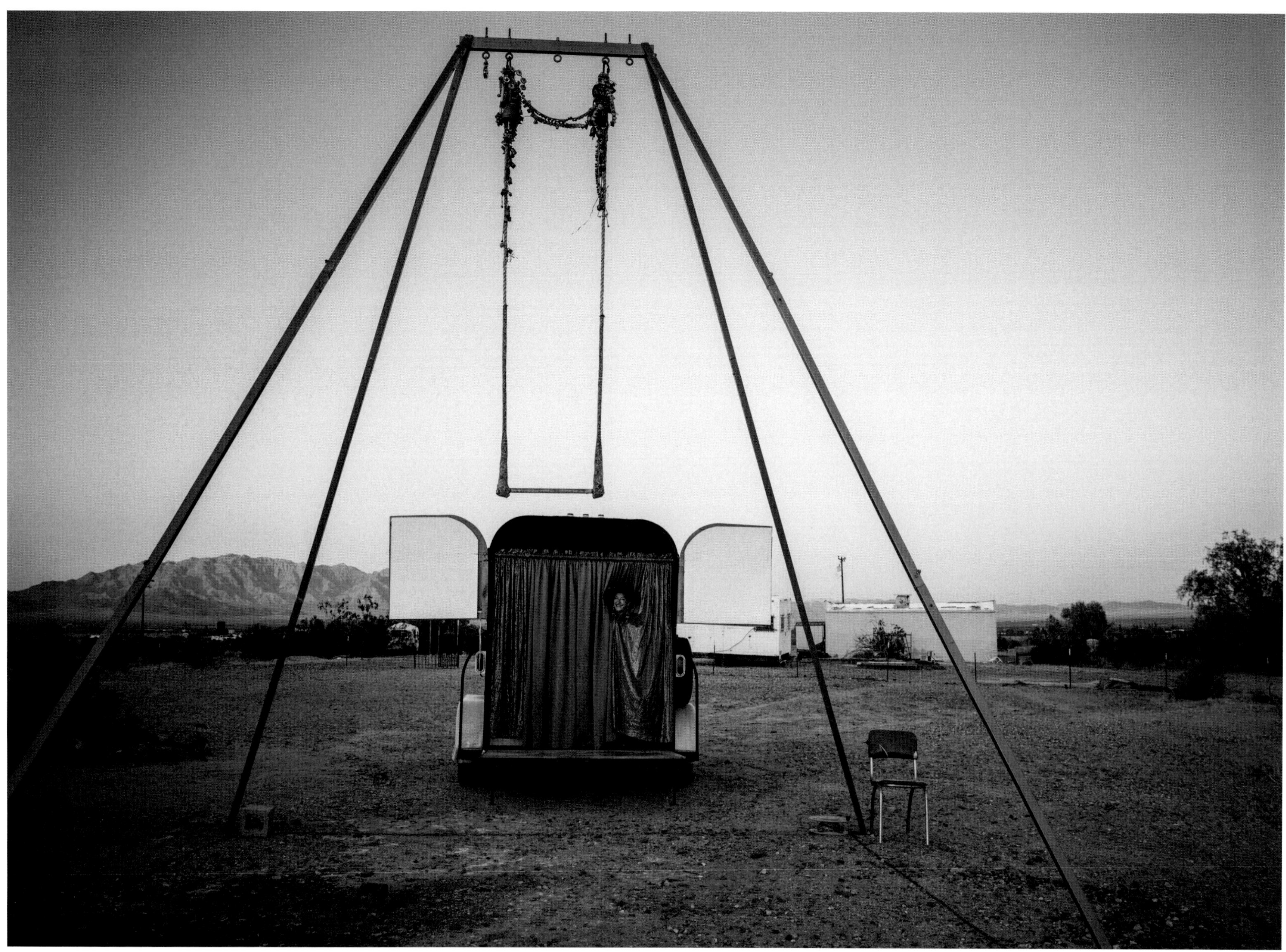

Aerial rig, California

N 34° 8' 8.0088" W 116° 3' 15.0084"

TWENTYNINE PALMS, CALIFORNIA

"I came to the desert to listen to my heart and clear my mind. Here it is so quiet that there's space to hear your soul talking to the stars. With solitude, time stretches and teaches you patience. The desert holds you and helps lighten your load. The heat and sky help absorb what is heavy within if you offer it to the endless expanse."

[Tanya]

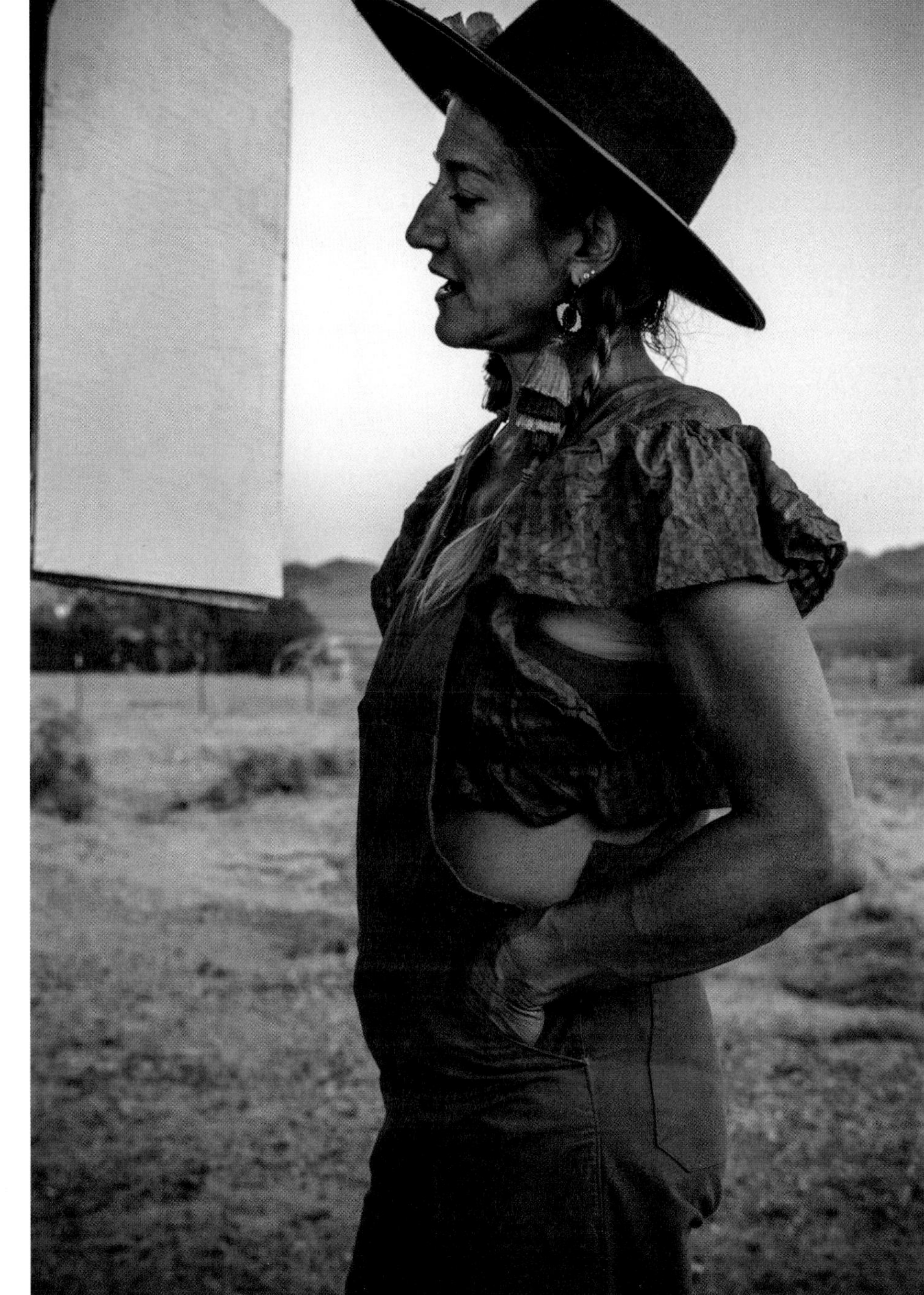

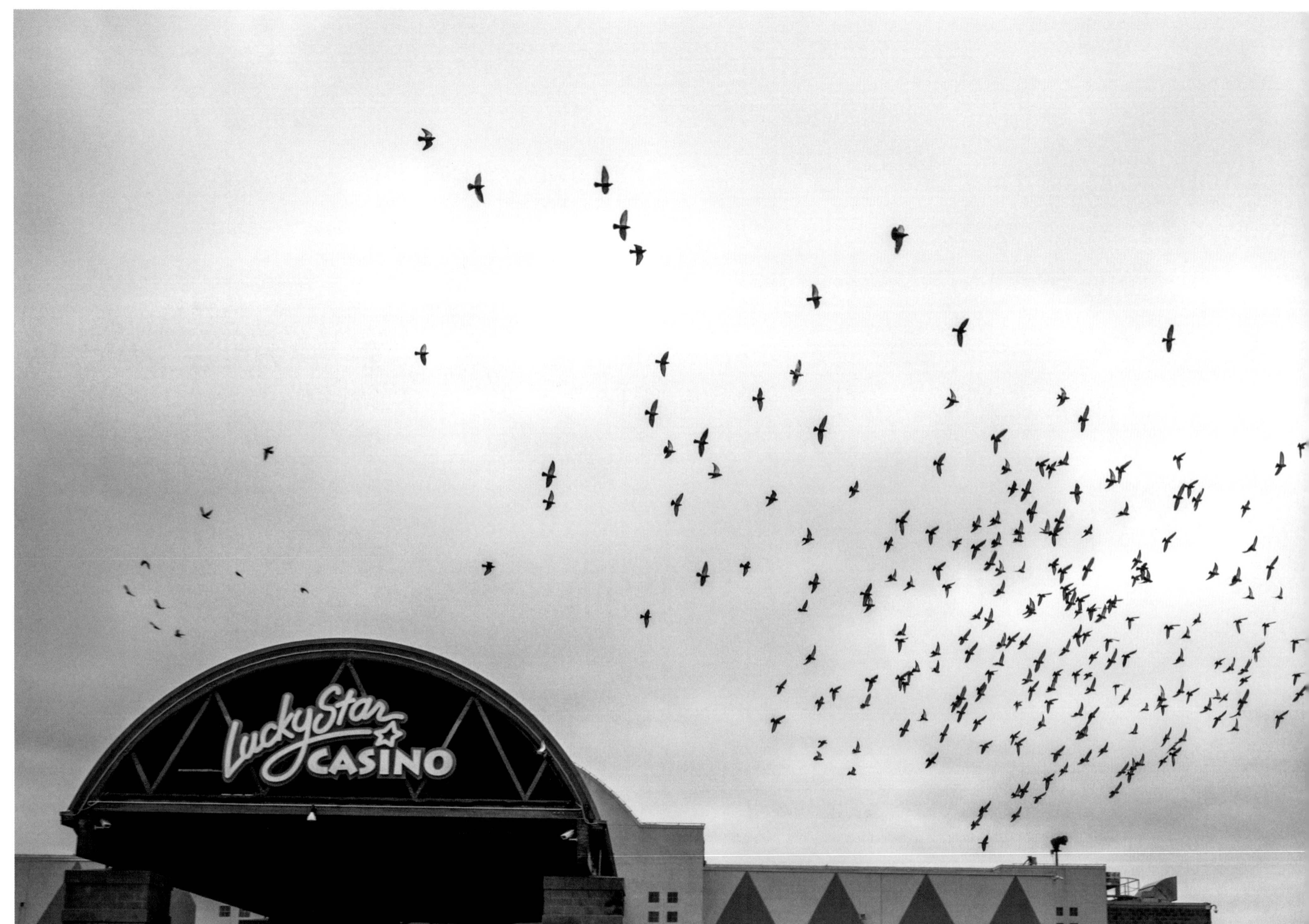

Lucky Star Casino, Oklahoma

"A lot of people come back to the casino over and over again. We have regulars, and I don't understand how they have money, but they come back. It's not always bad. There's people that seem to know what they do, and they seem to be on top of things. You get tired of hearing the bells and whistles, all the sound in here. Then we get off work, and some employees like to gamble too."

[Jeremiah]

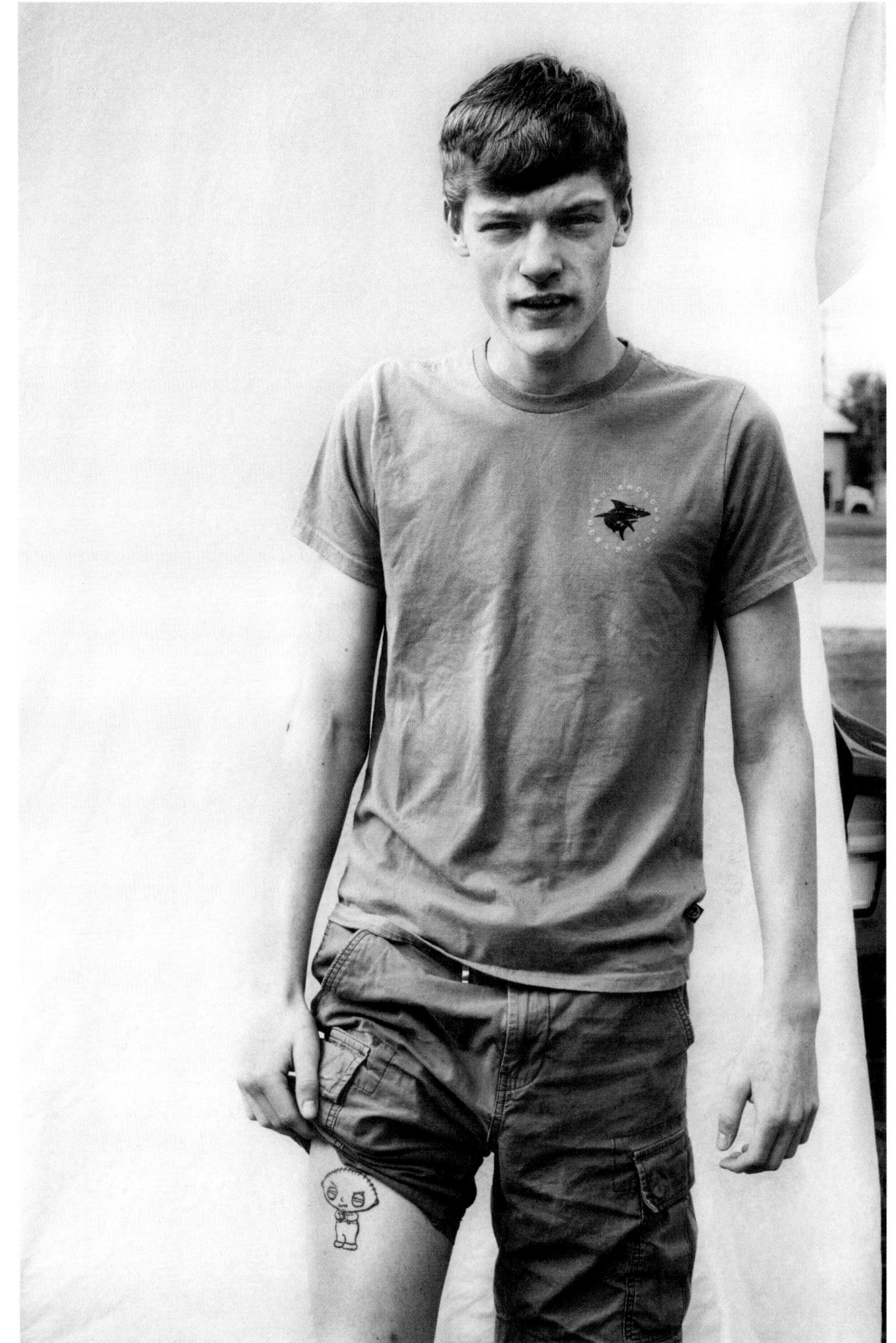

Josh with Stewie tattoo, Oklahoma

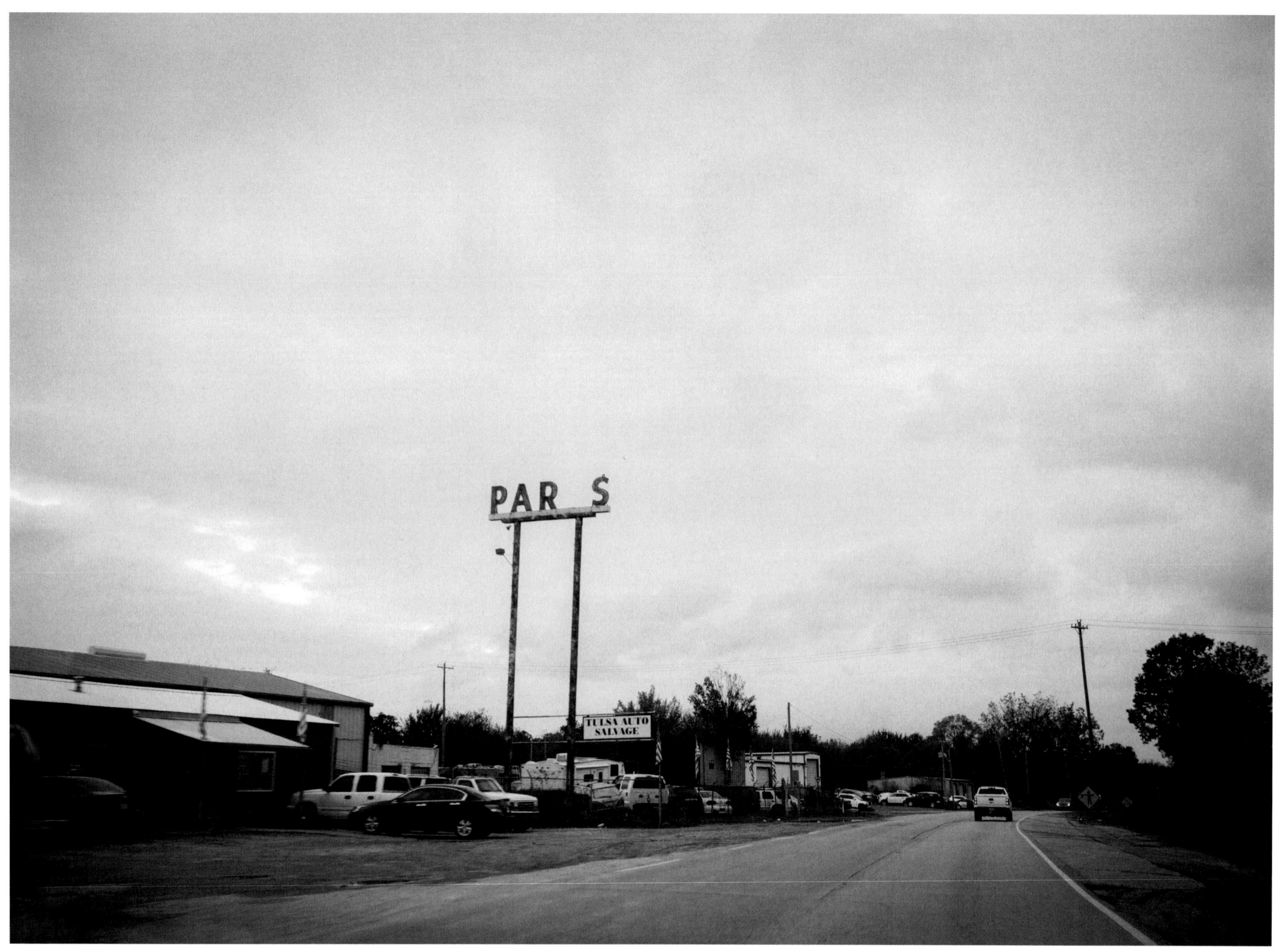

Par(t)s Tulsa, Oklahoma

N 40° 44’ 8.3652” W 74° 10’ 20.5212”

NEWARK, NEW JERSEY

“I was really depressed for months and months, and now I’m starting to get my juice back. I realize that it’s not gonna take anything other than just having faith and putting some work in myself to get back on my feet. I prefer the street. The shelter feels like jail.”

[Christian]

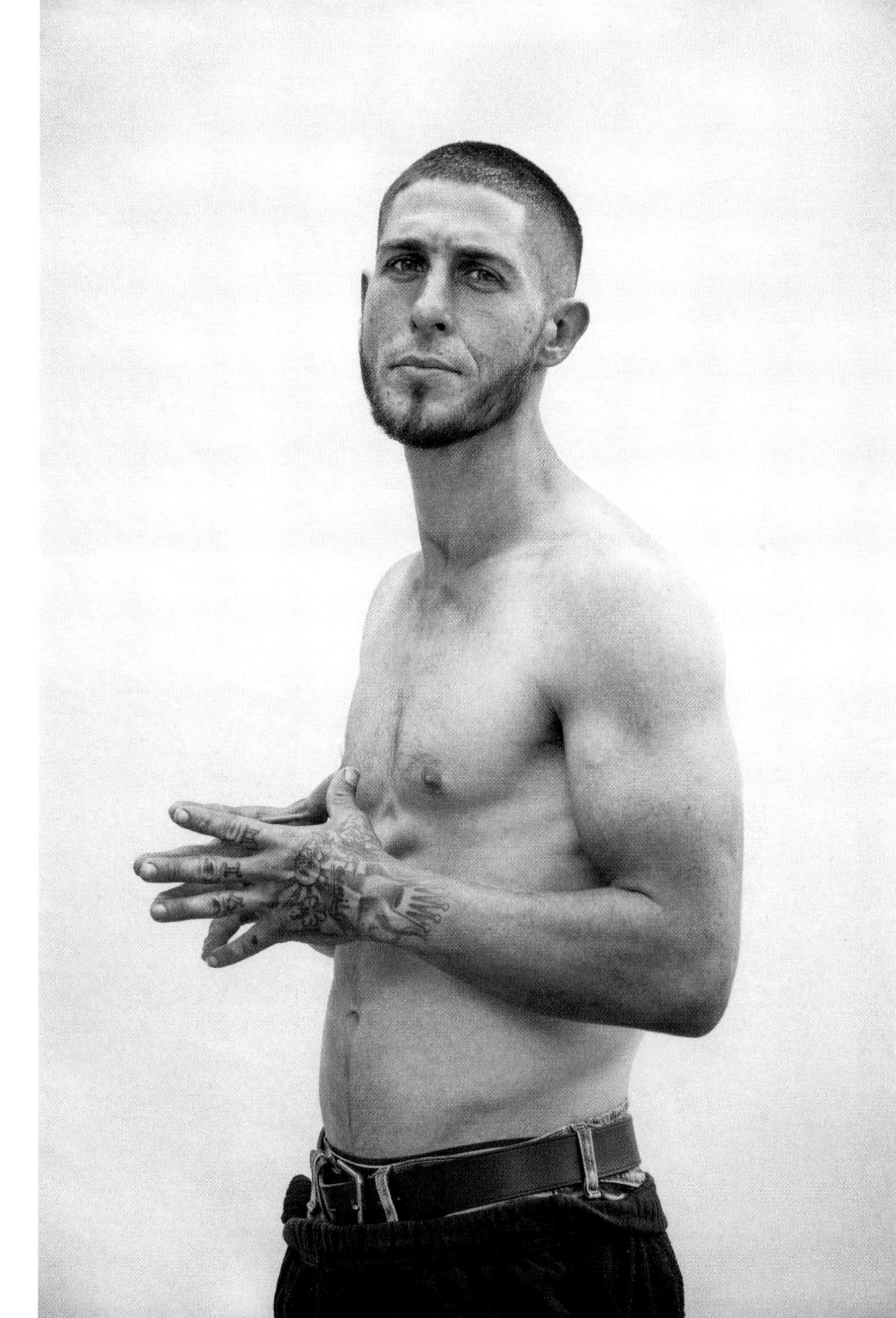

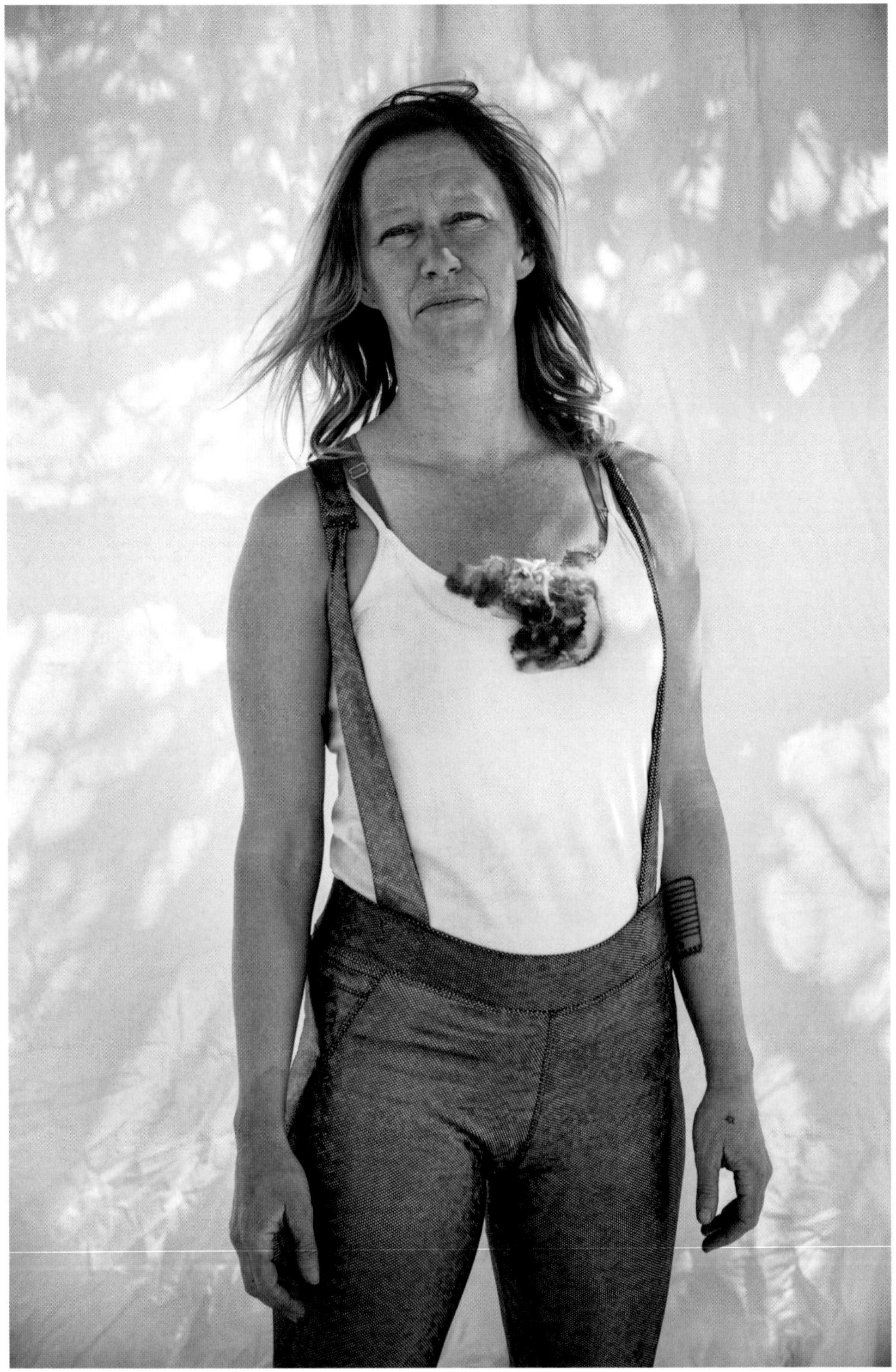

Sadye, California

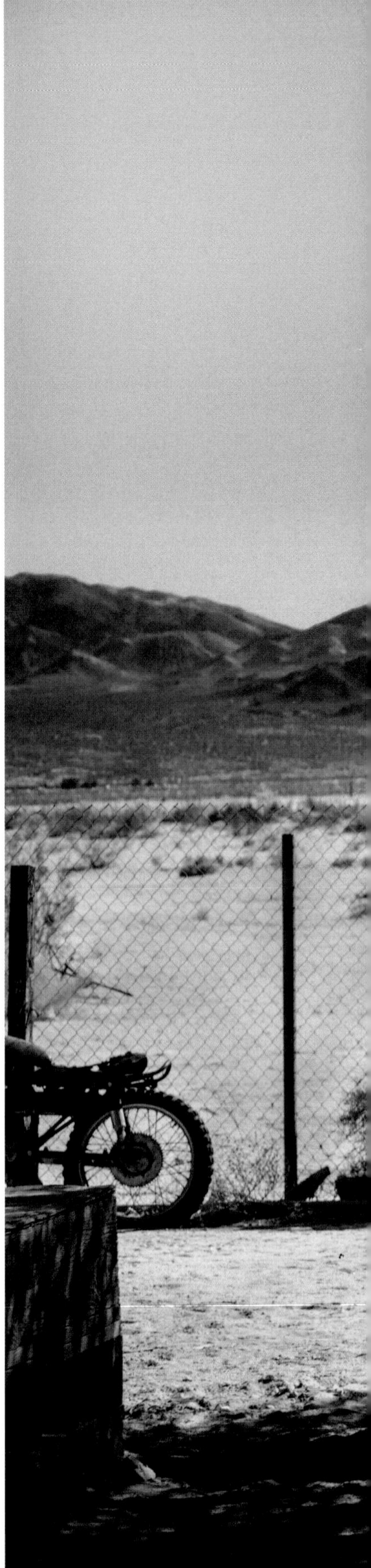

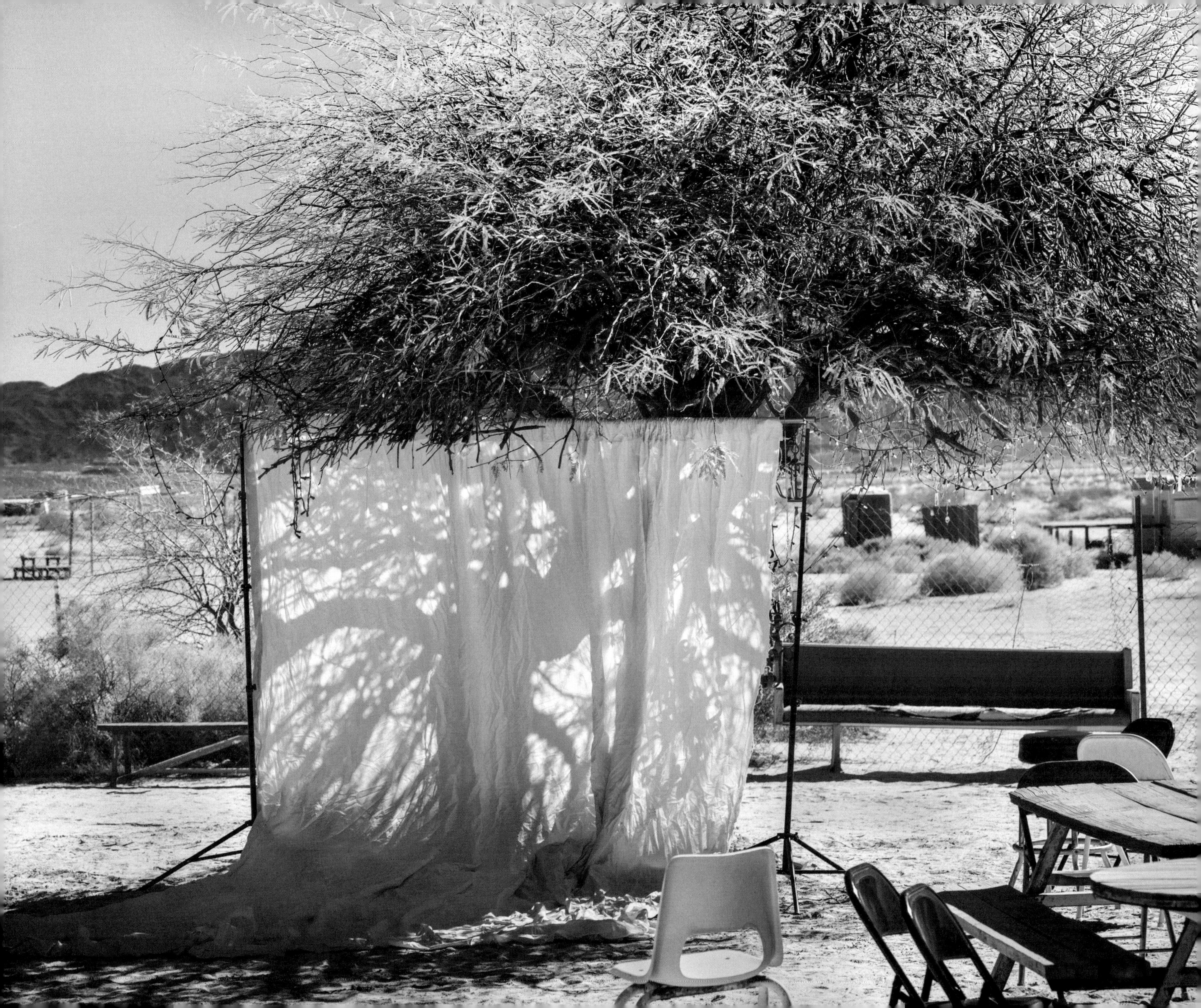

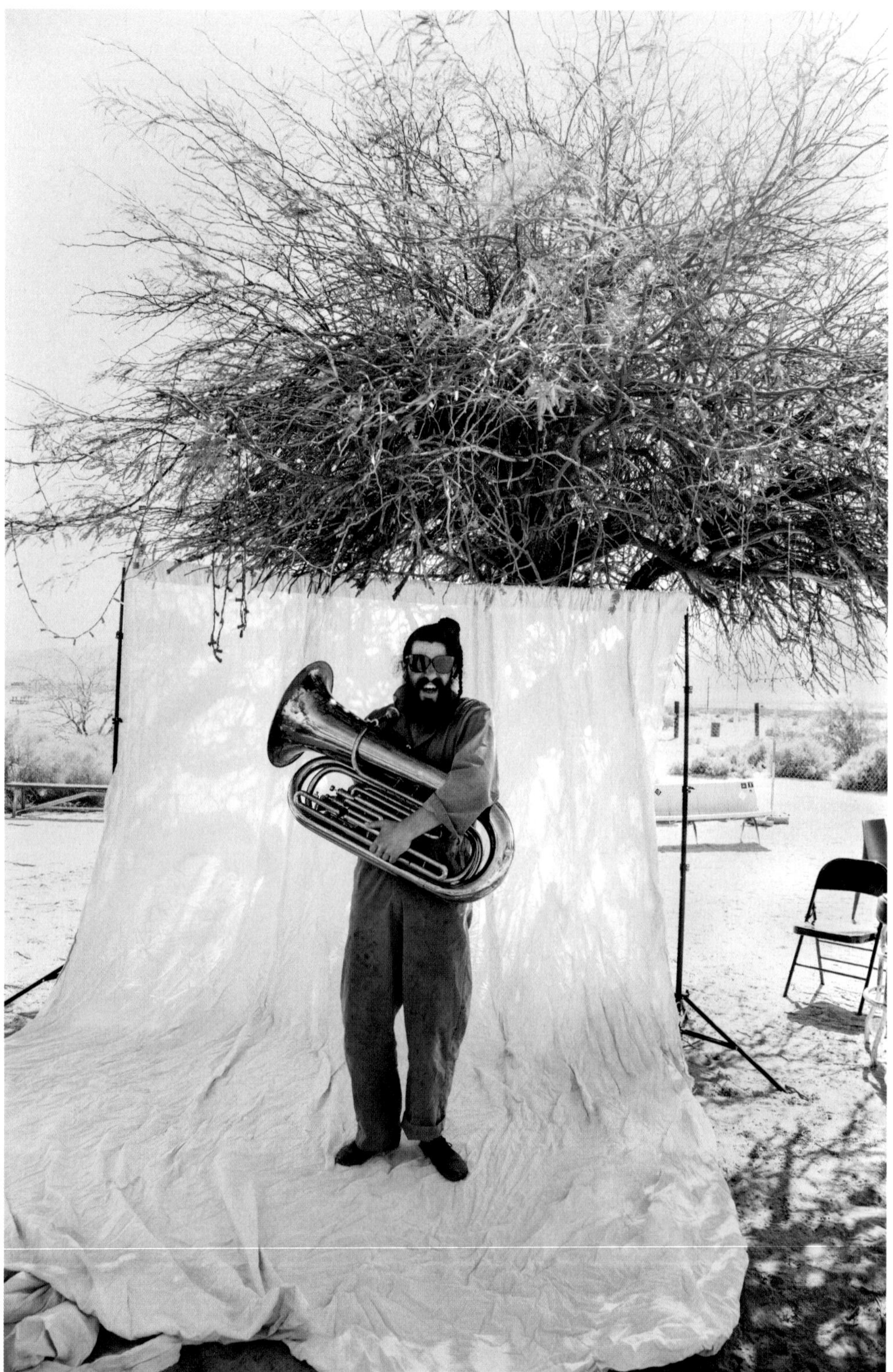

Tuba player, California

N 34°11’ 18.9672” W 115° 54’ 14.3064”

WONDER VALLEY, CALIFORNIA

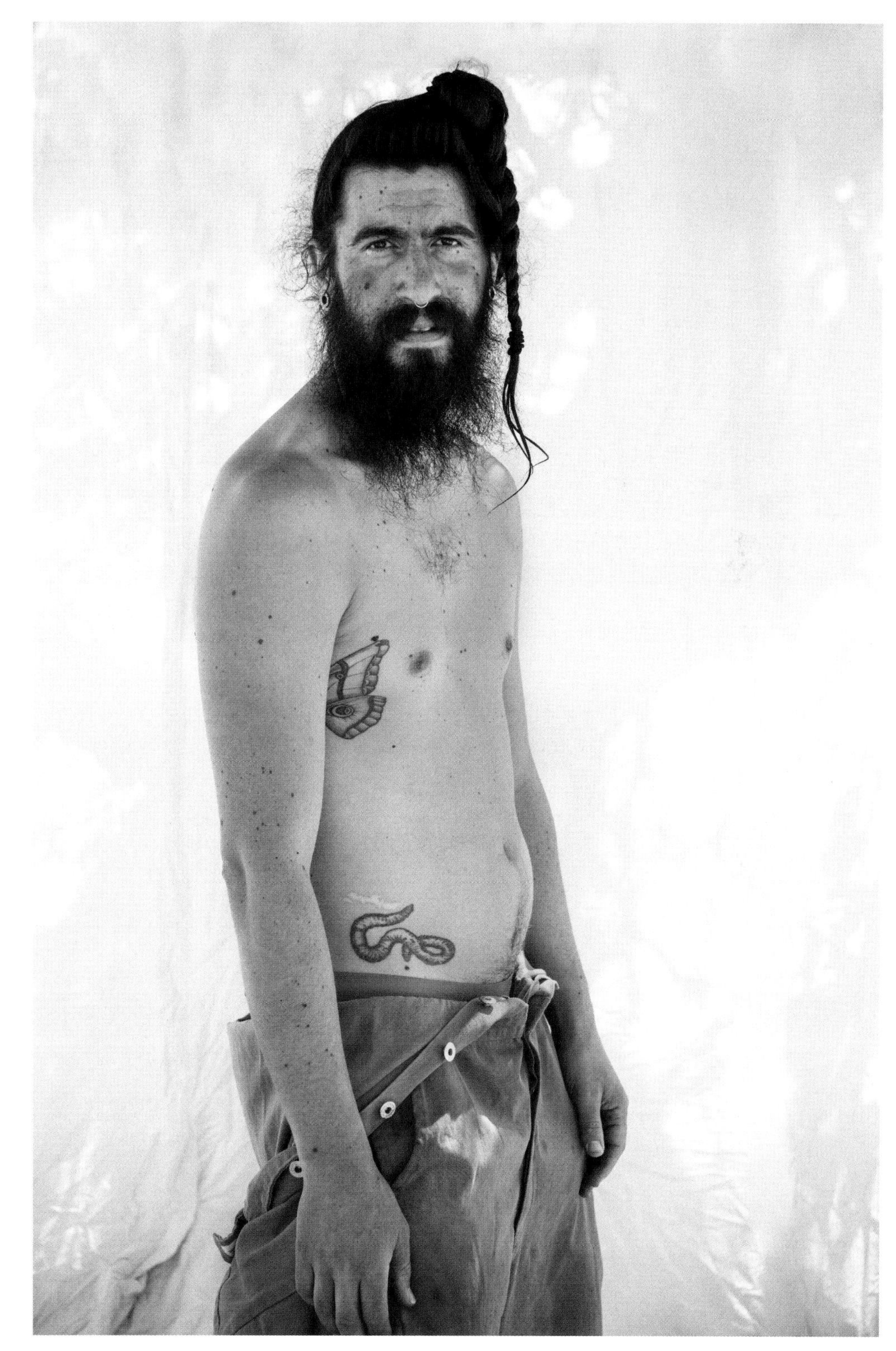

Poki, California

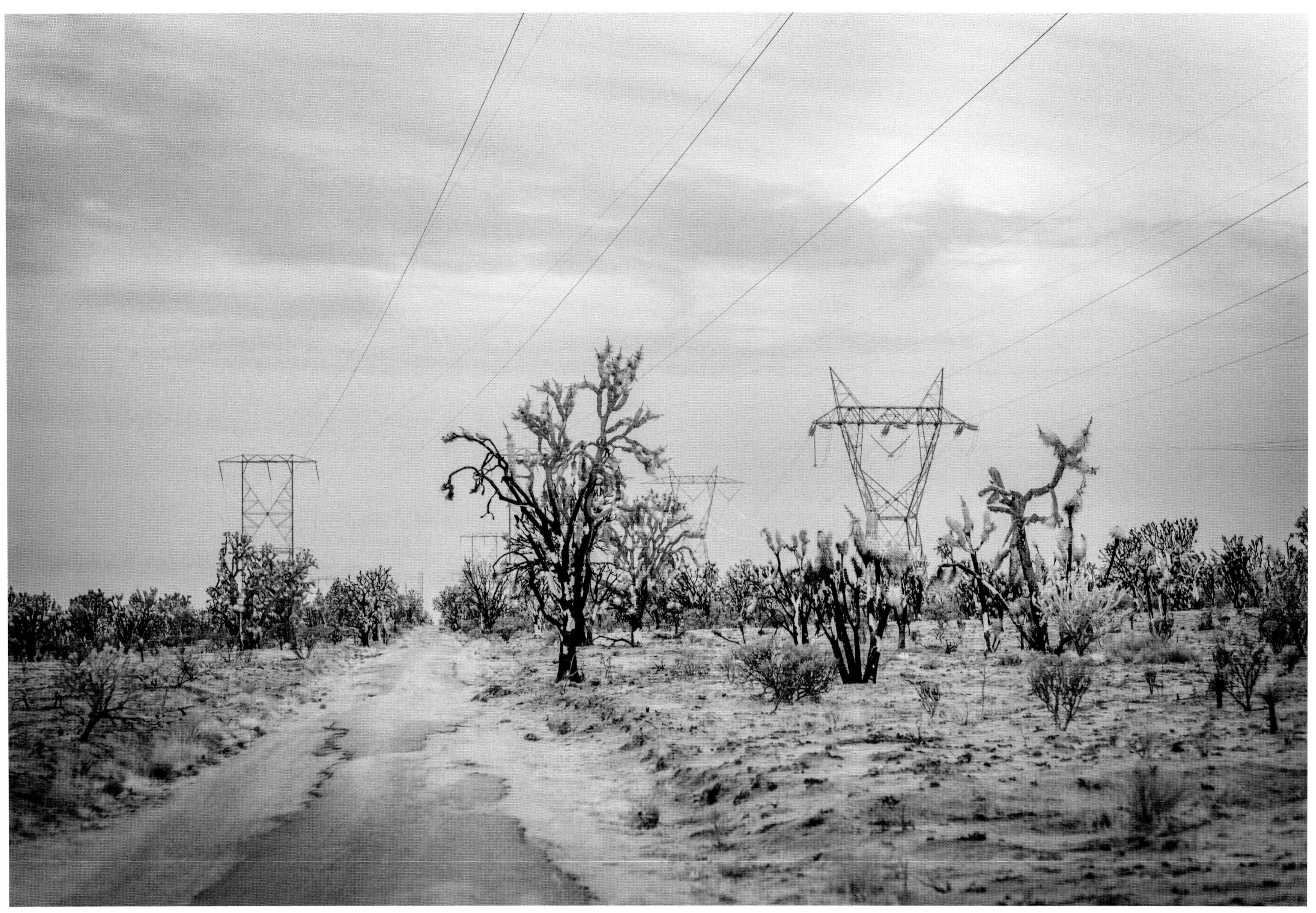

Charred Joshua trees, Nevada

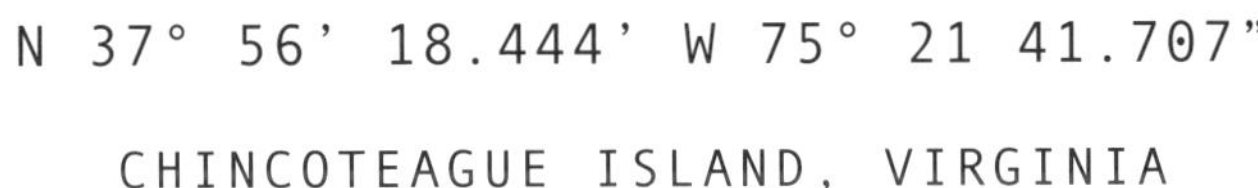

“We moved around a lot when I was a kid, but Girdletree, Maryland, is the town I claim. Last census it was around 112-120 people, so very small, pretty fields, and mostly tight knit. A lot of people live paycheck to paycheck, barely scraping by, and it’s been that way for a long time. People work very hard for very little, and lately they are scared of not being able to survive. Values are changing, and people are scared of that change. It’s such an insulated area.”

[Jessie]

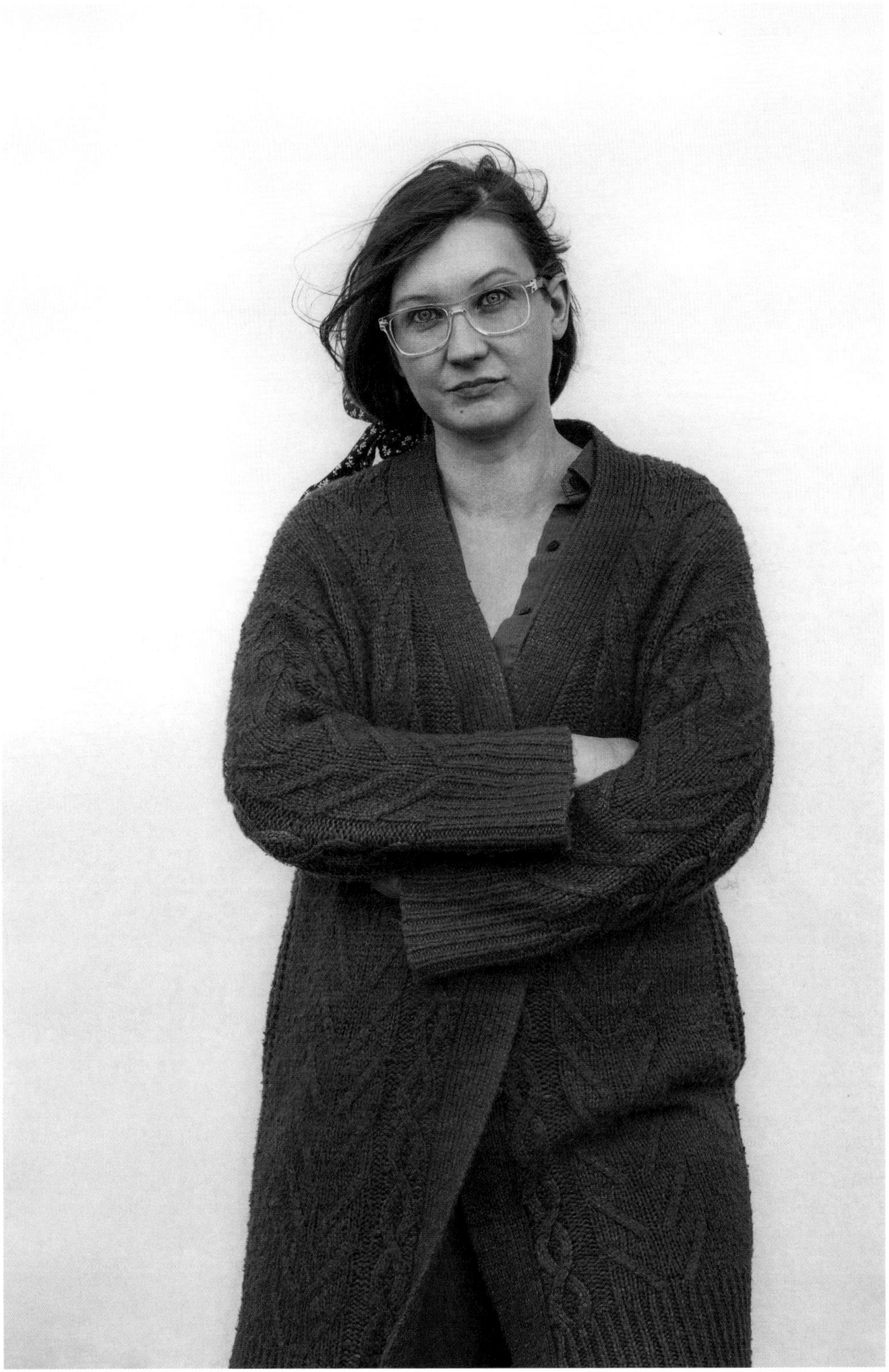

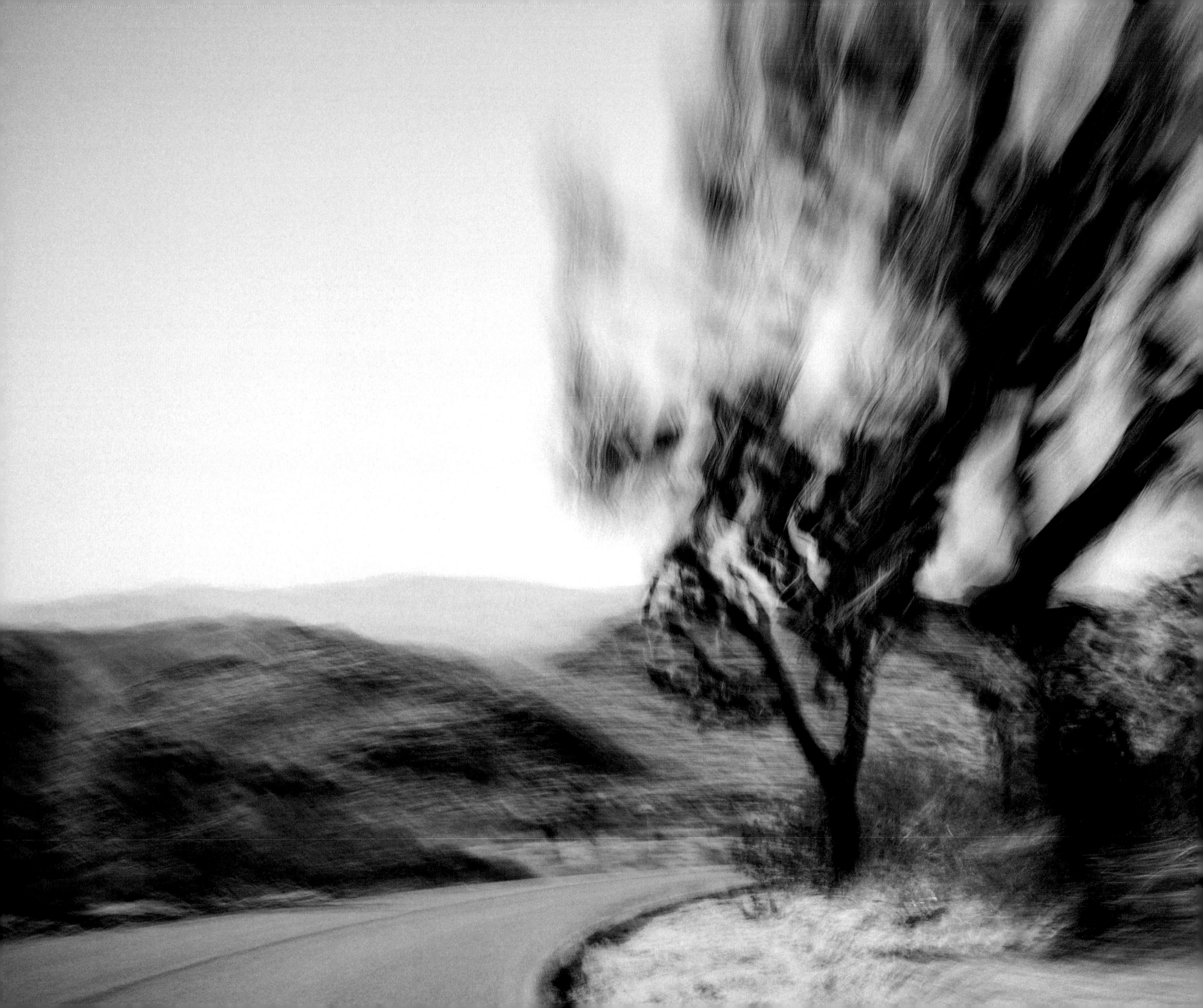

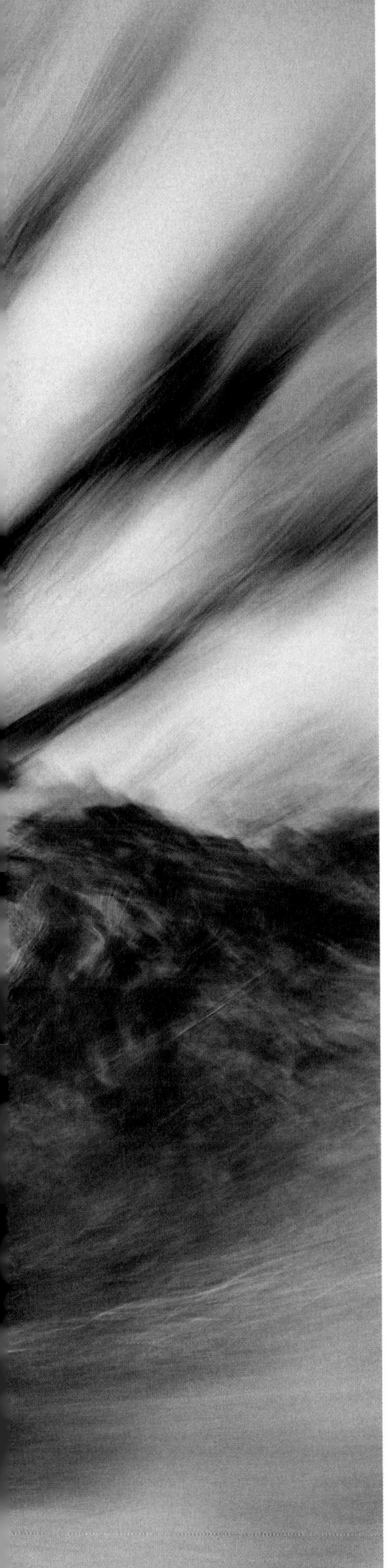

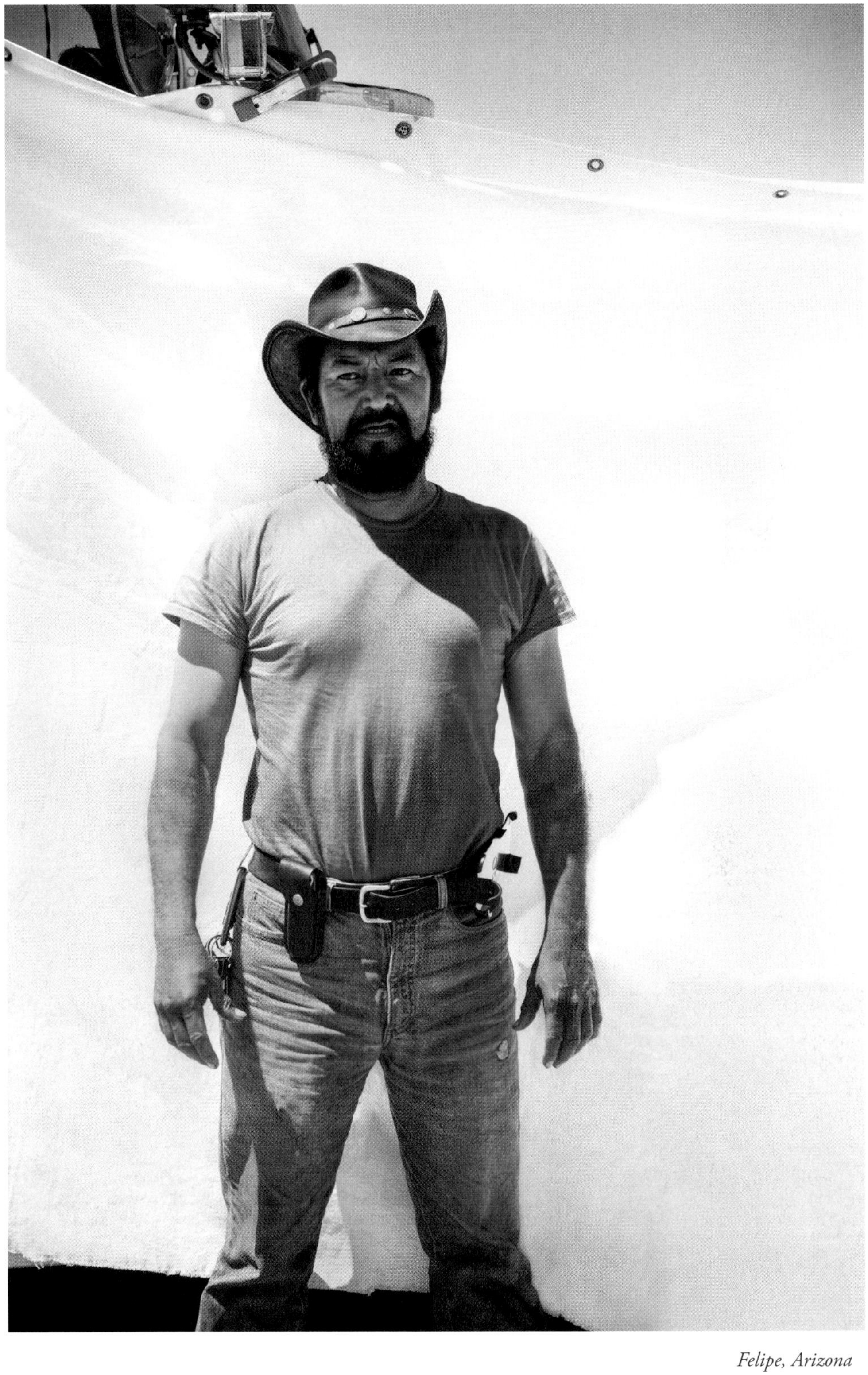

Felipe, Arizona

N 36° 13' 46.866" W 116° 46' 4.5084"

BADWATER BASIN, CALIFORNIA

"We are very similar with the haircut and all — we grew it for three years. Even our names are similar: Lalain and Lorrain."

[Lalain]

"Actually, even the computer gets confused with us, because our birthdays are similar too."

[Lorrain]

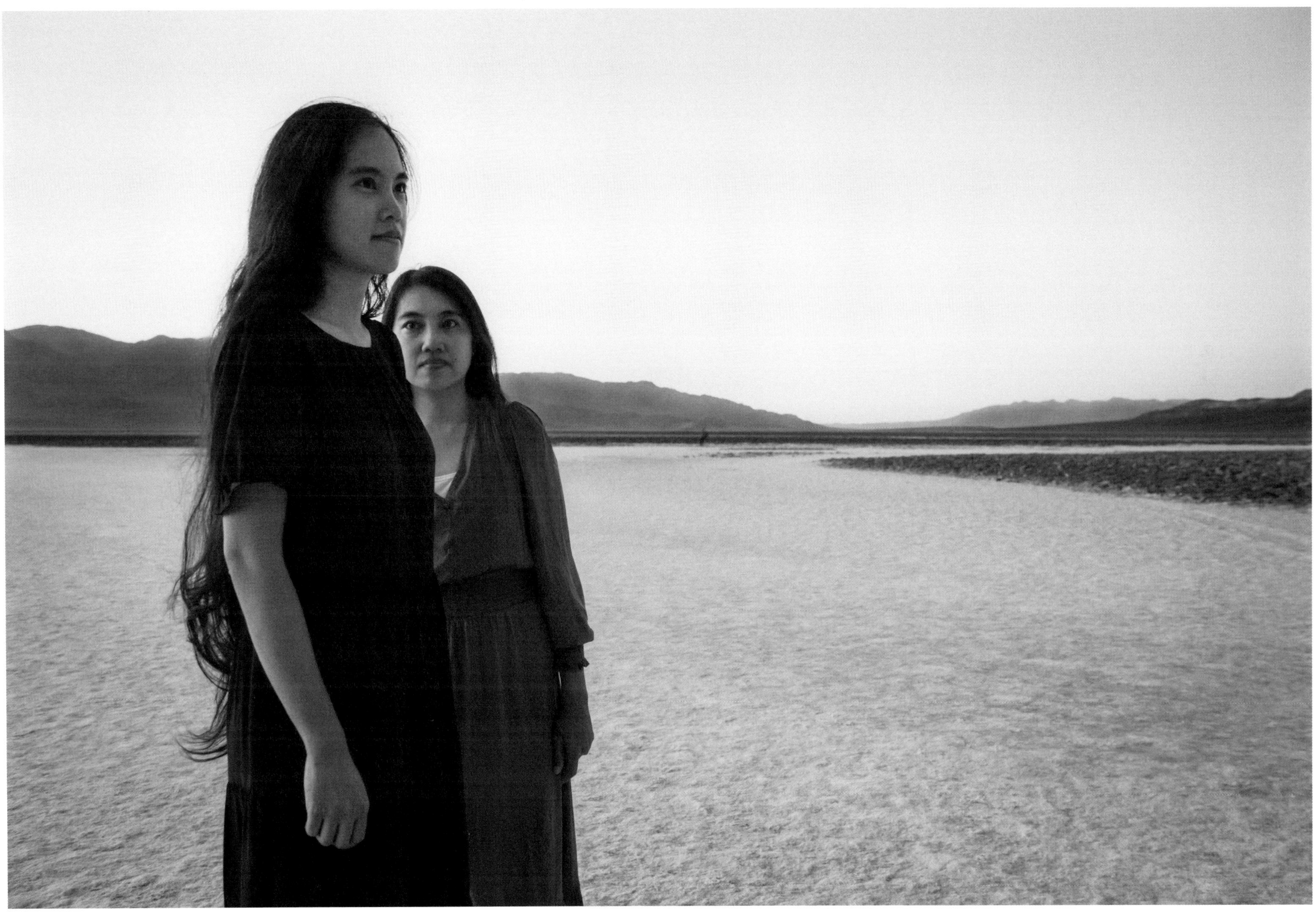

White Sands turn, New Mexico

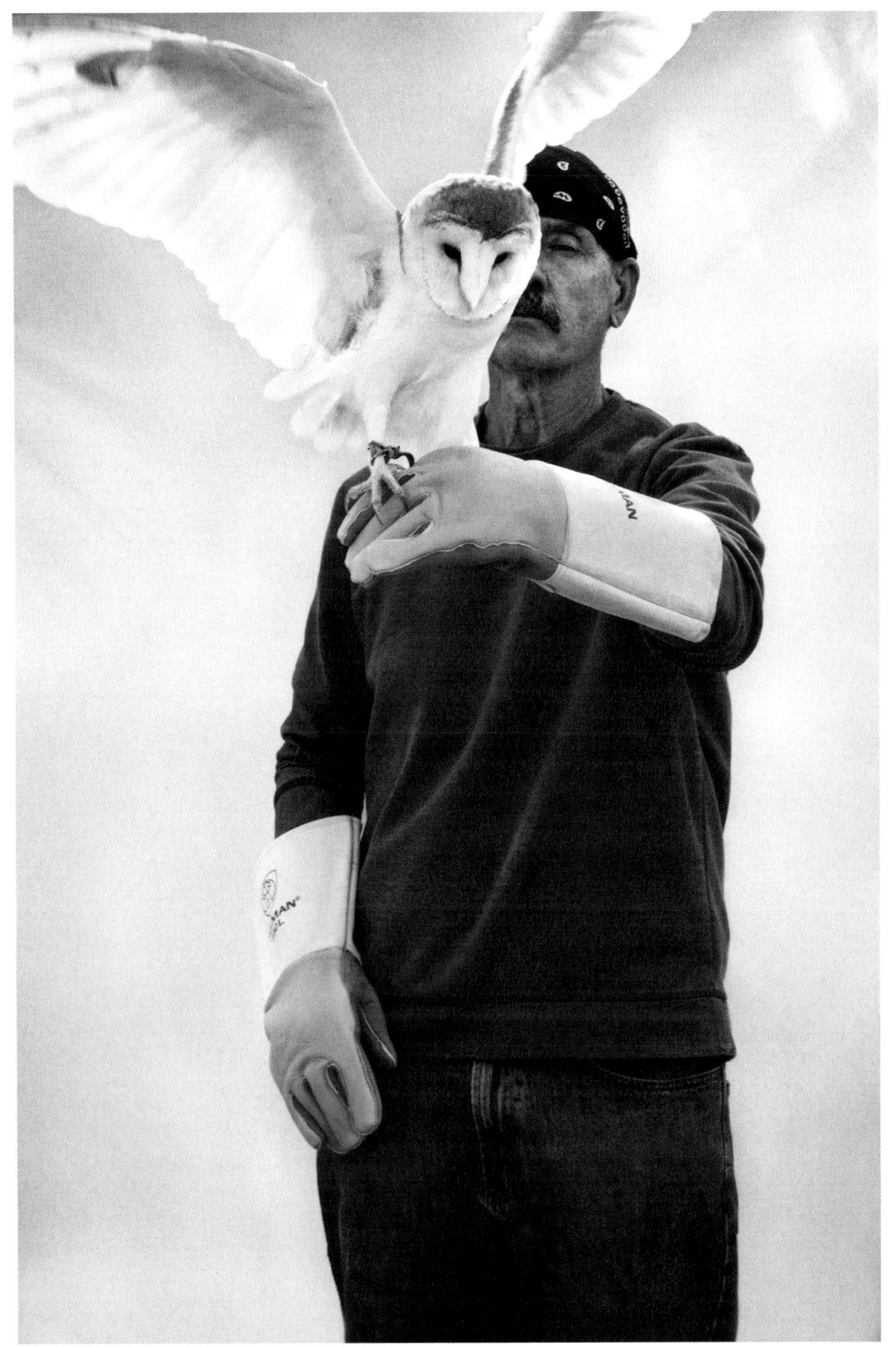

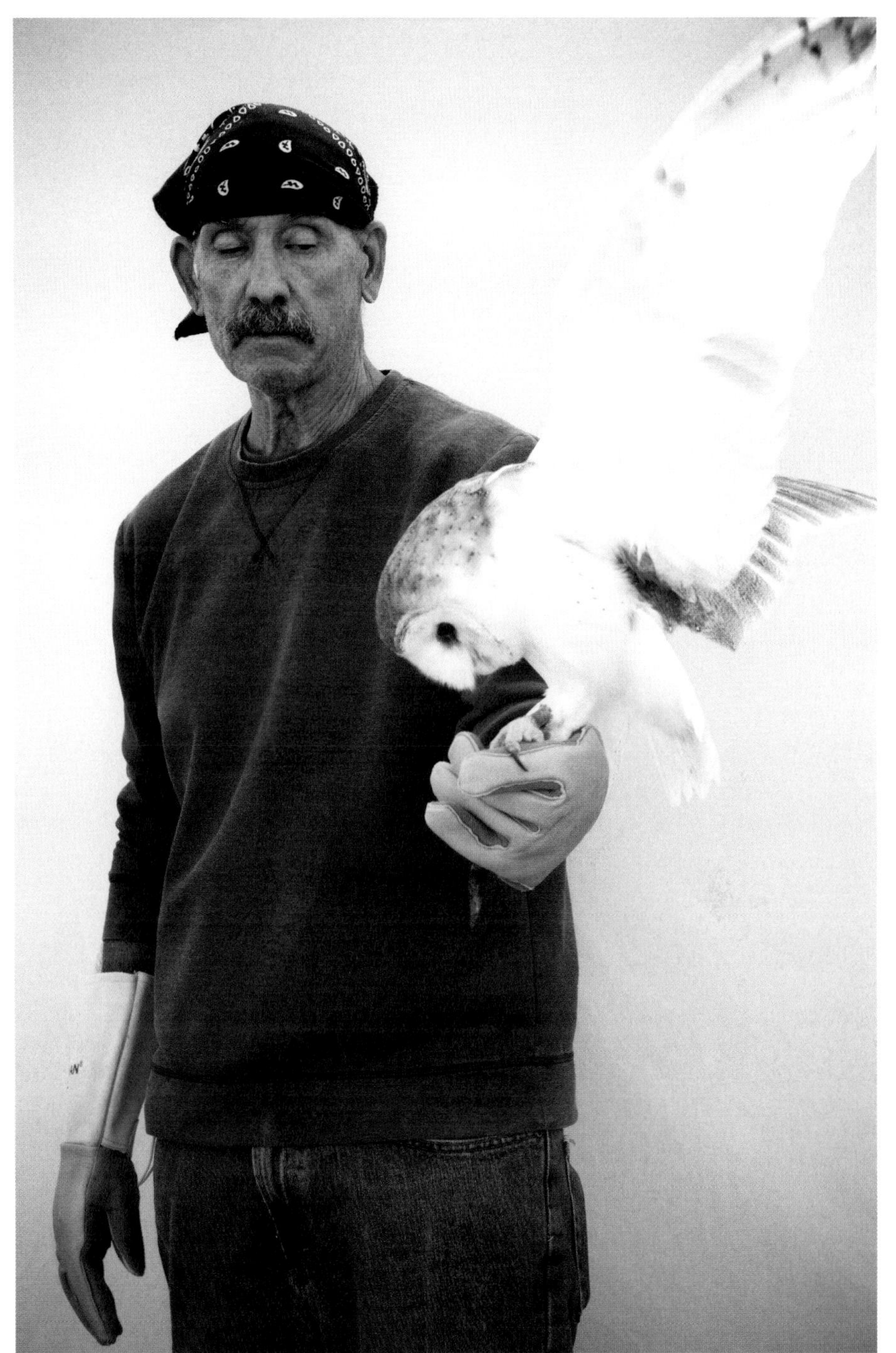

Michael and Luna, California

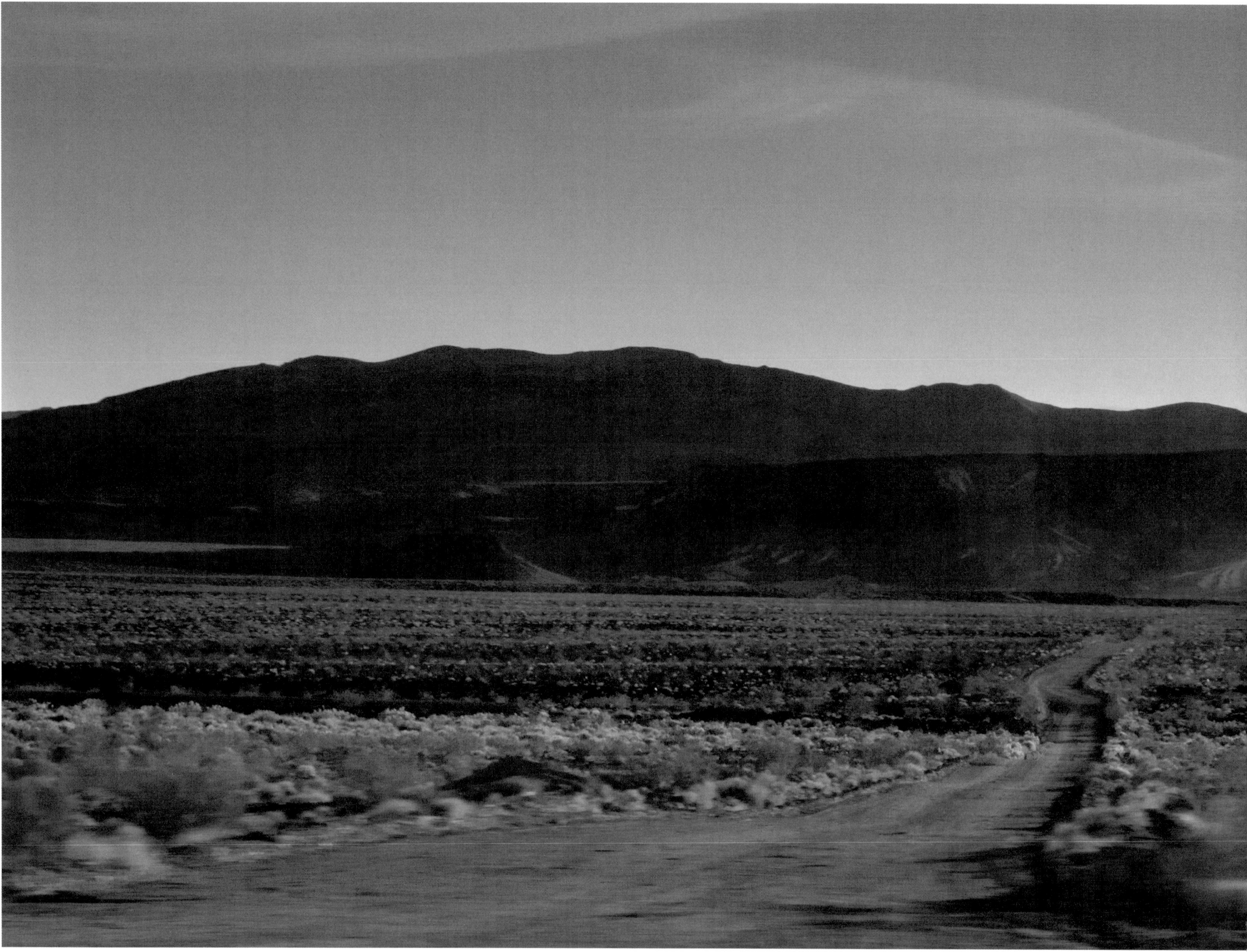

ACKNOWLEDGEMENTS

Ambrose Martos
Derek DiGuglielmo
Anders Weinar
Sam Samore
Robert Blake
Heather Clifton
Russ Wolske
Ford Motor Company
Polestar
Damiani Books

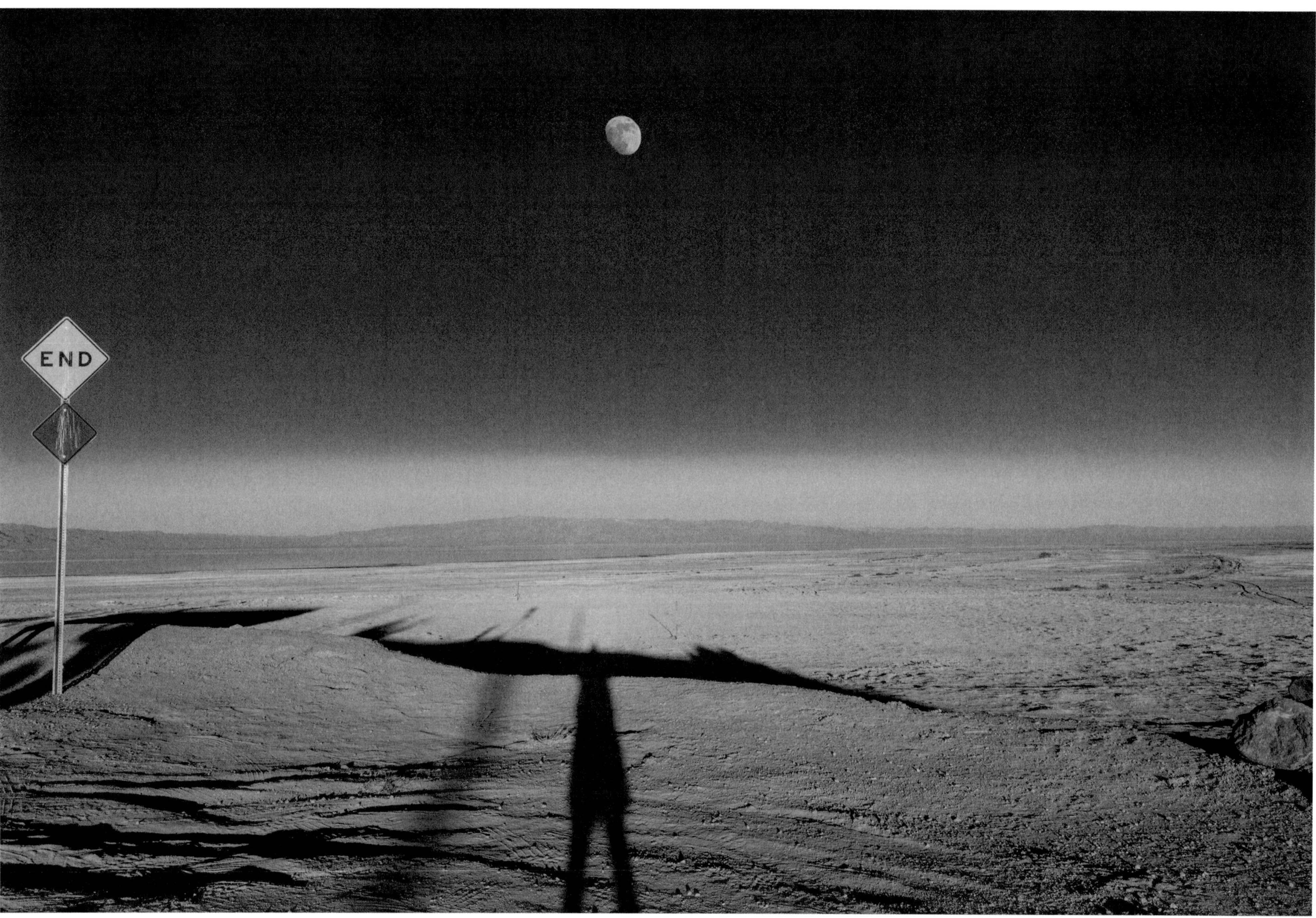
END

Florence Montmare
America Series

www.florencemontmare.com

Published by Damiani
info@damianibooks.com
www.damianibooks.com

Printed in May 2023, Italy

ISBN 978-88-6208-806-0